Keeping them in the family

Keeping them in the family

Outcomes for children placed in kinship care through care proceedings

Joan Hunt,
Suzette Waterhouse and
Eleanor Lutman

Published by British Association
for Adoption and Fostering
(BAAF)
Saffron House
3rd Floor, 6–10 Kirby Street
London EC1N 8TS
www.baaf.org.uk

Charity registration 275689 (England and Wales)
and SC039337 (Scotland)

British Library Cataloguing in Publication Data
A catalogue record for this book is available
from the British Library

ISBN 978 1 905664 52 8

Editorial project management by Shaila Shah
Cover photograph © Richard JE Anderson, www.flickr.com
Typeset by Avon DataSet Ltd, Bidford on Avon
Printed in Great Britain by Athenaeum Press

BAAF is the leading UK-wide membership
organisation for all those concerned with
adoption, fostering and child care issues.

Acknowledgements

Thanks must go first to the kinship carers, children and parents who felt able to participate in this study and tell their stories. We hope they feel their voices and experiences are accurately reflected through this publication and that the time they gave to us will help increase awareness of the need to use and support this form of care more effectively.

We are indebted to the two local authorities who participated in the research. Senior managers in both authorities were extremely patient, encouraging and committed in meeting with us often and helping us to persevere through many, many data access difficulties. Likewise administrative staff, team managers, social workers and kinship care specialist workers assisted at many points along the way. The positive and refreshing approach to research taken by the heads of the two legal services was also more than welcome at a point when our project seemed to be grinding to a halt.

We would like to thank the Department for Children, Schools and Families (previously the Department for Education and Skills and originally the Department of Health) for recognising the importance of kinship care in deciding to fund this research under the Quality Protects Initiative. Helen Jones and Caroline Thomas deserve special mention: Helen for her steadfast championing of this form of care, Caroline for her support throughout the difficulties the project encountered. Mike Stein, from the University of York, who shared the task of co-ordinating the research programme with Caroline, was also of enormous assistance.

Helen and Mike were both members of our Research Advisory Group which met regularly over several years and kept our spirits up in times of difficulty as well as providing invaluable expertise. The other members were: Bob Broad (then at De Montfort University); Elaine Farmer and Sue Moyers (Bristol University); Judith Harwin (Brunel University); Harriet Ward (Loughborough); Vivien Prior (Great Ormond Street Hospital); Lynn Chesterman (Grandparents Association); Jean Stogdon (Grandparents Plus); Anne Morgan and Cathy Ashley (Family Rights Group); Carol Edwards and Eddie Brocklesby (children's guardians and independent social work practitioners); Jenny Robson (Who Cares? Trust); Richard King (Birmingham Social Services); Rosie Smith, (Hampshire Social

Services); Vikki Swain (Fostering Network); Victoria Philippson (Cafcass). We are grateful to all of them for their contribution, whether they helped in the early stages, joined part-way through or were there for the duration. Special thanks are due to Elaine Farmer, Sue Moyers and Vivien Prior, all on our Advisory Group, who allowed us access to their research schedules, as did Jane Aldgate (of the Open University) and Ian Sinclair (York).

It was a matter of great sadness to us all that we lost one member of our Advisory Group, Alison Richards, because of her untimely death. We would like to take this opportunity to record our personal recognition of the huge contribution she has made to the development of kinship care in this country through her work for Family Rights Group. She is greatly missed.

Finally we would like to thank BAAF for publishing the report and, in particular, Shaila Shah for her excellent work as editor.

Joan Hunt, Suzette Waterhouse and Eleanor Lutman
May 2008

This work was undertaken by Joan Hunt, Suzette Waterhouse and Eleanor Lutman, who received funding from the government. The views expressed in the publication are those of the authors and are not necessarily those of the Department for Children, Schools and Families.

An overview of the studies in the programme entitled *Quality Matters in Children's Services: Messages from research* is being prepared by Professor Mike Stein, University of York.

About the authors

Joan Hunt is Senior Research Fellow in Oxford University's Centre for Family Law and Policy, part of the Department of Social Policy and Social Work. She has conducted many empirical research studies on children and families subject to court proceedings because of child protection concerns or parental disputes. In addition to contributing chapters on kinship care in several books, she is the author of an overview of research and policy commissioned by the government (*Family and Friends Carers: Scoping paper prepared for the Department of Health*; DH, 2003) and a research and practice briefing paper commissioned by Research in Practice (Briefing Paper 16: *Family and Friends Care*, Research in Practice, 2008). She is guest editor of a forthcoming special issue of the journal *Adoption & Fostering* on kinship care.

Suzette Waterhouse is a freelance social work practitioner and researcher. Her current professional practice includes court-based assessment work both as a children's guardian and as an expert social worker, and assessment/support work for the family placement agency Parents for Children. Her practice experience informed the development of the study and it was her original research on the proportion of children placed with kin as the result of care proceedings, which generated the research sample ('Keeping children in kinship placements within court proceedings', in Broad, B. (ed), 2001): *Kinship Care: The placement choice for children and young people*, Russell House Publishing). She has also conducted research for the (then) National Foster Care Association on the organisation of fostering services (NFCA, 1997) and children in temporary care (Brocklesby, E and Waterhouse, S. (2001) 'Placement choices for children in temporary foster care', *Adoption & Fostering*, Autumn 2001, 25:3)

Eleanor Lutman was Research Assistant at the Centre for Family Law and Policy, Department of Social Policy and Social Work, University of Oxford for the duration of the research project on which this publication is based. She currently works as a Research Associate at the School for Policy Studies, University of Bristol. Her research interests include child maltreatment and looked after children.

Contents

1 Introduction

Kinship care in the UK: under-researched, patchily utilised, poorly resourced and policy light

Where children are unable to be cared for by their birth parents, the Children Act 1989 stipulates that, unless it is not in the child's interests, priority should be given to placement with members of their extended families or social networks. Section 23(6) directs that when a child is looked after by the local authority and cannot be placed with a parent or others with parental responsibility, the local authority:

> '... shall make arrangements to enable him to live with a relative, friend, or other person connected with him, unless that would not be reasonably practical or consistent with his welfare'.

Guidance issued to accompany the Act pressed the message home, stating that:

> 'Possibilities for a child to be cared for within the extended family should have been investigated and considered as an alternative to the provision of accommodation by the responsible authority. However, even when it has become necessary for the responsible authority to arrange provision of accommodation, placement with a relative will often provide the best opportunities for promoting and maintaining family links in a familiar setting' (Department of Health (DH), 1991, p 27).

The Children Act was not, in fact, the first piece of UK legislation to emphasise the importance of the extended family. (See, for example, the 1948 Children Act and the Act for the Better Protection of Infant Life, 1872.) However, it did mark the rehabilitation of the extended family as potential carers after a lengthy period in which such placements had tended to be regarded with suspicion and had come to constitute a decreasing proportion of foster care placements (Rowe *et al*, 1984; Ryburn, 1998).

This change in official attitudes towards the extended family as

1

potential providers of care was, like much of the Children Act, based on research evidence. The specific UK knowledge base at the time, however, was not substantial – there was not a single major study which focused specifically on relative care, and only a few which included such placements at all. Nonetheless, all the studies came to similar conclusions – that relative care "worked" and had been unjustly relegated to the doldrums (Rowe *et al*, 1984; Millham *et al*, 1986; Berridge and Cleaver, 1987; Rowe *et al*, 1989; Farmer and Parker, 1991; Malos and Bullard, 1991).

In the event, kinship care was slow to take off. In March 1992, the first complete year for which the Act was in force, only nine per cent of all looked after children were placed with relatives, accounting for 15 per cent of all foster children (DH, 1992). By March 2000, such placements represented only 11 per cent of all children looked after and 17 per cent of foster children (DH, 2000). It currently represents 18 per cent of foster placements (Department for Education and Skills (DfES), 2005a). It is true that these figures indicate an increase on immediate pre-Act practice (in 1989 only six per cent of looked after children were fostered with relatives), but it was smaller than might have been expected. It was also a good deal less than the proportions reported from other countries such as Australia, New Zealand and the US which have also prioritised kinship care. While this might be taken to indicate differences in national conditions, there was mounting evidence of very different levels of use between local authorities within the UK (Hunt, 2003a; Sinclair *et al*, 2007; Farmer and Moyers, 2008). (Although these latter studies have only recently been published, we were fortunate to be given access to the draft reports by the authors.)

There were also indications that even where use was being made of kinship care, local policies were very patchy. Indeed, a survey of local authorities in 2003 found that only half had written policies on kinship care (Morgan, 2003). Broad (2001) considered that there was a 'policy vacuum' in some local authorities, while Waterhouse and Brocklesby (1999) reported that in the five local authorities in their study, kinship placements were seen as a contentious area of practice and there was no consistency in policy or practice.

Nor had kinship care become embedded in social work practice, as has been reported in other countries (Jantz *et al*, 2002). A recent study (Farmer and Moyers, 2008) found that even ten or more years after the Children Act, only four per cent of kinship placements were initiated by social workers.

With hindsight, what was clearly needed if the intentions of the Children Act were to be realised was a clear policy steer, underpinned with detailed guidance, from central government to local authorities charged with implementing the Act. However, for several years after the Act was passed, kinship care seemed to have a low profile in central, as well as local, government policy. The Social Services Inspectorate (DH, 1995) undertook a study of the use of residence orders by related and unrelated carers and made a whole series of recommendations with regard to the development of local authority policies. However, this seems to have had little impact.

The election of the New Labour government in 1997 seemed to herald a resurgence of central government interest in the extended family. The consultation paper, *Supporting Families* (Home Office, 1998), issued by the newly established cross-departmental Ministerial Group on the Family, highlighted the contribution the extended family, particularly grandparents, could make to strengthening families and declared an intention to introduce policies which would promote the role of kin and counter the tendency for them to be marginalised by service providers. The document also specifically stated that a grandparent could provide a very effective placement for a looked after child and invited views on best practice for grandparents as foster carers. Subsequently, the Home Office commissioned the Family Rights Group (Richards, 2001) to conduct a survey of grandparents bringing up grandchildren.

In the succeeding years there was what might best be described as intermittent and low key policy interest, largely sustained by the continued commitment of individual civil servants in the responsible government departments (first the Department of Health (DH), later the DfES, now the Department for Children, Schools and Families (DCSF)). Thus, one of the authors of this study was commissioned to prepare a "scoping paper" on kinship care to inform the development of policy (Hunt, 2003a). (This was submitted in 2001 though not published until 2003.) The Department of

Health issued a discussion paper (DH, 2002). A few pieces of developmental work were commissioned, for instance, work with two local authorities (Jordan, 2001; Doolan *et al*, 2004), including work on designing more appropriate assessment tools, and one piece of research (Richards, 2001). Work was commissioned on the training needs of kinship foster carers and a training pack produced (Waldman and Wheal, 1999). However, this fell far short of the clear policy framework which all commentators on kinship care were clear was needed (see the contributions in Broad, 2001 and Greeff, 1999; Hunt 2003a and Sinclair *et al*, 2007).

One central government initiative, however, does appear to have acted as a catalyst to the development of kinship care in local authorities. Although the Quality Protects Programme (DH, 1998) was not specifically focused on kinship care, this form of care could be seen as supporting many of the specific objectives set out for children's services, particularly in terms of reducing the number of moves children had in care. Perhaps more importantly, the programme made money available to local authorities to assist them in delivering the objectives. There is no precise data on how many local authorities used the money to develop their kinship care services but it is clear that many took the opportunity to create specialist posts, typically known as kinship care co-ordinators. Greater attention to kinship care was also reinforced by another government initiative – *Choice Protects* – which, as the name indicates, aimed to improve the quality of the care experience for children by increasing the range of placements available, thus ensuring that there is a better fit between what the child needs and what the placement offers.

Nonetheless, kinship care seemed to remain on the periphery of government thinking about child welfare services. It was not mentioned at all, for instance, in the Green Paper, *Every Child Matters* (DfES, 2003). It did manage to secure a few paragraphs in the subsequent Green Paper, *Care Matters* (DfES, 2006a), although it was obviously not considered important enough to make the Executive Summary. The draft version of our research report submitted to the DfES in January 2007 expressed disappointment at what appeared to be the continuing marginalisation of kinship care while expressing the hope that the Green Paper might provide the foundation on which a more strategic policy could be built. Many of the responses to the consultation on the Green Paper were similarly critical, including a joint response from an ad hoc group of voluntary agencies, academics and interested individuals, now formalised into the Kinship Care Alliance (www.frg.org.uk/policy_papers.html).

These efforts may have borne fruit: the subsequent White Paper, *Care Matters: Time for change* (DfES, 2007), did indeed seem to indicate that kinship care was at last going to get more attention:

'It is essential that carers in these circumstances receive proper support and recognition and we intend to provide this through a new framework for family and friends care which will set out the expectations of an effective service.' (para 2.36)

The White Paper *Care Matters: Time for change. Proposals for family and friends care*

These proposals are briefly summarised below:

The government's intention is to provide 'a new framework for family and friends care . . . which will set out the expectations of an effective service'. This is intended to address concerns about:

Variation across the country in the extent to which family and friends placements are used;

Absence of policy frameworks to underpin services to these families and, where they are in place, inconsistent application of the policy;

Lack of transparency of entitlements and services available and inequitable treatment of carers; and

Suitability of the approval process for family and friends carers.

Revised Children Act guidance will set out details of the 'gateway approach' which will be put in place to 'make sure that family and friends care is considered as an option at the first and every subsequent stage of decision-making', and is included in the initial care plans put to the court in care proceedings. Local authorities will be required to have transparent policies on supporting family and friends carers and this will be monitored through Ofsted inspections.

The government's commitment to family and friends care was reiterated in a policy briefing on the Children and Young Persons' Bill, introduced into Parliament in 2007:

'The provisions in the Bill relating to family and friends care form part of a strategy to enable more children to live with people they already know and trust if they cannot remain with their birth parents and to ensure that family and friends carers receive proper support and recognition . . . we recognise that in some areas of the country there is a lack of support and recognition for family and friends care. As well as encouraging greater use of family and friends care, where this is appropriate, we want to establish a more visible and strengthened framework which will set out the expectations of an effective serve to support these children and families.' (www.dfes.gov.uk/publication/childrenandyoungpersonsbill/docs/family)

Perhaps, therefore, these unequivocal commitments, if they are backed up with the promised frameworks, will at long last enable family and friends care to be the first placement option for children, as the Children Act 1989 intended.

There is now a rather more substantial knowledge base on which to build than there was in 1989, though again, it still falls far short of what is needed. It is to be regretted that for many years after the Children Act there was little interest by government in commissioning research into kinship care. The scoping paper prepared by Hunt (2003a) showed that while a number of studies had been conducted post-Act, they were typically small local projects, often carried out by practitioners with a particular interest in the subject. As a result, some aspects of the topic were better covered than others. Many of the studies had limitations, particularly in terms of evaluating outcomes. Hence, we were largely reliant on research from other countries, principally the US, whose applicability – given differences in social conditions – was questionable. Since that scoping paper was submitted to government in 2001, more studies have been completed, which help to fill in some of the gaps in the research picture. Perhaps most importantly, as an indication of government interest in the topic, two studies specifically focusing on kinship care were commissioned as part of the Quality Protects research programme, viz Farmer and Moyers (2008) and the present study. Other studies in the programme, notably Sinclair *et al* (2007) also provide valuable data.

The genesis of the study

The origins of this research are directly attributable to five, very real, small children whose cases were before the courts in the 1990s because of abuse or neglect and who needed to be placed away from their birth parents. In each case, the child's relatives (potentially competent carers) were determined to look after the child and the guardian *ad litem* (one of the authors of this study, Waterhouse) supported the placement despite the plan of the respective local authorities to pursue adoption. The social workers at that time put forward various arguments during proceedings to support adoption of these children – that the child needed a fresh start away from the extended family because of the abuse they had suffered, the parent might interfere with the placement, the carers were too old, too young, too unhealthy or potentially unstable and that the children would just 'do better' in adoption. The courts endorsed the guardian's recommendation for kinship placements, even in the two cases where the local authority remained, to the end, in active opposition.

These cases raised considerable practice issues for the guardian concerned. What thresholds did relatives have to cross to secure children within the extended family? Were the social workers right in their opinions that the children would have futures fraught with problems? Did other guardians favour using the kinship option as the first choice for a child? How commonly were such placements made when it was unsafe for children to return to their parents?

Encouraged and enabled by her guardian *ad litem* panel managers, Waterhouse analysed basic data on the use of kinship placements from local panels relating to care proceedings during 1995–1999 (and later 2000) (Waterhouse 1999 and 2001). Jean Stogden of the Grandparents Federation (who had at the time recently returned from a Churchill Fellowship to investigate the use of kinship care in the USA) was interested in the findings and made contact, later coming to talk to one of the panels about the experience in the USA. It was at this meeting, in 1999, that Waterhouse first met Hunt, who had separately developed an interest in kinship care in the course of researching care proceedings under the Children Act 1989 (Hunt *et al*, 1999; Hunt and Macleod, 1999) and had unsuccessfully tried to interest a range of funders in researching what was clearly going to be an important area of child care practice but where the knowledge base was frighteningly insubstantial.

After several further fruitless attempts to secure funding for various research studies, we were finally successful in our bid to the Quality Protects research programme. And gratifyingly, it was the work Waterhouse had done of her own initiative, in collecting data on kinship placements via the guardian panels, which provided a ready-made sample to follow up to explore outcomes for children.

The aims of the study

The study relates to Objective 1 of the Quality Protects programme: **to ensure that children are securely attached to carers capable of providing safe and effective care for the duration of childhood** (DH, 1998). It focuses specifically on outcomes for children who moved to kinship care at the end of care proceedings because of child protection concerns about parental care. Our specific aims were to:

1. measure placement stability over time, identifying the reasons for placement endings;
2. assess welfare outcomes for children in continuing placements, including their sense of permanency;
3. identify the factors which contributed to better or poorer outcomes in terms of placement stability and child well-being;
4. record the views of carers, children and, if possible, parents, about their experiences of kinship care and service provision;
5. consider what changes in policy or practice might be needed in relation to this placement option in order to deliver the objectives of Quality Protects and maximise child well-being.

Methods

The research used an existing four-year cohort sample of all the children from two local authorities who were placed with members of their extended family or friendship network at the end of care proceedings which were completed over the period 1.10.95 and 30.9.99 (Waterhouse, 1999, 2001). This was supplemented by children from two additional years of care proceedings, ending between 1999 and 2001 (the fifth and sixth-year cohorts), again from the same local authorities.

Data were collected for the study from the following sources:

- Case files held by Social Services departments in respect of 113 children;
- 37 interviews with kinship carers, including the completion of standardised measures of well-being for adults and children;
- 24 interviews with social workers in active or recently closed cases;
- 14 interviews with children and young people;
- two parent interviews;
- A standardised measure of well-being completed by teachers in relation to 25 children.

The research also involved a small **comparison group** of 31 children who had been the subject of care proceedings brought by the same local authorities but whose care plans were for placement in non-kin care (either fostering or adoption). These children formed part of the same cohort initially identified by Waterhouse (1999) and were drawn from the first three years of the initial set of data (1995–1998) to maximise follow-up time. Since most of the children placed with kin were very young, to facilitate comparison this "non-kin sample" was restricted to children who were under five years of age at the end of the proceedings. Because of resource constraints, information for these children was collected only from case files.

A detailed explanation of the methods and procedures used in this research is set down in Appendix A. A few limitations, however, should be noted. First, it proved virtually impossible to recruit birth parents to the study and in the end we were only able to interview two. Thus, an important dimension is missing. Second, we were only able to interview

12 children and two young people, and while this yielded rich material, those interviewed came almost entirely from continuing placements. The voices of children who had unsatisfactory placements are therefore largely absent. Third, much of the quantifiable data was file-based. This carries the risk that the more poorly recorded placements might come out better than they actually were, while others might appear more problematic simply because more information was recorded.

Structure of the report

Chapters 2, 3 and 4 of the report focus on outcomes. Chapter 2 considers placement outcomes and Chapter 3 examines how the children were faring in terms of their well-being. The outcome measures outlined in Chapters 2 and 3 are used in Chapter 4 to explore what factors explain better or poorer outcomes in kinship care.

Chapter 5 considers how decisions were made about kinship placements and the perspectives of the different parties involved. Chapter 6 outlines the challenges carers may face in caring for what were often very challenging children, the sacrifices they have to make and the stress they may experience. Chapter 7 looks at the question of support.

Chapter 8 presents the material from our interviews with children and young people and considers their perspectives on their placements. The maintenance of family links in terms of parental, sibling and extended family contact is covered in Chapter 9.

Finally, Chapter 10 draws out the implications for policy and practice.

We have used case studies throughout the report and usually given the children, and sometimes their carers, names. All names have been changed. Where cases appear more than once, we have usually not used the same names to ensure that the additional detail does not allow the families to be identified. In the chapter on children's perspectives, because of the small number of children involved, to avoid either possible breaches of confidentiality by using one name for each child or confusion by using more names than there were children interviewed, we decided not to use names at all.

2 How did placements work out?

Introduction

To address this question we first employed three outcome measures derived from Objective 1 of the Quality Protects programme (DH, 1998):

> *To ensure that children are securely attached to carers capable of providing safe and effective care for the duration of childhood.*

Outcome measure 1: *Placement stability*: did the placement last as long as needed/is the placement likely to last as long as needed?

Outcome measure 2: *Placement quality*: did the child receive safe and effective care while in placement?

Outcome measure 3: *Relationship quality*: did the child appear to have a close, emotionally supportive relationship with one or more carers while in placement?

All these measures are essentially proxy outcomes: i.e. they are conditions which research suggests should promote children's development. In the next chapter we look at a more direct measure – *child functioning* – which relates to the expected consequences of achieving the first three objectives; namely, how the child has progressed in placement. Chapter 4 then explores the factors which might help to explain differential outcomes.

Outcome measure 1: Placement stability

Evidence from previous research

Placement stability is often considered to be one of the key advantages of kinship care. It is true that kinship foster placements tend to be lengthy and to last longer than those with non-related carers.[1] Children have fewer

---

[1] Government statistics indicate that 42 per cent have lasted for two years or more compared to 29 per cent non-kin placements (DH, 2001); Farmer and Moyers (2008) report an average duration of four years and nine months, compared to three years 11 months. An average duration of four years has been reported for non-foster placements (Broad *et al*, 2001).

moves both overall and before entering placement (see Hunt, 2003a for summary). One large US study of children entering care under six and still in care eight years on, for example, found 71 per cent still in their first or second placement, compared to 48 per cent of other children (Webster *et al*, 2000).

In terms of placement disruption, however, the evidence is less clear. UK studies report very different breakdown rates, from less than 10 per cent (Rowe *et al*, 1984; Millham *et al*, 1986; Berridge and Cleaver, 1987) to a third or more (Rowe *et al*, 1989; Harwin *et al*, 2003; Hunt and Macleod, 1999; Sinclair *et al*, 2000). Sinclair *et al* (2007) report that only 15 per cent of placements with relatives were not successful (i.e. they either did not last as long as was needed or did not fully meet the child's needs).

Even the highest of these figures still appears to be lower than the 43 per cent average disruption rate for long-term fostering (Triseliotis, 2002). Indeed, a recent large study in the USA (Chamberlain *et al*, 2006) reports that non-kin foster placements were three times more likely to disrupt than kinship placements. However, in Farmer and Moyers' study (2008), the disruption rates for kin and non-kin-placed children were almost exactly the same (18% and 17% respectively). There is also recent research in the USA which indicates that, while kinship placements are more stable in the early years, after about three years kin and non-kin placements have the same chance of disrupting (Testa, 2001).

As one would expect, disruption rates are lower for adopted children. Before the adoption order is made, a breakdown rate of 18 per cent is reported (Cabinet Office, 2000). Averaging the disruption rates from a number of key studies, the rate is around five per cent for pre-school children and 15 per cent for those aged 5 to 12 (Triseliotis, 2002).

Findings from this study

Did placements last as long as needed?
Although the majority of placements in this study were intended to be long term, five were expected to be a prelude to rehabilitation[2] and two to non-kin adoption.[3] In the course of placement, 11 children returned to a parent although this was not the original plan.[4] By using the measure

'lasted as long as needed', we hoped to reflect this variability. The judgement in each case was based on the combined information from files and interviews with carers and social workers. The categorisation of lasted/did not last as long as needed was straightforward in cases where either the child was still in placement and had been continuously there since the proceedings or the placement ended in crisis. Any placement that ended in a planned way with no suggestion of breakdown was categorised as having lasted as long as needed, whether or not the move had been part of the care plan. Conversely, placements where the move was anticipated but precipitated by a problem in the kinship placement, whether or not the child's departure was carried out in a planned way, were coded as not lasting as long as needed.

Using these criteria, on the basis of the latest information available to us, 27 per cent of placements (31 of 113) did not last as long as needed[5,6]

---

[2] Three of these children returned to a parent who had previously had care following changes in parental circumstances (improved mental health, a father's release from prison, completion of counselling). These returns occurred, on average, 16 months after the end of proceedings. A fourth child spent nine months with his paternal grandmother before going to live, as planned, with his father, who had been unknown to him prior to the proceedings. Although in two of these four cases return was precipitated by problems in the kinship placement, there was no evidence that children were being returned to risky situations. In the fifth case the mother was unable to stay off drugs and the child remained with his kinship carer.

[3] The children (siblings) moved into their adoptive placements after a year. Unfortunately both broke down, as did a subsequent placement, and the children were returned to their original carer.

[4] Four of these returns were because a parent became able to care again and the placements (which lasted on average for 42 months after the end of proceedings) were deemed to have lasted as long as needed. The remaining seven, which all involved children with emotional/behavioural problems, were all placement breakdowns, although in five cases the problems in placement were clearly exacerbated by the child's desire to go back home. All the moves were achieved by consent, without the involvement of the court. There was no evidence that rehabilitation was placing any of the children at risk.

[5] Placement breakdowns will be explored in more detail in Chapter 4.

[6] On average, placements lasted for 36 months after proceedings before breakdown (minimum 7 months, maximum 79 months) with 50 per cent of placements breaking down before two years had elapsed.

(Table 2.1). These included one discontinuous placement[7] which had broken down because of the carer's inability to handle the child's behaviour. The child moved to a residential placement where his difficulties continued and after 14 months he returned to his carer, where he remains.

Table 2.1

Whether placement lasted as long as needed and whether continuing

	Did the placement last as long as needed?		Total
	Yes	No	
Placement continuing[8]	74	1[9]	75
Placement ended	8	30	38
Total	**82**	**31**	**113**

A 27 per cent rate of premature endings is obviously higher than one would wish, given the careful consideration which would have been given to the placement in the course of the care proceedings. Detailed examination of the circumstances in each case, however, suggests that from the children's point of view, the picture may be somewhat less bleak. While 16 placements would clearly be regarded as disruptions from any perspective, there were 15 which might not be considered as catastrophic endings in that often it was the child's decision to move, typically either to a parent or to another relative.

Indeed, of all the 31 children whose placements did not last as long as needed, only 14 went to carers outside the family, with nine going to other relatives (and the remainder to a parent). The extent to which some families rallied round to keep the child within the network was sometimes quite astonishing:

---

[7] By discontinuous we mean placements that were made as a result of care proceedings and were continuing at the date of last known information but where the child had spent time living elsewhere during this time.

[8] Includes discontinuous placements.

[9] This was a child who spent a period in residential care because his carers could not cope with his behaviour but subsequently returned to these carers and is living there currently.

Gina (11), Susie (9) and Corinne (7)[10] were removed from their mother because of the impact of her chronic drug abuse. Their father is dead. Their paternal grandmother had provided intensive support to the family for years and continued to do so when the children were placed, together, with their paternal aunt and uncle, who have three children of their own, of similar ages. Gina presented major behavioural difficulties from the start, which had adverse effects on the other children. She came to spend increasing amounts of time with her paternal grandmother, before moving to live there full time and eventually returning to live with her mother. This latter move destabilised Susie, the middle child, whose behaviour then deteriorated. She too asked to move and went to live with another paternal aunt and uncle. Corinne, the youngest child, remained in placement for six years before moving to live with her mother.

Another positive finding to set against the figures for premature endings is that, despite the fact that many of the placements ended in difficult circumstances, all of the carers we interviewed (6) found something positive to say about the placement. Moreover, all except one said that, knowing what they know now, they would still have made the same decision to care for the child/ren in the first place. All the carers were still in touch with the children and described quite positive current relationships. Indeed, it seems that, even where placements do not last the course, the kin carers may continue to offer support to children whether they are at home or in non-kin care. In one case where the placement ended because of the child's behaviour, for example, the carers now provide respite care for the child from her foster placement:

I do miss her if she doesn't phone, you worry if she's all right but if you ask a question she doesn't like being questioned – 'I've come to see you and not to answer questions'. I can manage her for 1–2 weeks respite. It's too stressful to have her back full time. We keep a lot of her stuff here.

---

[10]   All names have been changed.

Is kinship care more stable than other forms of care?

As described in Chapter 1, the study included a small comparison group of children, all aged under five at the end of proceedings, who were destined for non-kin care. At the point of data collection, 29 of these children had been placed for permanency, mainly through adoption (26). Only two of these placements had not lasted,[11] giving a disruption rate of seven per cent. In comparison, of the 54 children aged under five and placed with kin, six placements (11%) did not last as long as needed. However, the differences are not large, and, given the very different circumstances in which kin and non-kin carers take on children, might be regarded as surprisingly small. It should also be noted that, while most of our kin-placed children were in placement by the end of proceedings, 23 of the comparison group of children had to move. Since moves occurred on average nine months later, but could be anything between one and 32 months after the care proceedings, our follow-up periods for the non-kin-placed children were accordingly less.

Comparing our data on kinship placements which did not last as long as needed with disruption rates for non-kin foster care found in other studies, the overall figure of 27 per cent looks fairly positive, especially when compared with the 43 per cent average rate cited by Triseliotis (2002). However, when account is taken of the child's age at the outset, our outcomes for children under five appear to be worse than adoption (though considerably better than for long-term foster care) and for children aged 5–12 worse than both adoption and long-term foster care (Table 2.2).

---

[11] One because of poor care including inappropriate behaviour management and lack of warmth, the second because of conflict between the child and the carers' own child.

Table 2.2
Comparative disruption rates by age and placement type

	Kin (this study)	Adoption*	Long-term foster care*
Age	%	%	%
<5	11	5	33
5–12	43	15	35
13+	50	ND	50
All	27	ND	43

* (Triseliotis, 2002)

Farmer and Moyers (2008) report an almost identical disruption rate for under-fives (12%), but their figures for older children, although not strictly comparable, seem better (16% for children placed between the ages of five and 10 and 37% for those aged 10 or more). Their disruption rates for non-kin care were 13% for the youngest children; 35% for those placed between five and 10; and a surprisingly low 19% for those older than this.

In interpreting findings, however, it is important to bear the following considerations in mind, which suggest that like may not be being compared with like:

- Our follow-up period, between three and nine years, is likely to be much longer than most other studies. Farmer and Moyers (2008), for example, had a two-year follow-up. Half the premature endings in our study occurred after two years, with, on average, placements lasting for 36 months (minimum 7 months, maximum 79). At the two-year point only 13 per cent of the placements in our study had not lasted as long as needed.

- Our study used a cohort of children, tracked from the point they were placed. Farmer and Moyers, in contrast, used a snapshot of children in either kin or non-kin placements at a particular point in time. Their particularly lower disruption rates are therefore likely to be based on "survivor" placements. If we take into account both the cohort/ snapshot difference and the different follow-up periods, it is likely that the disruption rates in the two studies would not be very different.

- The children in our study were all placed as the result of decisions made in care proceedings, and the care given to them by their parents had therefore crossed the legal threshold of significant harm. They are, therefore, a "heavy end" group in terms of their early life experiences. While other studies will usually contain a good proportion of such children, they will be "diluted" with children who may have been somewhat less unfortunate. What is needed – and what unfortunately we did not have the resources to do – is a long-term large-scale follow-up of children of all ages who have been through care proceedings and been placed in a range of placements. The closest approximation is Hunt and Macleod's (1999) study which followed up a sample of 133 children for up to four years. This reports that of 21 children placed in long-term non-kin foster care after care proceedings, 11 placements (52%) terminated prematurely. Set against this figure, our 27 per cent disruption rate looks much more positive.

• Our criterion of whether the placement lasted as long as it needed to may be more rigorous than other studies. For instance, it included placements which had been intended to be long term but where the child went back to a parent and the move was driven by difficulties in the placement rather than positive changes in parental circumstances. It is possible that other studies would not have classed rehabilitation in these circumstances as a disruption.

For all these reasons we judge that, while on the face of it our figures suggest that kinship placements do less well than other forms of care, this would not be a reasonable conclusion to draw from the data.

Were the continuing placements likely to last as long as needed?

As reported earlier (Table 2.1), 74 placements were ongoing and had lasted as long as needed at the point of data collection.[12] We were able to rate the stability of all but two, again basing our assessment on all the information available to us.

Most continuing placements (54; 75%) were judged to be very stable and likely to last (Table 2.3). However, 13 were rated to be only reason-

---

[12] From our various data sources we have information for a mean of 56 months after proceedings, with 10 cases having information for less than one year, 23 cases for between one and five years, and 40 cases for more than five years.

ably stable and five fragile, typically because of the child's behaviour problems. In what was considered to be one of the most vulnerable placements, which had lasted for five years so far, the carer told us:

> *Some days I feel that I should hand him over. Something keeps me going. I believe in my heart he is just trying to see how far he can really go and some day soon it will all stop, maybe it's just a dream. I know as a family, as do my friends, neighbours and teachers, that we have gone over and beyond to help him. I feel he has to change himself and want to change. I am afraid that if changes are not made with him soon then I will have to give up and say we tried the best we could. I am crying as I say that because I do love him but can't stand the horrible life he is creating. He has no feelings, no remorse and a "don't care" attitude. He will do what he wants when he wants and does not care who he is hurting. I just pray he changes soon.*

Overall, then, taking the most pessimistic view of the data, giving what we have termed our "*worst case scenario*", only 62 of the 111 sample children on which information was available (56%) could be said to have unreservedly positive outcomes on this measure, in that their placements had either terminated but lasted as long as was needed or were continuing and there was no evidence to suggest that they might not last as long as needed. A rather more optimistic interpretation, in which "reasonably stable" placements continue, would give a figure of 68 per cent (the *best case scenario*).

Local authority A had rather poorer results on the placement stability outcome than Authority B, with only 48 per cent of placements lasting as long as needed or continuing and stable compared to 65 per cent in Authority B. Thirty-one per cent of Authority A's placements terminated prematurely (compared to 25% of Authority B's) and 13 per cent of their continuing placements were fragile (compared to 3%). However, these differences did not reach statistical significance.

Table 2.3
Placement stability for all placements

	Authority A		Authority B		All cases	
	No.	%	No.	%	No.	%
Continuing and stable	24	41	30	58	54	49
Continuing but vulnerable	13	22	5	10	18	16
Ended but lasted as long as needed	4	7	4	8	8	7
Did not last as long as needed	18	31	13	25	31	28
(N=)	(59)		(52)		(111)	

Comparison with children under five placed with non-kin carers

As reported earlier, only six per cent of our comparison group of *non-kin* placements of children aged under five did not last as long as needed, compared with 11 per cent of our *kinship* sample of under-fives. This group also fared somewhat better in terms of whether the placement was likely to last, but again, the differences were very small (16% compared to 19% being regarded as vulnerable [Table 2.4]). Overall, 77 per cent of the non-kin sample were in stable placements compared to 65 per cent of the kin-placed group. Again, we would emphasise that, given the differences in the circumstances of related and non-kin carers, one should not be unduly pessimistic about these outcomes.

Table 2.4
Placement stability in kinship and non-kin care of under-fives

	Non-kin		Kin under five	
	No.	%	No.	%
Continuing and stable	24	77	35	65
Continuing but vulnerable	5	16	10	19
Ended but lasted as long as needed	0	0	3	6
Did not last as long as needed	2	6	6	11
(N=)	(31)		(54)	

Outcome measure 2: Placement quality

Unlike placement stability, quality of care is not usually advanced as an argument for promoting kinship care. Indeed, it is more likely to be identified as a possible defect, to be weighed against potential advantages (Rittner, 1995; Ehrle *et al*, 2001; Sinclair *et al*, 2007). A common theme in the international literature is that many kinship carers would not meet the standards required for non-kin foster carers. This may be for a variety of reasons: age; physical capacity and health; parenting capacity and style; accommodation; or family relationships (Hannah and Pitman, 2000).

Outcome measure 2 looks at the ability of the carers to provide 'safe and effective care' in six domains: protection from child abuse and neglect; provision for basic needs; meeting the child's emotional needs; behaviour management; environmental factors and the child's experience of change. Inevitably, there is some overlap between these categories and some individual items could arguably be located in other domains. The aim, however, is to provide data on the range of factors which are likely to affect children's development and well-being. The items[13] have been influenced by the, admittedly limited, literature on quality issues in kinship care (notably Wells, 1999; Shlonsky and Berrick, 2001). We end the section with two more summary measures: any assessment by Social Services of the carer's parenting capacity, and our own overall assessment of the quality of placement based on all the evidence available to us.

Protection from abuse and neglect

Previous research
Relatives do, on occasion, abuse children in their care, as the Climbié inquiry (Laming, 2003) showed all too clearly. There are references in a

---

[13] In addition to the factors mentioned, we also looked at the following factors but no occurrences were found: abuse of another child in the household; child being afraid of anyone in the household; concerns about level of supervision of the child; concerns about ability to deal with issues related to reasons for child's placement; criminal behaviour by carer or others in the household; child protection case conference held about any child in the household.

small number of research studies (see Hunt, 2003a), perhaps the most chilling being a US study of sexual abuse involving grandparents, which found that 10 per cent of the children had been living permanently with their abuser (Margolin, 1992).

There is, however, surprisingly little focused research on incidence and findings are mixed in relation to whether children are more or less at risk than in non-kin care. In one large US study (Dubowitz *et al*, 1993), allegations of maltreatment, half of which involved the relative carer, were made in 12 per cent of cases. Twenty-one per cent of all reports were substantiated. Although the research did not use a comparison group of children in non-related care, these figures for both report and substantiation were noted to be higher than those found in other studies of foster care. However, other American studies have found lower rates of confirmed abuse (see Hunt, 2003a).

In the UK, Farmer and Moyers (2008) found a four per cent rate of substantiated abuse in both kinship and non-kin placements, although there were rather more unsubstantiated allegations in the former (4% compared to 1%). Nixon and Verity (1996, cited in Nixon, 1999) found that, in one year, there were allegations of abuse in four per cent of non-kin foster placements with half of these being substantiated.

Findings from this study

It is a tragedy when any child is abused or neglected. It is perhaps particularly to be regretted where children have been removed from home because of concerns about the standard of parental care and placed, after careful consideration by a range of professionals, with carers who have been scrutinised and judged safe.

This study does not indicate that there are substantial grounds for concern about kinship placements. However, 10 per cent of cases did raise issues in this domain (Table 2.5). Just under half of these placements were continuing.

Table 2.5
Protection from abuse and neglect

	Occurrence		Placement continuing		Placement[14] ended	
(N=)	No.	%	No.	% (where identified)	No.	% (where identified)
Substantiated abuse						
(111)	4	4	2	50	2	50
Neglect of the child						
(111)	8	7	4	50	4	50
Exposure to sexual activity						
(108)	2	2	0	0	2	100
Any of these issues						
(111)	11	10	5	45	6	55

- There were allegations of abuse or exposure to substantial risk in six cases, of which four (4% of all cases) were substantiated.[15]
  - Two of the four substantiated incidents involved serious sexual abuse. In one case the child was removed because of abuse by the carer. In the other the child told the carer about abuse by a visitor to the household. The carer took immediate action and the child remained in placement.
  - The third case involved the carer hitting the child with a belt (the placement continued) and the fourth a child being put at risk by being repeatedly left in the care of a relative with a history of sexual abuse. This child was removed.

---

[14] Although these placements have ended we are not inferring that they ended due to the issues identified in the table. They may have ended in crisis or lasted as long as needed and ended in planned moves.

[15] One case where the alleged abuse was not substantiated involved a girl who made an allegation of sexual abuse against the kinship carer's son. This was fully investigated by the police but the case was dropped due to inconsistencies in her story. As the child wanted to live with other relatives, Social Services concluded that the allegation was invented to engineer the move (which did subsequently happen). The other unsubstantiated allegation was that the carer left the child in the care of a grandfather who had previously sexually abused the child's mother. This allegation was deemed to be malicious and part of the mother's repeated attempts to disrupt the placement.

Two sisters were reported to have watched "adult" videos whilst in their kinship placement. The placement subsequently terminated but not for this reason.

In eight cases (7%) there were concerns about neglect. In one placement of three siblings the family support worker was so concerned about the standards of care, which included the children being scruffy and wearing shoes which were too small for them, that she made an official complaint. Half these placements continued.

Meeting basic needs

Previous research
Unlike non-kin foster carers, who are likely to be recruited because of their above-average parenting skills, kinship carers tend to be just normal people, with all the variability that entails. International research paints a picture of a spectrum of standards in kinship placements (see Hunt, 2003a) with one US study describing care ranging from excellent to grossly inadequate (Dubowitz *et al*, 1993). Two American surveys of social workers reported that between a half to just under a quarter did not consider that kinship carers provided competent parenting (Beeman and Boisen, 1999; Chipungu and Everett, 1998). Another study reported that 29 per cent of kinship homes fell below the standard of the average non-kin foster home (Berrick *et al*, 1999). The level of concern generated by these findings prompted the US government to commission an investigation, which reported that, in more than 90 per cent of both related and non-related foster care, almost all parenting tasks were carried out adequately (GAO, 1999).

The limited amount of UK research has tended to be positive (Rowe *et al*, 1984; Hunt and Macleod, 1999; Harwin *et al*, 2003). Farmer and Moyers (2008) are slightly more cautionary, finding that family and friends carers were less likely to have very good parenting skills than non-related carers (47% compared to 81%); and significantly more likely to have poor parenting skills (25% compared to 12%). Substantially more were struggling to cope (45% compared to 30%). Sinclair reports that, although social workers saw many advantages in kinship placements, on average they were judged to be of poorer quality than non-kin placements (Sinclair *et al*, 2007).

Findings from this study

There were concerns about some elements in this domain in 25 cases, 23 per cent of the 111 for which data was available (Table 2.6). Most of these placements (64%) are continuing.

Table 2.6
Meeting basic needs

	Occurrence		Placement continuing		Placement ended	
(N=)	*No.*	*%*	*No.*	*% (where identified)*	*No.*	*% (where identified)*
Ability to care impeded by age/physical disability						
(111)	13	12	10	77	3	23
Abuse of drugs/alcohol by carer						
(111)	5	5	2	40	3	60
Domestic violence in the household						
(111)	1	1	1	100	0	0
Ability to care impeded by mental illness						
(111)	2	2	1	50	1	50
Concerns that the family was socially isolated						
(111)	4	4	3	75	1	25
Unsatisfactory care of the child when carer not available						
(111)	4	4	2	50	2	50
Carers' attitude to school						
(100)	2	2	1	50	1	50
Any of these issues identified						
(111)	25	23	16	64	9	36

The most common problem was the carers' ability to care being compromised by age or physical disability (13 cases; 12%). These figures are much lower than those reported in other studies,[16] probably because all the placements in our study had been made through the court process. It

---

[16] Richards (2001): 48 per cent of grandparents had long-standing health problems or disabilities which limited their activities; Farmer and Moyers (2008): 31 per cent of carers had severe health difficulties; Aldgate and McIntosh (2006): 58 per cent of carers had a long-term illness or disability.

should be noted that, while in seven of these cases the problem had been identified as a potential issue at the time of the proceedings, in another 15, problems which had been anticipated in terms of the carer's age/ disability did not materialise.

Other problems were rare:

- *Alcohol misuse by the carer* (5 cases). For one carer, who was arrested for being drunk and disorderly and assaulting another woman in the street, this was only one of a multitude of deficits in care which culminated in the local authority beginning care proceedings.
- *Domestic violence* (1). This was a single reported incident which the child was not thought to have witnessed.
- *Ability to care impeded by mental illness* (2). In one case this was identified at the time of proceedings as being a potential concern. In the other the carer's partner developed dementia. Neither of these placements were with sole carers at the time of placement but one carer with mental illness concerns was widowed during the placement.
- *Social isolation* (4). These families were described as lacking support networks although this had not been identified as an issue during proceedings. The carers were all grandparents; two being lone carers, which chimes with concerns arising from our interviews with children about the more restricted social networks of some children placed with grandparents (Chapter 9).
- *Unsatisfactory arrangements for care in the carer's absence* (4). These concerns related to children being cared for by teenagers or by too many different people.
- *The carer's attitude to school* (2). One set of carers were reported to be uninterested in the child's schooling. The other instance was more complex with the carer finding it difficult to interact with the school, being perceived as unco-operative and blaming the school for the difficulties.

Meeting the child's emotional needs

Children who have suffered abuse and neglect, particularly in their early years, are likely to have special needs and present carers with serious challenges (Murphy, 1988; O'Reilly and Morrison, 1993; Cox, 2000). Love, commitment and levels of parenting skills which would be adequate in ordinary circumstances, may not be enough. Such children may need exceptional skill and patience (Smith *et al*, 1999) from carers who can understand difficult behaviour and have the skills to repair some of the damage the children have experienced (Broad *et al*, 2001).

Previous research
Kinship carers may lack this skill and understanding. Gebel (1996), for instance, found that kin carers had significantly lower levels of empathy towards children's needs than non-kin foster carers. In a survey of practitioners in the US (Terling-Watt, 2001), workers stated that many relative carers were simply not equipped to deal with the issues, that they were uninformed and unrealistic about their ability to address the children's problems, believing, mistakenly, that time and love would be sufficient. In the UK, Berridge and Cleaver (1987) reported that many carers were clearly unprepared for the demands that emotionally deprived children would make on them.

On the other hand, there are some positive indicators. For instance, Malos and Bullard (1991) noted the high degree of sensitivity displayed by carers. Le Prohn (1994) considered that kinship carers were more willing than non-related carers to focus on the child's experience of separation and loss; and Flynn (2001) writes that carers wanted to help children deal with painful feelings and support them through life changes.

Findings from this study
Meeting the child's emotional needs was an issue in 15 of the sample cases. This included lack of bonding, rejection, or negative interactions. There were also 11 cases where the child was moved at the carer's request, either permanently or for temporary relief, and another eight where the carer asked for this at the point of crisis but subsequently relented. In all there were 27 cases (24%) where one or more of these conditions applied (Table 2.7). Most of these placements (70%) terminated.

Table 2.7
Meeting the child's emotional needs

	Occurrence		Placement continuing		Placement ended	
(N=)	*No.*	*%*	*No.*	*% (where identified)*	*No.*	*% (where identified)*
Failure to meet child's emotional needs						
(109)	15	14	5	33	10	67
Carers requested removal of child						
(111)	19	17	5	26	14	74
Either of these issues identified						
(111)	27	24	8	30	19	70

Behaviour management

A closely related issue is the capacity of kinship carers to manage difficult behaviour.

Previous research

Several writers have commented that kinship carers are less likely than non-related carers to see children as problematic and difficult to handle (Farmer and Parker, 1991; Gebel, 1996; McFadden, 1998). While this may indicate a degree of carer naivety, it could also reflect a greater readiness to tolerate "problem" behaviour and persevere despite difficulties. For instance, one US study (Hatmaker, 1999) found that compared to non-kin placements, kin-placed children tended to be viewed more positively; carers found it easier to provide care; children seemed to be better understood; and negative traits were more frequently balanced with positive aspects of behaviour or personalities, with carers being more tolerant of shortcomings and willing to overlook discipline problems because the reasons for them were well understood. On the other hand, some kinship carers are reported either to be over-indulgent (O'Reilly and Morrison, 1993) or to resort to methods of discipline which professionals consider inappropriate (Gebel, 1996; Berrick, 1997; Osby, 1999).

Findings from this study

Twenty-nine cases (26%) raised concerns in this domain. More than half these placements had terminated (Table 2.8). The issues were:

- concerns over ineffective discipline or control (15 cases; 14%) – these mostly related to the carer's perceived failure to set appropriate boundaries.
- child judged to be beyond control (13 children; 12%) – (only seven of these were also those where effective discipline/control was an issue).
- concerns about excessive or inappropriate punishment, for example, taking away all a boy's best clothes because he wore a T-shirt under his football kit (eight cases; 7%).

Table 2.8

Behaviour management

(N=)	Occurrence		Placement continuing		Placement ended	
	No.	%	No.	% (where identified)	No.	% (where identified)
Ineffective discipline						
(111)	15	14	8	53	7	47
Child beyond control						
(110)	13	12	5	38	8	62
Inappropriate punishment of the child						
(111)	8	7	3	38	5	62
Any of these issues identified						
(111)	29	26	13	45	16	55

Environmental factors

When traditional foster carers take on the care of a child they will normally do so after careful consideration as to whether they have the financial and material (as well as physical and emotional) resources to do so. Kinship carers, in contrast, often take on care despite the strain this may put on capacity which may be already limited. This domain examines three factors within the child's environment which may have a negative impact on the child: financial hardship, accommodation problems, and substance abuse by people within the household other than the carer. In all, concerns about one or more of these issues were noted in 23 per cent of cases (25, Table 2.9). More than half the children in these cases (56%) were still in placement.

Table 2.9
Environmental factors

	Occurrence		Placement continuing		Placement ended	
(N=)	No.	%	No.	% (where identified)	No.	% (where identified)
Serious financial issues						
(111)	9	8	3	33	6	67
Inadequate housing provision						
(111)	13	12	7	54	6	46
Abuse of drugs/alcohol by anyone else in the household						
(111)	5	5	3	60	2	40
Any of these issues identified						
(111)	25	23	11	44	14	56

Financial hardship

The financing of kinship care is a major issue, which we look at in more detail in Chapter 7. Taking on additional dependants, usually unexpectedly, would challenge most households and there is a great deal of research indicating that many kinship carers struggle to manage financially (see Hunt, 2003a). A UK study of grandparent carers, for example, found that 72 per cent had experienced financial hardship as the result of taking on care; with 43 per cent either giving up work or reducing their hours (Richards, 2001). Farmer and Moyers (2008) report that 75 per cent of carers experienced financial hardship.

It was therefore somewhat surprising to find that in our study, while there was evidence of some financial strain in many cases, there appeared to be only nine (8%) where financial hardship was ever serious enough to have an impact on the care given to the child, although in one case it did threaten to disrupt the placement. While all these nine families were receiving some kind of financial support at the point the file data/placement ended, it does beg the question of how well financial need had been assessed in the first place in those cases. On the other hand, the relatively low proportion of cases with serious financial hardship may reflect the nature of our sample and the involvement of the courts.

Housing

Previous research has also highlighted accommodation as a serious problem for kinship care households (Pitcher, 1999; Laws, 2001; Richards, 2001). Farmer and Moyers (2008), for example, estimated that 35 per cent of kinship households were overcrowded.

The proportion in our study was lower, with concerns about inadequate housing provision, typically involving overcrowding, in 13 cases (12%). Again this probably reflects the nature of our sample. In ten cases the problem was identified at the point of placement while in two it resulted from other people joining the household or the family moving and staying temporarily with relatives. In six cases the problems were resolved during the placement with house moves. In seven cases, however, the problem remained at the point the file data ends or at the point the placement ended. For example:

- A child living with his carer in a one-bed flat in a complex for the elderly. This situation continued for the duration of the six-year placement. Re-housing was offered but refused by the carer.
- Two siblings living, for over two years, with four other children and two adults in a three-bedroom house.
- One placement ended at least partly because of overcrowding. Sadly, although Social Services had agreed funding for an extension, the plans were rejected by the planning authority.

Substance misuse by other members of the household

As reported earlier, there were a small number of cases where there were concerns about the carer's abuse of alcohol. There were also five cases where others in the household, either adult children of the carers or the child's older siblings, were misusing drugs or alcohol.

The child's experiences of change in the placement[17]

The lives of many of the children in this study prior to placement were marked by substantial turbulence (see next chapter). We therefore felt it was important to assess how far the placement provided them with a more stable experience.

Change, of course, is an unavoidable part of life. Children go to school or move up to a senior school; adult children leave home; babies are born; families move house. All these might be regarded as *normative* changes. Fifty-two of the children in this study experienced at least one of these changes (Table 2.10):

- Almost a quarter (23%) moved house, typically to obtain more space/ more suitable accommodation. Most of the moves were single moves or, averaged over the period of time we have data for, were not frequent occurrences.
- Only five children (6%) changed school for reasons other than the normal transition between school levels. These moves either related to house moves or were due to children moving from mainstream school to special educational provision.
- Forty-three children (44%) experienced some movement of persons in and out of the household (adults in 24% of cases; children in 20%). Most of the movement of adults is explained by carers' children reaching maturity and moving out, adult children of the carers' moving in and out and elderly relatives moving elsewhere or dying. A number of children were born to kinship carers and this resulted in additional children in the household.

Even normative changes, of course, might be problematic for insecure and vulnerable children. *Non-normative* changes are potentially even more difficult. Eighteen children (17%) experienced at least one such change and five per cent more than one.

---

[17] Excludes all discontinuous placements as by definition these children had experienced a great deal of change unique to their circumstances.

Table 2.10
The child's experiences of change in the placement

(N=)	Occurrence		Placement continuing		Placement ended	
	No.	%	No.	% (where identified)	No.	% (where identified)
Changes in the placement						
Normative changes:						
House moves						
(102)	23	23	20	87	3	13
School moves						
(84)	5	6	3	60	2	40
Adults left/joined/both						
(99)	24	24	22	92	2	8
Children left/joined/both						
(103)	19	18	12	63	7	37
Children experiencing any of these changes						
(104)	52	50	39	75	13	25
Children experiencing one of these changes						
(104)	37	36	25	68	12	32
Children experiencing two or more of these changes						
(104)	15	14	14	93	1	7
Non-normative changes:						
Carer relationship breakdown						
(104)	6	6	3	50	3	50
Absence of main carer						
(101)	10	10	4	40	6	60
Placement breakdown of sibling						
(103)	5	5	1	20	4	80
Difficult house moves						
(102)	2	2	0	0	2	100
Children experiencing any of these changes						
(104)	18	17	8	44	10	56
Children experiencing one of these changes						
(104)	13	13	8	62	5	39
Children experiencing two or more of these changes						
(104)	5	5	0	0	5	100

Partnership breakdown

The risk of partnership breakdown in kinship placements has been high-lighted in a number of studies (Burton, 1992; Jendrek, 1994; Worrall, 1996). This affected six children in our study. Two experienced the perm-anent breakdown of their carer's relationship and two temporary separation and reconciliation. Two children had to cope with even greater change with the breakdown and formation of multiple relationships by the carer.

Absence or loss of main carer

Ten children (10%) had to cope with the loss or absence of their main carer. Sadly, two children were bereaved. Seven experienced the hospital-isation of their main carer and one child's carer was absent because of an army posting abroad.

Breakdown of sibling placement

Five children witnessed a breakdown of a sibling's placement in the kinship household. In one sibling group of three, each child's placement consecutively broke down, with the youngest sibling witnessing place-ment breakdowns for two of his siblings.

Non-normative house/school moves

Two children experienced moves which may have been difficult for them. In one case this resulted from the breakdown of the carer's relationship. Another child experienced multiple house moves and changes of school because of the carer's army postings.

Placement quality issues: a summary

In all, as can be seen from Table 2.11, in 41 per cent of cases there appeared to be no concerns whatsoever about the quality of the place-ment, while a further 23 per cent had concerns in only one area. Most of these placements were still continuing. However, 36 per cent raised concerns in more than one area. While more of these tended to have ended (half of those with issues in two and 64 per cent of those with more than this), 17 children were still in placement.

Table 2.11
Summary of incidence of issues within placement quality domains

	Occurrence		Placement continuing		Placement ended	
(N=)	*No.*	*%*	*No.*	*% (where identified)*	*No.*	*% (where identified)*
Placement quality issue						
Abuse/neglect						
(111)	11	10	5	45	6	55
Basic needs						
(111)	25	23	16	64	9	36
Meeting emotional needs						
(111)	27	24	8	30	19	70
Behaviour management						
(111)	29	26	13	45	16	55
Environmental factors						
(111)	25	23	11	44	14	56
Non-normative change						
(104)	18	17	8	44	10	56
All domains						
No issues in any domain						
(111)	46	41	38	83	8	17
Any issues in any domain						
(111)	65	59	35	54	30	46
Any issues in 1 domain						
(111)	25	23	18	72	7	28
Any issues in 2 domains						
(111)	18	16	9	50	9	50
Any issues in 3+ domains (max 4)						
(111)	22	20	8	36	14	64

Social worker assessment of carer capacity

In addition to the detailed analysis of these various placement quality domains, we also looked for and categorised, any assessment of the carer's parenting by Social Services. The carers of 78 per cent of children were rated as having good parenting capacity (Table 2.12). Fifteen per cent were judged acceptable and seven per cent marginal. Four of these latter (seven) placements are no longer continuing and one has been discontinuous, having ended initially because the carers could not cope with the child's behaviour.

Table 2.12

Assessed parenting capacity by whether the placement had ended

		Occurrence		Placement continuing		Placement ended	
	(N=)	*No.*	*%*	*No.*	*% (where identified)*	*No.*	*% (where identified)*
Assessed parenting capacity							
Good	(102)	80	78	53	66	27	34
Acceptable	(102)	15	15	10	67	5	33
Marginal	(102)	7	7	3	43	4	57

Researcher rating

Finally, as a team we collectively rated the placements using the information available to us from the files, the carer interviews and the social worker interviews. We rated all the placements using the same criteria regardless of whether they were continuing or not.

Table 2.13

Researcher rating and whether the placement is continuing or has ended

		Occurrence		Placement continuing		Placement ended	
	(N=)	*No.*	*%*	*No.*	*% (where identified)*	*No.*	*% (where identified)*
Researcher rating							
Positive							
	(111)	63	57	57	90	6	10
Some concerns							
	(111)	21	19	12	57	9	43
Seriously problematic							
	(111)	27	24	4	15	23	85

Fifty-seven per cent of placements were rated as positive, 19 per cent were rated as having some concerns and 24 per cent as seriously problematic (Table 2.13). Almost all the latter group of placements had terminated although four (15%) were continuing, as were more than half the placements where we judged there were some concerns.

Overall rating of placement quality

To sum up this section, in 41 per cent of cases no concerns were raised in any of the placement quality domains, while at the other end of the spectrum 20 per cent had issues in three or more. Seventy-eight per cent of carers were rated by social workers as having good parenting capacity, with seven per cent being marginal. The research team rated 57 per cent of placements as positive but 24 per cent as seriously problematic (Table 2.14).

We combined these ratings to give an overall measure of placement quality:

- *Problem-free*: 40 placements (36%) raised no issues in any of the placement domains, parenting capacity was rated as good and the researcher rating was positive.
- *Some concerns*: for 49 placements (44%) there was at least one problematic area in terms of either issues in the placement quality domains, or assessed parenting capacity, or researcher rating.
- *Major concerns*: 22 placements (20%) had three or more issues in any of the placement domains, parenting capacity was rated as only acceptable or marginal and the placement had some concerns or was seriously problematic according to the researcher rating.

On the harshest interpretation of these findings – the *worst case scenario* – just over a third of placements were of unimpeachable quality. In the *best case scenario*, however, only a fifth were seriously worrying. Our findings are not directly comparable to those of Farmer and Moyers (2008) who used only two categories – satisfactory (66% of kin placements) and problematic (34%), although they also report that 10% of placements were extremely poor. However, the messages from the two studies would seem to be the same: the majority of kinship placements are probably good enough, but there is a not insubstantial minority which raise serious quality issues.

Table 2.14

Summary of placement quality issues

(N=)	Occurrence		Placement continuing		Placement ended	
	No.	%	No.	% (where identified)	No.	% (where identified)
Placement quality issue						
Placement domains						
No issues in any domain						
(111)	46	41	38	83	8	17
Issues in 1 or 2 domains						
(111)	43	39	27	63	16	37
Issues in 3+ domains						
(111)	22	20	8	36	14	64
Assessed parenting capacity						
Good						
(102)	80	78	53	66	27	34
Acceptable						
(102)	15	15	10	67	5	33
Marginal						
(102)	7	7	3	43	4	57
Researcher rating						
Positive						
(111)	63	57	57	90	6	10
Some concerns						
(111)	21	19	12	57	9	43
Seriously problematic						
(111)	27	24	4	15	23	85
Overall rating						
Problem-free						
(111)	40	36	36	90	4	10
Some concerns						
(111)	49	44	29	59	20	41
Major concerns						
(111)	22	20	8	36	14	64

Local authority differences

As noted earlier, Local Authority A had rather poorer outcomes on the placement stability measure than Authority B, with fewer placements lasting as long as needed or being continuing and stable. We wondered whether this might mean that Authority B had a higher proportion of placements which were continuing but of poorer quality. However, the reverse proved to be the case, with 16 per cent of the continuing placements in Authority A being judged to be of poorer quality, compared to only six per cent in Authority B. When all placements were considered, however, there was little difference between the two authorities with regard to any of the placement quality domains, the researcher rating, perceived parenting capacity or overall placement quality rating.

Comparison with children placed with non-kin carers

When we compared our sample of children under five in non-kin care with the sub-group of under-five kin-placed children, it was found that the non-kin placements fared better than the kinship placements in three of the five placement quality domains for which we had information (Table 2.15). The largest differences were in the domains of basic needs and environmental factors – which is scarcely surprising as most of the non-kin placements would have been through a thorough adoption assessment. Interestingly, however, the kinship placements fared better in their ability to meet the child's emotional needs. Therefore, it appears that although there are a number of specific aspects of placement quality where non-kin placements fare better than kinship placements, in terms of meeting the child's emotional needs the outcome in kinship placements may be better. This is despite the assessed parenting capacity of the non-kin carers being slightly higher than that of the kinship carers (6% difference).

Farmer and Moyers (2008) report that although non-kin placements were most likely to be rated satisfactory (73% compared with 66%), the difference was not statistically significant.

Table 2.15
Placement quality in kin and non-kin placements

Placement quality issue	Non-kin		Kin <5	
	No.	%	No.	%
Abuse/neglect	1	3	5	9
Basic needs	2	6	11	20
Failure to meet emotional needs	6	19	6	11
Behaviour management	5	16	9	17
Environmental factors	0	0	5	9
Assessed parenting capacity				
Good	28	90	41	76
Acceptable/marginal	3	10	8	15
(N =)	(31)		(54)	

Placement stability and placement quality

Our earlier analysis of placement stability indicated that 73 per cent (82) of placements had lasted as long as was needed or were still continuing. Of those which were still continuing and had lasted as long as needed, 54 (75%) were judged to be very stable and likely to last. However, 13 were rated to be only reasonably stable and six fragile, typically because of the child's behaviour problems.

As Table 2.16 shows, of the 62 placements which had achieved the Quality Protects objective in terms of stability on our most rigorous measure (lasted as long as needed and were likely to last), 39 (63%) also did so in terms of placement quality (problem-free). Only one of the 18 continuing but more vulnerable placements was problem-free in terms of placement quality and none of the placements which did not last were free of any placement quality concerns. Therefore, the less stable placements and those that did not last also tended to be poorer in terms of placement quality.

Table 2.16
Overall placement quality rating by placement stability

Placement stability	(N=)	Overall placement quality					
		Problem-free		Some concerns		Major concerns	
		No.	%	No.	%	No.	%
Lasted as long as needed/likely to last	(62)	39	63	23	37	0	0
Continuing but reasonably stable/fragile	(18)	1	6	10	56	7	39
Did not last as long as needed	(31)	0	0	16	52	15	48

Overall, of the 111 placements for which information was available on both our first two outcome measures, 39 placements (35%) could be described as entirely positive, in that they were continuing and stable, or had lasted as long as needed and did not raise any concerns about quality (Table 2.17). At the other end of the spectrum, 15 placements (14%) had not lasted as long as needed *and* had had major quality issues. This provides our *worst case scenario*, i.e. the outcome produced by using the harshest measures of both placement stability and placement quality.

Table 2.17
Placement stability and placement quality, worst case scenario

Placement stability	Overall placement quality					
	Problem-free		Some concerns		Major concerns	
	No.	%	No.	%	No.	%
Lasted as long as needed/likely to last	39	35	23	21	0	0
Vulnerable	1	1	10	9	7	6
Did not last as long as needed	0	0	16	14	15	14

N = 111

41

A more positive picture is produced if we take as our measure of stability whether a placement was continuing/had lasted as long as needed and whether a placement had *major* quality issues as our measure of quality. In this *best case scenario*, 59 per cent of placements would be deemed to meet the Quality Protects objective in terms of both stability and quality.

Continuing placements of poor quality

Farmer and Moyers (2008) found that unsatisfactory kin placements continued for significantly longer than poor non-kin foster placements, with 67 per cent of the former lasting for more than two years (compared to 34% of the latter) and 27 per cent for more than six (5%). They suggest two explanations for this: infrequent monitoring and referrals about concerns being ignored and social workers allowing standards to fall considerably below those that would be accepted in non-kin foster care.

Our figures are rather similar – 73 per cent of poor quality placements which ended (and all of those which were continuing) lasted for more than two years, although only one went on for more than six years. (It should be noted, however, that this does not necessarily mean that placements had been poor for all that time.) Some of the social workers we interviewed also commented on the dilemmas practitioners can face. One put it in general terms.

> *With foster care (we are) more inclined to remove, it's clearer when a placement is not good for a child. With kinship, do we maintain the placement at any cost?*

Another social worker, who had been involved in one of the poor quality placements which had recently terminated, when asked whether the approach would have been different if the child had been in a non-kin placement, told us:

> *With hindsight yes, he probably would have been moved earlier but because it was with kin and he had been there a long time . . .*

We looked in detail at the five continuing poor quality placements where there was current social worker involvement. In two, the most likely reason for the placement being allowed to continue was the lack of any viable alternative. Indeed, in one case this had been amply demonstrated because the child had actually been removed and then returned to the placement.

Freddie, aged seven, already had serious behavioural problems when he was removed from his mother's care after years of neglect, exposure to domestic violence and parental drug addiction and placed with his paternal grandparents. Although his presentation improved, there was no sustained improvement in his behaviour and he was diagnosed with ADHD and learning difficulties. His grandmother, now also having to look after a husband with dementia, struggled to cope with Freddie's behaviour and on at least one occasion over-chastised him. When he was 14, Freddie was moved to residential care. However, over the next 18 months his behaviour worsened with self-harm, risky behaviour and aggression to peers. After further assessment it was decided that he would fare better if, in accordance with his wishes, he was returned to the care of his grandmother, with a support package in place.

The lack of a viable alternative may become more salient as the children get older, with a much poorer success rate in non-kin foster care for older children (Sinclair, 2005). Also, it is more likely that the young people themselves may reject alternative placements and vote with their feet about where they want to live.

In another case, a difficult dilemma was posed by a sibling placement where one sibling's placement was of better quality because she had far fewer difficulties. This placement was likely to be continuing because of the sibling's positive placement and because to end the poor quality placement would result in either splitting the siblings or disrupting the other successful placement.

In one further case with current local authority involvement, it was more difficult to identify why the placement was still continuing. The concerns were about neglect and the basic parenting ability of the kinship carer. Three of the child's siblings had already left the placement (two because the children ran away, one moved to improve the child's emotional well-being) and the concerns had been identified whilst the siblings were in placement. The remaining child, placed at 10 months and now seven years old, and a later-born sibling (not part of our cohort) was also now living there. This may explain, to some extent, why this placement was still continuing.

Thus, it appears that in our sample of continuing poor quality placements with current local authority involvement, there was some kind of explanation other than lack of monitoring or the acceptance of lower standards. It is also important to remember that more of the terminated placements were of poor quality, so it appears that most unsatisfactory placements were not being left to continue. At what point placements cease to be good enough and the disadvantages to the child of poor care outweigh the advantages of staying in the family will continue to be one of the most difficult issues with which social workers have to grapple. However, the evidence from this study does not suggest that simply letting poor quality placements continue was a widespread problem in our study authorities.

Outcome measure 3: Relationships within the household

This measure was an attempt to estimate the extent to which our kinship placements met the Quality Protects objective that children should be securely attached to their carer. The ideal, of course, would have been to complete validated attachment measures with all the children, and/or with their carers, or at least with social workers familiar with the child. This was not possible. The available data only allow us to make an approximation using information about relationships within the household.

Previous research

Assessing relationship quality is difficult and has not been systematically addressed in kinship research. However, a number of researchers and practitioners have commented on the warmth and loving nature of relationships in most kinship placements (Adamson, 1969; Rowe et al, 1984; Altshuler, 1999; Smith et al, 1999). Wilson and Conroy (1999), for instance, report that children in kinship care were more likely to say they 'always' felt loved compared to children in non-kin care. Even in Poland, where social workers, it is reported, generally have a poor view of kinship placements, the strong emotional bonds between carers and children are acknowledged (Stelmaszuk, 1999). Farmer and Moyers (2008) report that 99 per cent of kinship children were close to at least one of their carers.

Comparative data is limited. In a study of children late-placed for permanence in adoption or long-term foster care, Quinton *et al* (1998) found that, after one year in placement, 43 per cent of children had "good" attachment (mutual attachment to both new parents), 30 per cent had "intermediate" attachment (showing signs of attachment to one parent) and 27 per cent had "poor" attachment (few signs of attachment to either parent). Comparing adoption and long-term fostering, Selwyn and Quinton (2004) found that 73 per cent of adopted children in the sample were described as close to their carer with the figure being only about half for fostered children.

Findings from this study

Relationship with carer(s)
The available data indicate that almost all kin-placed children (96; 92%) had developed close relationships with at least one carer. Most (87; 91%), were either close to their sole carer, or to both carers, although there were nine children (9%) who were close to only one of their two carers. The majority of the children (80; 92%) who had a close relationship with a carer were also thought to be definitely attached to them. The remaining eight children were thought to have some attachment to a carer.

Most of the carers we interviewed reported that they were, or had been, very close to the child or children:

We are extremely close. Clearly, you get a child for the first time it takes a while even with your own baby. It's gone at a normal pace the way it should do.

More like a mother's feeling for a child. He has changed, he is more caring.

We are so close to him, we all are. Always have been.

Some of these close relationships had developed during the placement and some had existed even before the child moved to the carers. Almost all carers also considered that the children saw/had seen themselves as part of the family, with only two having some reservations about this, and all but one that the child felt secure.

We also asked social workers to describe the relationship between the child and the carer(s). Most workers (19) said only positive things about the relationship between the carer(s) and the children: 'loving, nurturing, warm, protective', with only five being negative: 'critical, ambivalent, stifling, cold, blaming'.

Despite predominantly close relationships, tension between the child and the carer was noted in nine cases (8%). In seven of these the child was recorded as being beyond control so the tension may have been a product of this. Farmer and Moyers' (2008) figure was much higher (40%). Moreover, having a close relationship with a carer did not preclude a child wanting to live elsewhere. According to the files, 20 children (21%) had expressed this desire at some point; mainly children wanting to return to their parent/s.

To produce an overall measure to establish if there were problems with the child's relationship with the carer, we looked at whether there was tension between them and whether the child was thought to be close and definitely attached to the carer. By combining these indicators we concluded that 24 per cent of children had some problems with their relationship with the carer(s) during placement. As can be seen from Table 2.18, and as one would expect, such problems were mainly a feature of placements which had ended, although they also featured in almost a third of the continuing placements.

Table 2.18

Relationship problems by whether the placement lasted as long as needed/is likely to last

	Occurrence		*Placement continuing*		*Placement ended*	
(N=)	*No.*	*%*	*No.*	*% (where identified)*	*No.*	*% (where identified)*
Problems with relationship with the carer						
(111)	27	24	8	30	19	70
No problems with relationship with the carer						
(111)	84	76	65	77	19	23

Local authority differences

There was a statistically significant difference between our two local authorities in the child–carer relationship, with 34 per cent of children in Authority A having problems compared to only 12 per cent in Authority B.[18]

Comparison with children placed in non-kin care

There was virtually no difference between the two groups on this outcome measure (11 per cent of kin-placed under-fives had some problem in their relationship with their carer compared to 13 per cent of those placed in non-kin care).

Relationship with other outcome measures

Placement stability

Table 2.19

Placement stability and relationship with carer

Placement stability	Problem-free		Difficulties	
	No.	%	No.	%
Lasted as long as needed/likely to last	59	53	3	3
Vulnerable	13	12	5	5
Did not last as long as needed	12	11	19	17

N = 111

Overall, in our *worst case scenario*, of the 111 placements for which information was available on both these outcome measures, 59 placements (53%) were both continuing and stable/had lasted as long as needed *and* did not raise any concerns about the child's relationship with the carer (Table 2.19). At the other end of the spectrum, 19 placements (17%) had not lasted as long as needed *and* there were concerns about relationships.

In our *best case scenario*, 72 placements (65%) were continuing/had lasted as long as needed and there were no relationship issues.

---

[18]   X2 = 7.7, df = 1, p = 0.006

Placement quality
The findings in terms of relationships and placement quality were understandably poorer, given that the sample produced more concerns over quality than stability. Overall (Table 2.20), in our *worst case scenario*, only 33 per cent of placements had no issues about quality or relationships. However, in the *best case scenario*, only 12 per cent had both major concerns about quality and relationship difficulties.

Table 2.20
Relationship with carer and placement quality

| | Overall placement quality | | | | | |
| | Problem-free | | Some concerns | | Major concerns | |
Relationship quality	No.	%	No.	%	No.	%
No problems	37	33	38	34	9	8
Some difficulties	3	3	11	10	13	12

N=111

Relationships with other children in the household – a note
Relationships with other children in the household were not part of our measure of relationship quality. However, we did feel it was important to report our data on this. In the main, the findings are positive: in 79 per cent of the cases where there were other children in the household, relationships with the kin-placed child were judged to be close. Most of these close relationships were with siblings (36 of 58), but some children were close to the carer's children (21) or (one case) another related child in the household. However, there was also evidence of tension in over a quarter of cases (28%). While this is lower than the 45 per cent reported in Farmer and Moyers' (2008) study, it is a substantial proportion, and in some cases contributed to placement breakdown. There was no particular pattern to the difficulties: in seven cases, the tension was with the child's sibling, in six cases with the carer's children, while in six cases the child had good relationships with some children in the household and experienced tension with others. In one sad case, relationships between the child and all the other children in the household appeared to be difficult.

Conclusion

Table 2.21

Summary of positive ratings on each outcome measure

		Occurrence	
	(N=)	*No.*	*%*
Placement stability			
Lasted as long as needed/likely to last	(111)	62	56
Placement quality			
No issues about quality	(111)	40	36
Relationship quality			
No problems	(111)	84	76
Overall outcomes			
Positive ratings on all 3 outcome measures	(111)	37	33
Positive ratings on 2 out of 3	(111)	24	22
Positive ratings on 1 out of 3	(111)	27	24
Positive ratings on none	(111)	23	21

The information presented here gives a reasonably positive picture of kinship care in terms of meeting Quality Protects Objective 1. In our *worst case scenario* (Table 2.21), over half the placements (56%) were either continuing and stable or had lasted as long as needed, while our *best case scenario* (no table) gives a figure of 68 per cent which were continuing or had lasted as long as needed. Forty placements (36%) were problem-free in terms of our overall rating of placement quality and only 20 per cent had major quality issues. Problems in the child's relationship with the carer were evident in less than a quarter of cases.

Overall, in our *worst case scenario* (Table 2.21), 37 placements (33%) had positive ratings on all three of the outcome measures while 23 (21%) had none. Of the remainder:

- 27 (24%) had positive ratings on only one measure. In almost all cases (25/27) this was relationship quality. In one case the placement was stable but there were concerns about quality and relationships, and in another there were no issues about quality, but the placement was vulnerable and relationships were strained.

• 24 (22%) cases had positive ratings on two measures. Placement stability was the missing dimension in all but two (22/24). In both exceptions, placements were stable and there were no quality issues but there were some difficulties in the relationship with the carer.

While there was no significant difference between the two local authorities in the overall rating on the three outcome measures, there was a trend: Authority B had more placements with positive ratings on all three outcome measures (40% cf. 27%) whereas Authority A had more placements which lacked positive ratings on any measure (27% cf. 14%). The proportion having positive ratings on between one and two measures was the same, but Authority B had more cases with a positive rating on two measures (25% compared to 17%) whereas Authority A had more cases with a positive rating on only one. The mean rating for Authority B was 1.9, that for Authority A 1.5.

In the next chapter we look at how the children themselves fared.

Summary

Three outcome measures were derived from Objective 1 of the Quality Protects Programme: placement stability, placement quality and relationship quality.

Placement stability

Fifty-six per cent of placements were continuing and stable or had ended but lasted as long as needed; 16 per cent were continuing but vulnerable and 28 per cent had not lasted as long as needed. A comparison of under-five children placed with kin or non-kin carers showed only slightly higher disruption rates for kin-placed children (11% compared to 7%).

A comparison of our disruption data on kin-placed children with that from other studies of foster care and adoption indicates that, when account is taken of the child's age at the outset, our outcomes for children under five appear to be worse than adoption (though considerably better than for long-term foster care) and for children aged 5–12, worse than both adoption and long-term foster care.

A number of mitigating factors offset this, on the face of it, rather negative conclusion. Our follow-up period is likely to be much longer than other studies. The children in the cohort were at the "heavy end" in terms of adverse life experiences and difficulties. Less than half of the placements which did not last as long as needed could be considered as clear disruptions from the child's point of view. More than half the children were retained in their family network and the original carers often maintained a positive relationship with the child.

Placement quality

Thirty-six per cent of placements were assessed as problem-free, 44 per cent had some problems and 20 per cent major concerns.

Comparing our two under-fives groups, kinship care scored somewhat poorer on most measures than did non-kin-placed children. However, it was more likely to meet the child's emotional needs and there was little difference regarding behaviour management. This was despite the assessed parenting capacity of the non-kin carers being slightly higher than that of the kinship carers.

Most poor quality placements ended and there was little evidence that there was a widespread problem of local authorities allowing such placements to continue. Usually the continuation of poor placements could be explained, by, for example, reluctance to move a child where they were placed with a sibling who was doing better in that placement.

Relationship quality

Twenty-four per cent of children had some problems in their relationship with the carer. In most of these cases the placement had ended, although relationship problems were evident in a third of continuing placements. There was little difference between the kin and non-kin under-fives groups with regard to relationship quality.

Combining these three outcome measures gives a fairly positive picture of kinship care in terms of meeting the Quality Protect objectives. A third of placements (33%) had *positive* ratings on all three of the outcome measures with 21 per cent having *problematic* ratings on all three. Of the remainder, 24 per cent had positive ratings on only one measure (in almost all cases this was relationship quality) and 22 per cent had positive ratings on two measures, with placement stability usually being the missing dimension.

3 How did the children fare?

As indicated earlier, the three measures we have used so far are proxy rather than direct outcomes. In this chapter, in contrast, we examine the data on various aspects of children's well-being, namely: physical health; learning difficulties; schooling; peer relationships; sexual behaviour; and emotional and behavioural development. Again, we draw on all the available information from files, interviews with carers, social workers and children. We have also used information from a standardised measure of child functioning, the Strengths and Difficulties Questionnaire (SDQ), completed by carers and teachers about the child.

The context: pre-placement adversities

Before examining how the children were faring, it is important to high-light the difficulties they were likely to be bringing to placement because of the prior adversities they had experienced. We categorised these adversities as: parental circumstances; environmental adversities; instability; experience of bereavement or loss; child protection concerns; and child difficulties. Full details of these are given in Appendix C. In summary, however, we found that, on average, children had been exposed to 15 different adversities, ranging from a low of three to 30. Only 15 children (13%) had experienced fewer than 10 adversities, with 75 (66%) having between 11 and 20. There was little difference between our two local authorities in the level of pre-placement adversity experienced by the children.

Table 3.1

Pre-placement adversities

Adversity domain	Mean	Range	Incidence		
			No.	*%*	*(N=)*
Parental circumstances	4.2	0–8	112	99	(113)
Environmental factors	4.7	0–8	111	98	(113)
Instability	1.7	0–4	103	91	(113)
Child difficulties	1.6	0–8	78	70	(112)*
Abuse/child protection concerns	2.5	0–6	111	98	(113)
Bereavement	0.3	0–1	36	32	(113)
All adversities	15.1	3–30	113	100	(113)

* *details on one case not available*

Parental circumstances

The vast majority of children had lived with parents whose circumstances put them at risk of poorer outcomes.[19] Only one child had experienced no parental adversities. Sixty-six per cent experienced four or more adversities in this domain, with a maximum of eight. For example:

- 88 per cent of mothers and half the fathers had no educational qualifications.[20]
- 58 per cent of children had a parent with psychological or psychiatric problems.
- 58 per cent had a parent with addiction problems.
- 68 per cent had a parent whose own early experiences of care were poor; 36 per cent had a parent who had been in care as a child.
- 45 per cent had lived with a parent involved in criminal activity, typically drug-related.
- 48 per cent were born to mothers under 21 years old.

---

[19] These figures will underestimate the extent of parental difficulties because we excluded parental problems to which the child was not exposed.

[20] In the general population, only 13.6 per cent of women of working age and 12.2 per cent of men have no qualifications (DfES, 2006c).

Environmental factors

Only two children were not exposed to any adverse environmental factors. Seventy-four per cent experienced four or more. For example:

- 81 per cent of children had lived in a one-parent family.
- 89 per cent had a parent on benefits.
- 66 per cent had lived in a household where there was domestic violence.
- 50 per cent lived in a household with three or more children.
- 50 per cent had lived in substandard housing and 56 per cent in temporary accommodation.

Instability

Children's lives prior to placement were characterised by unstable care or household arrangements. For example:

- 29 per cent had experienced multiple substantial separations from their main carer and 41 per cent many changes in the composition of the family household.
- Only 12 per cent of children had had stable care arrangements prior to the index placement. Of the remainder, 40 per cent were characterised as very unstable.[21] On average, children had experienced four different care arrangements prior to the index placement and had lived in an average of five residences; 53 per cent had been looked after.

Bereavement and loss

Twenty-seven per cent of children had experienced parental separation; five the death of a parent and one the death of a sibling.

Child protection concerns

Almost all the children (90%) were believed to have experienced abuse or neglect: 76 per cent were considered to have been neglected; 28 per cent physically abused; 32 per cent emotionally abused and five per cent sexually abused. Forty-two percent had experienced multiple forms of abuse.

---

[21] Child had had serial disruptions, moves, previous care spells.

Child difficulties

Given these levels of adversity, it is not surprising that many children were already displaying a range of difficulties prior to placement. While the proportions suffering from chronic ill-health, physical disability or learning difficulties were quite low, 58 per cent were already manifesting emotional, and 48 per cent behavioural, problems.

Comparison with children going into non-kin foster care

One of the key issues in kinship care is to what extent the children them-selves are "easier" than those placed in non-kin care. Clearly the answer to this affects the evaluation of outcomes. Much of the previous research, although not definitive, suggests that though kin-placed children have higher levels of difficulty than the general child population, they may have had slightly less damaging pre-placement experiences than those placed with non-kin (see Hunt, 2003a for summary). However, while Farmer and Moyers (2008) found some differences, their striking finding was how similar the two groups were.

Our study, though using a more limited comparison group (children under five at the end of the proceedings), lends weight to the view that the children are extraordinarily similar (see Appendix E for details). Only a few differences were identified, most of which suggested that if anything, the kin-placed children had experienced rather more pre-placement adversities. Thus:

- They were significantly more likely to have: been born to a mother under 21 years old; lived with a parent who had been in care as a child; lived with a parent who was on benefits; and been abused or neglected. The children in non-kin care were significantly more likely to have lived with a parent with physical problems and been in close contact with a Schedule 1 offender.
- They were slightly more likely to have experienced higher numbers of adversities in the domains of: parental circumstances; environmental factors; bereavement and loss; child protection concerns; child diffi-culties; and the total number of adversities experienced. The non-kin sample children experienced a slightly higher number of adversities in the domain of instability.

Child functioning in placement

It will be clear from the data presented in the preceding section that the life chances of most of the children in the sample had probably already been seriously compromised. How did they fare in placement? To assess this we looked at a range of factors, grouped into six broad domains: physical health; learning difficulties; emotional and behavioural development; schooling; peer problems; sexual behaviour (Table 3.2).

Table 3.2
Incidence and classification of problems within child well-being dimensions

(N=)	Occurrence		Placement continuing		Placement ended	
	No.	%	No.	% (where identified)	No.	% (where identified)
Child well-being dimension						
Physical health						
(111)	9	8	8	89	1	11
Learning difficulties						
(111)	29	26	20	69	9	31
Emotional/ behavioural development: global measure						
(111)	39	35	19	49	20	51
School problems						
(84)	27	32	9	33	18	67
Peer problems						
(91)	18	20	9	50	9	50
Sexual behaviour						
(91)	7	8	2	29	5	71

Physical health

Previous research on kin-placed children has produced very different estimates of their health, at least in part because of differences in definitions of ill-health and methods of assessment. The only study to use medical evaluation (Dubowitz *et al*, 1992) found that 90 per cent of children had health problems. Another US study, based on administrative records (Benedict *et al*, 1996), found that 24 per cent of the children had chronic conditions.

UK data are much sparser but similarly varied. Thus Harwin *et al* (2003) found that only seven per cent of children in kinship placements made as the result of care proceedings were recorded as having any health deficit, while Farmer and Moyers (2008) report that 42 per cent had at least one long-term health condition.

Our data are more in line with Harwin's, with only nine children (8%) known to have long-term health conditions or physical disabilities[22] (Table 3.2). Most of these problems (6) were diagnosed pre-placement. These figures are much lower than those recorded for looked after children in general, two-thirds of whom were reported by their carers to have at least one physical complaint (Meltzer *et al*, 2003). They are also lower than estimates of national prevalence which indicate that 19 per cent of boys and 17 per cent of girls have a long-standing illness or disability (Office for National Statistics, 2004). While there may be a degree of under-recording in our data,[23] it does not suggest that children placed with kin are likely to fare worse in terms of their health than other children nor that children with health problems are disproportionately likely to be placed with kin, at least where the courts are involved.

Learning difficulties/developmental delay

Kinship placements do, however, appear to have higher proportions of children with learning difficulties or developmental delay than in the general population. While national estimates of the prevalence of learning difficulties are not available, only 2.9 per cent of children in England and Wales have a statement of special educational need (SEN) (DfES, 2005b). In contrast, Farmer and Moyers (2008) found that 23 per cent of kin children had SEN statements. The proportion in our study was slightly higher (28 per cent of school-aged children), which is close to the prevalence in the looked after children population overall (27%, [DfES, 2006b]). In total,

---

[22] Conditions included eczema, cystic fibrosis, hearing problems, talipes, asthma and mild cerebral palsy.

[23] However, in the cases where we interviewed carers, a comparison of the data recorded on files with that reported by the carer did not indicate major discrepancies.

29 children in our study (26%) had problems in this domain. Eight were in a non-mainstream school to meet their educational needs.

Schooling

Twenty-nine per cent of the school-aged children in our study had some form of difficulty with their schooling.

The most common problem was *underachievement*, which was reported for 20 children (27 per cent of those where data were available). This is very similar to Harwin's sample (29%; Harwin *et al*, 2003); but higher than Rowe's (15%; Rowe *et al*, 1984) and lower than Farmer and Moyers (52%; Farmer and Moyers, 2008). The US literature suggests a rate of between 36 per cent and 50 per cent (Berrick *et al*, 1994; Inglehart, 1994; Sawyer and Dubowitz, 1994). Our figures are also much lower than those reported for children in non-kin care: Farmer and Moyers (2008) found that 48 per cent of children in non-kin foster care were under-achieving and cite a finding by Skuse *et al* (2001) that over half the looked after children in six local authorities were underperforming in English and mathematics.

Non-attendance at school was surprisingly rare, being a major problem for only five per cent of school-aged children (4) and something of a problem for three (4%). This is lower than US data would suggest: Benedict *et al* (1996) found that 33 per cent of children in kinship foster care had problems with school attendance. It also appears to be lower than UK figures for looked after children, 13 per cent of whom missed at least 25 days of school per year (DfES, 2006b). Farmer and Moyers (2008) report similar rates of non-attendance for both groups (15%).

For many children, moreover, school attendance had improved after placement (61%) and did not deteriorate for any. Farmer and Moyers (2008) report improvement for 48 per cent of children but also deterioration for a small proportion (6%).

Only 11 children (13%) had ever been excluded from school, either temporarily (8) or permanently (3). There does not appear to be any comparative data on this but since one per cent of children in the looked-after population are permanently excluded each year (DfES, 2006b) and our data covers many years of children's lives post-placement, these figures do not seem inordinately high.

Peer and sexual problems

Eighteen children (20 per cent of those for whom sufficient data were available [91]) were judged to have peer problems and seven (8%) problems with sexual behaviour.

Emotional and behavioural development

The national prevalence of clinically recognisable mental disorders (including emotional disorders, conduct disorders and hyperkinetic disorders) is 10 per cent of 5–16-year-olds (Green et al, 2005). Looked after children are recognised to be at greater risk of such impairments: Meltzer et al (2003) report that 45 per cent of those in the UK had a clinically recognisable mental disorder (either emotional, conduct or hyperkinetic). Similar rates are noted by Richards et al (2006).

Previous research has also reported increased risk for children in kin placements, with UK rates ranging from 17 per cent (Rowe et al, 1984) to 57 per cent (Harwin et al, 2003). A Norwegian study (Holtan et al, 2005) reports that 36 per cent of kinship children scored above borderline on a standardised test. In the US a similar proportion (35 per cent) had scores in the clinical range in a study by Dubowitz and Sawyer (1994), while Benedict et al (1996) found 53 per cent of children in kinship foster care had behavioural problems and 39 per cent had mental health problems.

We obtained 40 completed Strengths and Difficulties Questionnaires (Goodman, 1997) through our carer interviews. Thirty-five per cent of the children concerned had a total difficulties score that fell into the abnormal range (the proportion in the general child population is 10 per cent). We also obtained 25 completed questionnaires from teachers, which put 20 per cent of the children in the abnormal range.

Combining information from the files, carer interviews and social worker interviews, we produced a global rating of emotional and behavioural development. This indicated that just over a third of the children in our sample (39) had more than minor problems with some aspect of emotional and behavioural development.[24] Seventeen children (15%) had problems which needed remedial action and nine (8%) had serious

---

[24] The children identified as having only minor problems at the point the file data ceases were not included in this group.

problems needing specialist input.[25] Fourteen of the children in the latter two groups were receiving some sort of treatment. The behaviour of 15 per cent of children was considered to be unacceptable to children and/or adults.[26]

We were also able to rate whether there had been a change in the child's behaviour during the placement. Twenty-five (23%) were considered to have improved, 13 (12%) to have deteriorated while 20 (18%) changed for both the better and the worse. No noticeable changes were recorded for the remainder.

Virtually all the children were considered to have made progress by the carers we interviewed:

I'm extremely pleased with her progress. She has come along as a normal child would, which is what we aim to do. She's such a lovely child. She is really, really talented. Able in many ways.

She's a changed child. And it's not just me saying that, it's the school, my mother, my friends, anyone who is associated with the past and the present. She's doing better than I ever thought she would.

Nonetheless, some were reported to have problems, mostly emotional or behavioural:

Constant lying, stealing, getting suspended from school, fighting, talking back.

She's very withdrawn at times. And she only looks at her own needs. She is unable to understand other people.

Emotionally I would like to see more progress. She has issues she hasn't laid to rest.

I still think he's got a troubled mind but he's dealing with it a lot better now.

---

[25] Farmer and Moyers (2008) found the figures of 27 per cent and 25 per cent respectively.

[26] Farmer and Moyers (2008) report that the behaviour of 80 per cent of children was acceptable to both children and adults.

Comparison with children placed with non-kin carers
The non-kin sample had higher levels of physical health problems and school problems than the children in the kinship under-fives sample. These differences are likely to be explained by higher levels of physical health problems in the non-kin sample pre-placement (see Appendix E) and the fact that we had school data on the entire non-kin sample and only for a proportion of the kinship under-fives sample. Levels of learning difficulties, emotional and behavioural problems, peer problems and sexual behaviour problems were not dissimilar between the two samples. It appears, therefore, that the levels of child well-being were fairly commensurate between the two samples.

Overall levels of child well-being
In the previous chapter we concluded that the findings of our study indicate that kinship care can make a positive contribution to children's welfare by delivering on Objective 1 of the Quality Protects Initiative. The information presented in this chapter also suggests that many of the children were doing well. In 47 per cent of cases there were no concerns in any of the child well-being and development dimensions, while a further 16 per cent were presenting difficulties in only one area and only

Table 3.3
Overall levels of difficulty in child well-being dimensions

	(N=)	Occurrence No.	Occurrence %	Placement continuing No.	Placement continuing % (where identified)	Placement ended No.	Placement ended % (where identified)
No difficulties							
	(111)	52	47	38	73	14	27
One dimension only							
	(111)	18	16	15	83	3	17
Two	(111)	20	18	11	55	9	45
Three	(111)	14	13	6	43	8	57
Four	(111)	5	5	2	40	3	60
Five	(111)	2	2	1	50	1	50

19 per cent in three or more (Table 3.3). This is a substantial achievement given the levels of adversity these children had suffered prior to placement.

Local authority differences

The children in Authority B had very slightly higher levels of difficulty in the domain of well-being (mean of 1.25 difficulties compared to 1.1 in Authority A). Authority B had very slightly fewer children with no difficulties at all (46% cf 48%) and more with difficulties in three or more domains (23% cf 15%). However, these differences were not statistically significant.

Child well-being in relation to other outcome measures

Placement stability and child well-being. In our *worst case scenario*, only 33 per cent of placements had lasted as long as needed/were likely to last *and* there were no problems with child functioning (Table 3.4). At the other extreme, 12 per cent of placements had not lasted and the child had major difficulties. Interestingly, however, even where placements had disrupted, more than half the children had done well, or reasonably well (16 of 31; 52%) while in placement. Similarly, of the 18 vulnerable continuing placements, only five children had difficulties in more than three of the domains of well-being.

Table 3.4
Placement stability and child well-being

Placement stability	No difficulties		Difficulties in 1–2 domains		Difficulties in 3+ domains	
	No.	*%*	*No.*	*%*	*No.*	*%*
Lasted as long as needed/likely to last	37	33	22	20	3	3
Vulnerable	8	7	5	5	5	5
Did not last as long as needed	7	6	11	10	13	12

N = 111

In our *best case scenario*, 65 per cent were continuing/had lasted as long as needed *and* the children had problems in no more than two domains.

Placement quality and child well-being. In our *worst case scenario*, only 23 per cent of the children did well and there were no issues about placement quality (Table 3.5). In 10 per cent, there were poor outcomes on both the quality and child well-being measures. Again, however, a sizeable proportion appeared to be doing very well (24%) or quite well (23%) despite concerns about quality.

Table 3.5
Placement quality and child well-being

Placement quality	No difficulties		Difficulties in 1–2 domains		Difficulties in 3+ domains	
	No.	%	No.	%	No.	%
Problem-free	26	23	13	12	1	1
Some concerns	21	19	19	17	9	8
Major concerns	5	5	6	5	11	10

N = 111

Our *best case scenario* produces a much more optimistic result, with 71 per cent of children having problems in no more than three domains of well-being and there being no major quality issues about the placement.

Relationship with carer and child well-being. In the *worst case scenario*, 41 per cent of children did well and there were no difficulties in the relationship with their carer. In eight per cent of cases, there were relationship difficulties and major problems with the child's functioning. In 16 per cent of cases, children were doing well or fairly well despite relationship problems, while in 11 per cent, children were struggling despite what appeared to be good relationships.

Table 3.6
Relationship with carer and child well-being

Relationship with carer	No difficulties		Difficulties in 1–2 domains		Difficulties in 3+ domains	
	No.	%	No.	%	No.	%
No difficulties	46	41	26	23	12	11
Some difficulties	6	5	12	11	9	8

N = 111

In the *best case scenario*, 65 per cent of children had problems in no more than two domains *and* enjoyed a good relationship with their carer.

Conclusion: overall outcomes

The picture presented in these two chapters indicates that kinship care *can* be a positive option for many children. Fifty-six per cent of placements were continuing and stable or had lasted as long as needed and a further 16 per cent were continuing though vulnerable. Forty placements (36%) were problem-free in terms of our overall rating of placement quality and only 20 per cent had major problems. Problems in the child's relationship with the carer were evident in less than a quarter of cases. In 47 per cent of cases, there were no concerns in any of the child well-being and development dimensions, while a further 16 per cent were presenting difficulties in only one area and only 19 per cent in three or more.

Nonetheless, it has to be said that, in *our worst case scenario*, only 23 per cent of cases (25) achieved positive ratings on all four of our outcome measures and 17 per cent (19) did not score positively on any (Table 3.7). Of the remaining 67 cases (60%) which fall into what we might term the "middling" category:

• 19 cases (17% of the total) scored positively on only one outcome measure. Typically this was the relationship with the carer (15 cases) but in four cases it was child well-being.

• 25 cases (23%) scored positively on two of the four measures. The most common combination was either stability and carer relationships (11) or well-being and relationships (10). Less usual pairings were

Table 3.7

Summary of positive ratings on each outcome measure

	Occurrence	
	No.	*%*
Placement stability		
Lasted as long as needed/likely to last	62	56
Placement quality		
No issues	40	36
Relationship quality		
No problems	84	76
Child functioning		
No problems in any domain	52	47
Overall outcomes		
Positive ratings on all 4 outcome measures	25	23
Positive ratings on 3/4 measures	23	21
Positive ratings on 2/4 measures	25	23
Positive ratings on 1/4 outcome measures	19	17
Positive ratings on no measure	19	17

N = 111

stability and quality (2); stability and well-being (1) and well-being and quality (1).

- 23 cases (21%) scored positively on all but one measure. In 12 cases the missing dimension was child well-being, and in 11, placement quality.

As we have already indicated, it is possible to produce a more positive picture by using more generous measures. In this *best case scenario*, 58 per cent of placements scored positively on all four measures and only five per cent scored positively on none. Of the remainder:

- 11 cases (10% of the total) scored positively on only one outcome measure: child well-being (6); placement quality (4); relationship with carer (4); placement stability (3).

- 17 cases (15%) scored positively on two of the four measures: child well-being and placement quality (8); child well-being and relationship quality (3); placement quality and relationship with carer (3); well-being and stability (2) and relationship with carer and stability (1).
- 14 cases (13%) scored positively on all but one measure. The missing dimensions were: child well-being (5), relationship with carer (4); placement stability (3) and placement quality (2).

Local authority differences

There was no significant difference between our two local authorities in the overall rating of the four outcome measures (*worst case scenario*). However, there was a trend: Authority B had more placements with positive ratings on all four outcome measures (27% cf. 19%) whereas Authority A had more placements that lacked any positive ratings on any measure (22% cf. 12%).

Table 3.8
Outcomes by local authority

| | Number of dimensions with positive rating (%) | | | | | |
	None	One	Two	Three	Four	(N=)
Authority A	22	17	25	17	19	(59)
Authority B	12	17	19	25	27	(52)

In the next chapter we look at what might help to explain why some children appear to do very well in kinship care and others do less well or even poorly.

Summary

The children were likely to be bringing to placement not insignificant difficulties because of the prior adversities they had experienced. Most children had experienced some kind of adversity in each of the areas of parental circumstances, environmental factors, instability and child protection concerns. Seventy per cent of children had some kind of difficulty themselves i.e. ill-health, physical or learning difficulties, emotional or behavioural problems. A comparison of kin-placed children aged under five at the end of proceedings with our small sample of children placed with non-kin found very few differences, most of which suggested that, if anything, the kin-placed children had experienced rather *more* pre-placement adversities.

A range of factors were used to assess how the children fared in placement. These were grouped into six broad domains: physical health; learning difficulties; schooling; peer problems; sexual behaviour; and emotional and behavioural development. The children most commonly had difficulties in the domains of emotional and behavioural development and schooling (35% and 32% of children respectively). Overall, almost half of children (47%) were functioning well and had no difficulties in any of the domains. At the other end of the spectrum, 20 per cent of children had difficulties in three or more domains.

These outcome data were combined with that presented in the previous chapter on placement stability, placement quality and relationships to give an overall outcome measure. In our *worst case scenario*, 23 per cent of placements scored positively on all four of the outcome measures but 17 per cent did not score positively on any. In the *best case scenario*, the figures were 58 per cent and five per cent respectively.

4   Explaining outcomes

What explains why some children appear to thrive in kinship care and others do not? Why do some placements last and others terminate prematurely? Is it possible to improve outcomes through better decision-making at the outset or is it all the luck of the draw? In this chapter we explore these questions quantitatively, by investigating the relationship between our four outcome measures and a range of different factors relating to the child and the placement, viz:

- *Characteristics of the child and their pre-placement history*: age; gender; ethnicity; prior adversities; acceptance of placement;
- *Characteristics of the placement*: relationship of carer to child; single or couple carer/s; age of carer; other children/adults in household; sibling placement; child cared for previously by this carer;[27] assessed parenting quality;
- *Decision-making and support*: Social Services involvement prior to proceedings; who instigated the placement; route to placement; assessment; disagreement about placement or order; concerns/ reservations about the placement expressed by professionals during proceedings; legal order; post-placement support while the case was open.

The quantitative analysis is complemented, wherever relevant or feasible, by qualitative material drawn from all our data sources.

Outcome measure 1: Placement stability

Factors associated with placement stability
As described in Chapter 2, our measure of placement stability was whether a placement had lasted or was likely to last as long as was needed.

---

[27] Figures were very small for whether the carer previously knew the child (2 = hardly knew, 3 = little opportunity, child newborn) so it was not possible to test for this factor in the analysis.

Sixty-two children (56% of the 111 for which data were available) were in placements which had either terminated but had lasted as long as needed or were ongoing and judged to be likely to continue; 18 (16%) were continuing but there were concerns about their stability, and 31 (28%) had terminated prematurely.

Of all the factors tested, only four were found to have any explanatory power, viz: the child's age at the end of the proceedings; the child having previously been cared for full-time by the kinship carer; the carer being a grandparent; and the child not having asked to live elsewhere at any point. Regression analysis indicated that all four factors were independently significant and together explained 50 per cent of the variance in placement stability.

We look at each of these factors in more detail in the following sections.

Child's age at the end of the proceedings

Previous research has highlighted the significance of the child's age to placement stability in kinship care as well as in non-kin foster care and adoption (for kinship care see Altshuler, 1998; Hunt and Macleod, 1999; Webster *et al*, 2000; Terling-Watt, 2001; Harwin *et al*, 2003; Farmer and Moyers, 2008; for adoption and fostering see Triseliotis, 2002; Sinclair, 2005).

Our study confirms these findings, with the child's age at the end of the proceedings being the most important explanatory factor (Table 4.1). The children whose placements did not last as long as needed were significantly older (mean 7.97 years) than those whose placements lasted as long as needed/were continuing and stable or were continuing but less stable (means 3.87 years and 4.67 years respectively).[28]

We tested the hypothesis that this relationship between age at the end of proceedings and instability was illusory, and that what was really happening was that placements were simply coming under greater pressure as the children got older. However, this did not prove to be the case: children in continuing placements were actually slightly older[29] than

---

[28] F = 13.28, df = 2, p < 0.001;linear contrast: t = –4.54, df = 108, p < 0.001

[29] Calculated at point data collection began (March 04) for all placements known to be continuing at that point.

Table 4.1

Placement stability rating by child's age at the end of proceedings

	0–4 years		5–9 years		10–14 years	
	No.	*%*	*No.*	*%*	*No.*	*%*
Lasted as long as needed/ continuing and stable	38	70	20	53	4	21
Continuing but vulnerable	10	19	5	13	3	16
Did not last as long as needed	6	11	13	34	12	63
(N=)	(54)		(38)		(19)	

those whose placements had ended (11 years 5 months vs. 10 years 11 months).

As might be anticipated, the child's age at the end of proceedings was significantly associated with a number of factors, which might help to explain why this proved to be such a potent variable:

- Total number of adversities experienced prior to placement – older children had experienced significantly more adversities;
- Older children were more likely to have difficulties (e.g. emotional and behavioural problems) that pre-dated the placement;
- Length of Social Services involvement prior to the start of proceedings – longer involvement was found for older children.

However, none of these variables, *on their own*, were predictive of placement instability. Farmer and Moyers (2008) similarly found that the number of parental or child adversities was not associated with placement survival in kinship care, although, interestingly, they were in non-kin foster care.

Previous full-time care by the index carer

Thirty-one per cent of children had been previously looked after on a full-time basis by the relative they were placed with as the result of the proceedings (the index carer). This was significantly associated with placement stability,[30] with 87 per cent of such placements having

---

[30] X2 = 12.13, df = 2, p = 0.002

lasted/being likely to last as long as needed or to be continuing though vulnerable compared to 60 per cent of placements where the index relative had not previously had full-time care. This factor was not significantly related to the child's age at the end of proceedings.

Relationship of carer to the child

There is scant previous research on this. However, Hunt and Macleod (1999), Harwin *et al* (2003) and Farmer and Moyers (2008) all suggest that placements with grandparents may be less vulnerable to breakdown than those with aunts and uncles.

Our research provides further support for these findings. Eighty-four per cent of placements with grandparents either lasted as long as needed or were continuing (either stable or more vulnerable) compared to only 46 per cent of those with an aunt or uncle.[31] It is true that, in our sample, younger children were more likely to be placed with grandparents. However, this does not explain away the importance of who the relative is, which remains a significant factor even when age is taken into account.[32]

An unusual case illustrates the different outcomes of placements with different relatives.

> Carley, only a year old at the end of proceedings, was placed with her grandparents with an agreement that an aunt and uncle would take over if the grandparents found it too difficult to cope because of their age and health problems. After being with her grandparents for four years, Carley duly moved to her aunt and uncle. However, this placement only lasted for four months as they could not cope with her aggressive behaviour towards their own toddler. Carley returned to her grandparents, where she remains.

What might explain why grandparent placements are more successful? It was significantly more common for aunts/uncles to have children other

---

[31] Overall X2 = 17.48, df = 2, p < 0.001

[32] The ethnicity of the child was not independently related to placement stability but was significantly related to the type of relative the child was placed with. Children of minority ethnic origin were more likely to be placed with aunts or uncles than with grandparents.

than the child's siblings in the household (typically their own children) and certainly there were cases where tension in the children's relationships led to placement breakdown. It may be that the children of aunts and uncles were quite similar in age to the placed children, which can be a risk factor (Wedge and Mantle, 1991).[33] Also, on average, placements with aunts/uncles had significantly larger overall numbers of children in addition to the index child compared to grandparent placements (1.2 and 2.2 respectively). This may mean that the resources of aunts/uncles were spread much more thinly.

Aunts/uncles were slightly more likely to be in work and the index children in their care had slightly higher levels of difficulty in the area of child well-being (though neither trend was statistically significant). These two factors may put additional pressure on a placement. Alternatively, it could be that grandparents have the greatest sense of obligation/continuity of the family and are therefore more likely to persist in the face of difficulties. However, our dataset does not enable us to explore this further.

Child's acceptance of care

Research into placement stability in non-kinship foster care has highlighted the importance of the child's acceptance of the need for care (Sinclair, 2005; Sinclair *et al*, 2007). Our criterion was somewhat different – whether the child had ever said they wanted to live somewhere other than with the index carer. However, our findings – that in almost half the placements that did not last (48%) the child had asked to live elsewhere at some point, compared to 13 per cent of those which had lasted/were continuing and stable and six per cent of those which were continuing but more vulnerable – suggest that this may be an important factor in kinship care too.[34] As one of the young people we interviewed put it:

> *That's the bottom line of it really. You don't want to be with your auntie and uncle or Nan or granddad, you want to be with your mum . . . whatever she does, however bad she is. If that's your natural parent you will defend them down to the ground. They (the kinship carers)*

---

[33]   We do not have sufficient data to explore this possibility.

[34] $X2 = 14.88$, df = 2, p = 0.001

could have been nice to me 24 hours a day and it wouldn't have worked out as I didn't want to be there, I wanted to be with my mum.

One striking example of this was Megan, who was seven years old at the end of proceedings and was placed with a second cousin on the maternal side. It was clearly noted at the time of proceedings that Megan did not want to be in this placement but wanted to be with her maternal grandparents. Professionals felt that this would not be suitable as there was conflict between Megan and her brother, who was already living with the grandparents. A year and seven months after proceedings had concluded, Megan made an allegation of sexual abuse against her carer's son and was moved to her grandparents. On investigation it was felt that the allegation was made to engineer a departure from the placement.

Again, it is true that the children who had said they wanted to live elsewhere were significantly older than those who had not. However, regression analysis reveals that, taking account of the effect of the child's age, whether the child had asked to live elsewhere remains a significant factor in predicting placement stability.

The picture is somewhat complicated by the fact that we included in our analysis any report that the child had asked to live elsewhere, not just whether these sentiments were expressed prior to placement. Thus, in some cases the child's expressed wishes may reflect, rather than be a contributory factor to, placement breakdown. If, for that reason, we exclude this factor from the regression analysis, the amount of variance explained by the three remaining factors is reduced to 46 per cent.

Factors not found to be associated with placement stability

As discussed earlier, the level of adversity the child had experienced prior to placement was not *independently* predictive of placement stability. It was, however, *associated with* placement stability as a consequence of its relationship with the child's age at the end of proceedings.

The following additional factors were not significantly independently related to placement stability and no trends were identified:

- child's gender or ethnicity, previous adversities;
- the carer's age; which parent they were related to; whether there were one or two carers;
- whether the child had siblings in the same placement; whether there were other children or adults in the household;
- length of Social Services involvement prior to proceedings; who instigated the placement; type of order;
- whether the carer was assessed prior to placement; the type of assessment; whether the child went straight from home to kinship care; whether the child was in placement prior to proceedings;
- concerns expressed about placement during proceedings; parenting capacity as assessed during the proceedings;
- which local authority the case was from; whether the placement was within or outside the authority boundary;
- level of support for the placement from Social Services while the case was open.

Farmer and Moyers (2008) found a wide range of factors with a statistically significant association with unplanned placement disruption, including some which showed no association in our data such as no siblings in placement. Most related to post-placement factors. Regression analysis, however, indicated that the model which best predicted disruption was the child being 10 or more at placement; there was low carer commitment; the child was beyond control; and contact was not supervised. As the authors note, the only one of these which could be known in advance is the child's age, although assessment may give an indication of the level of carer commitment.

Why did some placements end prematurely?

The foregoing analysis has suggested a small number of factors which might explain why some placements last as long as necessary and others do not. Analysis of the circumstances in which placements ended prematurely provides some further clues (Table 4.2).

It is notable that only two carers (6%) concluded that they had made a mistake in offering to care and only one was unable to carry on caring because of ill-health (3%). Four placements (13%) ended because of child protection concerns. However, over half the placements which broke down (55%) did so either because the carer was unable to cope with the child's behaviour or the child indicated they wanted to leave/voted with their feet. The importance of behavioural difficulties to placement stability is also highlighted by Farmer and Moyers (2008), who report that 20 per cent of placement endings (not necessarily breakdowns) were due to the child's behaviour and that placements where children had emotional or behavioural problems at a level which required remedial help were more at risk of termination in both kinship and non-kin foster care.

Table 4.2
Main reason for placement not lasting as long as needed

	No.	*%*
Alleged or substantiated abuse or neglect/child put at risk	4	13
Child's behaviour	9	29
Child wanted to leave	8	26
Relationship difficulties child and other children in household	4	13
Relationship difficulties child and carer	3	10
Carers no longer wanted to care	2	6
Carer's poor health	1	3
(N=)	(31)	

In almost another quarter of cases (23%) placements disrupted because of relationship difficulties between the child and either the carer or other children in the household. The importance of the impact of the placed child on other children in the family has been highlighted in the literature on disruption in foster care (Farmer *et al*, 2004; Sinclair, 2005). There were several examples in our study which indicate this is also an important factor in kinship care. Indeed, in one case, the placement was only continuing because the carers had decided to live apart, one caring for the kinship children, the other for the children of the marriage.

A carer in one of the placements which had terminated told us that she had not anticipated the conflict between the child and her own children and wished she had been forewarned:

I didn't know, obviously. Not about my own children and how it would affect them . . . That's the main change in my own children, emotionally, emotional difficulties, it's still ongoing. (You) could be told that your children might be affected by another child coming into the house.

Might at least some of these placements have been saved had the families had help in dealing with the stresses on their relationships or dealing with the child's emotional and behavioural problems? We look at this further in Chapter 7.

Outcome measure 2: Placement quality

Factors associated with placement quality

In Chapter 2 we combined a number of different measures of placement quality to produce an overall rating. In 40 placements (36%) there were no reported concerns about placement quality; in 49 (44%) some concerns and in 22 (20%) major concerns. Again, we tested a range of factors to see whether any of them explained placement quality.[35] Only four proved to be significant: whether there were children other than siblings in the household; whether the carer was assessed prior to placement; the parenting capacity of the carers as assessed during the proceedings; and whether there was disagreement or conflict during the proceedings. Regression analysis including these four variables explained 43 per cent of the variance in placement quality, with all four factors retaining significance.

The presence of children other than siblings in the household
The overall quality of the placement was significantly related to whether or not there were children other than siblings in the household.[36] Only 21 per cent of placements where there were other children were problem-free compared to 50 per cent of placements where there were only siblings or the child was placed alone. As mentioned above, it was much more

---

[35] Factors which relate to the characteristics of the child and pre-placement adversities have not been used as explanatory variables as they should not logically have an influence on this particular outcome measure.

[36] $X2 = 11.35$, df = 2, p = 0.003

common for children other than siblings to be present in placements with aunts/uncles than in placements with grandparents.

Having to manage conflicting loyalties between birth children and kinship children proved an overwhelming task for one carer couple we interviewed.

It has had a huge impact. We always thought about the physical side, not the tensions in our family. We hardly speak to each other now, we're so worn out. I do feel guilty because now our children are suffering and want to leave because of the boys. Zoe (birth child aged 17) is really, really quite depressed and low. She says, 'You've had five years now to make your decision. You've made your choice who you want to keep and I've got to go.' So it's really hard. So we have come to the conclusion now that my husband is going to leave with the boys and I'll stay here with the other children. We were so worn out with the care of just those two let alone . . . I suppose we did neglect our own children, not intentionally but they (kinship children) were destructive children and it took all your time without thinking about anything to make any rational decisions.

Whether the carer was assessed prior to the placement

In all other forms of substitute care, prospective carers undergo a thorough assessment before they are approved to look after a child. In kinship care the children may often already be with their carers before Social Services become involved or, in order to minimise disruption to children, place-ments are made with only the most rudimentary checks. Rowe *et al* (1984) found, surprisingly, that whether or not kinship placements were made after a full assessment made little difference to their success. Our analysis of the factors associated with placement *stability* also did not reveal any significant relationship. However, we did find a relationship with placement *quality*,[37] with half of the placements where there had been a prior assessment being rated as problem-free compared to 27 per cent of the rest. There was little difference, however, between the proportions rated as having major problems (assessed prior 17%; not assessed prior 19%).

---

[37] $X2 = 6.22$, $df = 2$, $p = 0.045$

Assessed parenting capacity at the time of proceedings[38]

The parenting capacity of the carer/s as assessed by professionals at the time of proceedings was significantly related to the overall quality of the placement.[39] Thirty-nine per cent of placements where the carer was considered to have a good level of parenting capacity were problem-free and 41 per cent had some concerns. The figures for placements where assessed parenting capacity was only acceptable or marginal were five per cent and 70 per cent respectively. This was not related to the point at which the child was placed, i.e. before, during or after proceedings.

Disagreement/conflict during proceedings

Finally, and surprisingly, we found a significant association between over-all placement quality and whether there was any disagreement or conflict during proceedings about placement plans or final orders.[40] Paradoxically, where there had been disagreement, 45 per cent of placements were rated as problem-free compared to only 23 per cent where there was no disagreement. Also, only 10 per cent of placements with disagreement had major concerns with placement quality compared to 34 per cent of placements where there had not been disagreement. This could be due to more intense scrutiny of the placement prompted by the disagreement, with only the better quality placements surviving opposition. It could also be that the more committed relatives with a greater sense of obligation were more likely to weather the conflict.

Factors not associated with placement quality

Although not significant, there was a trend in the association between placement quality and who instigated the placement. There was little difference in the rate of problem-free placements between those instigated by relatives and by Social Services (36% and 28% respectively) but more placements made by mutual agreement were problem-free (65%).

---

[38] To rectify small group numbers, assessed parenting capacity was divided into two groups: good and acceptable or marginal.

[39] X2 = 8.63, df = 2, p = 0.013

[40] X2 = 11.09, df = 2, p = 0.004

These remaining factors were not significantly independently related to placement stability and no trends were identified:

- child's age, gender, ethnicity or level of adversity experienced prior to placement;
- the carer's age; their relationship to the child; which parent they were related to; whether there were one or two carers; previous substitute care of the child;
- whether the child had siblings in the same placement; whether there were other adults in the household;
- length of Social Services involvement prior to proceedings; type of order;
- the type of assessment; whether the child went straight from home to kinship care; whether the child was in placement prior to proceedings;
- concerns expressed about placement during proceedings;
- which local authority the case was from; whether the placement was within or outside of the authority boundary;
- level of support for the placement from Social Services while the case was open.

Two pre-placement factors reported to be associated with placement quality in Farmer and Moyers' study (2008) were not found in ours viz: the parents not being drug users and the child not having a history of behavioural problems prior to placement.[41] Their regression analysis indicated that the factors which best predicted poorer quality placements were: the identity of the placing authority; the child having truanted pre-placement; lower carer commitment; and the carer struggling to cope.

---

[41] We were unable to test the remainder of the factors that Farmer and Moyers (2008) found were related to placement quality either because our dataset did not provide us with adequate data or because we had used the information from the variable already to inform our placement stability categorisation and therefore any significant relationships would be because of this.

Outcome measure 3: Relationship quality

Factors associated with relationship quality

As reported in Chapter 2, 24 per cent of children were judged to have had some problems with their relationship with the carer/s during placement. Three variables proved to be significantly related to this: the child's age at the end of proceedings; whether the child was living with a lone carer or a couple, and who was the main instigator of the placement. Regression analysis shows that together these variables explain 45 per cent of variance, with each factor retaining significance.

Child's age at the end of proceedings

Children who had problems in their relationship with their carer were significantly older (mean 8.26 years) at the end of proceedings than children who did not (mean 4.14 years).[42] Again, although there were a number of factors related to the child's age which might help to explain this, for instance, the level of pre-placement adversity, the length of Social Services involvement and the level of the child's difficulties prior to placement, these were not independently predictive.

Lone carer or couple

Problems in the relationship with the carer were significantly associated with whether the child was cared for by one carer or a couple,[43] with problems recorded in only seven per cent of placements with single carers compared to 31 per cent of those with couples. Why this should be is not known. It was not linked to whether the carers were grandparents or other relatives. It could simply be that with two carers there is more potential for difficulties or more need to invest in a relationship with a sole carer.

Main instigator of placement [44]

The main instigator of the placement was significantly related to whether or not there were problems in the child's relationship with the carer during

---

[42] $t = 5.13$, df = 109, $p < 0.001$

[43] X2 = 6.36, df = 1, $p = 0.012$

[44] To rectify the problem of small group numbers, only placements instigated by relatives, Social Services and by mutual agreement were included in this analysis. This excludes six placements instigated by either parents, the child or de facto placements.

the placement.[45] In 39 per cent of placements instigated by Social Services there were problems, compared to only 11 per cent of placements insti-gated by relatives and 12 per cent of placements made by mutual agree-ment. To some extent, this is related to whether or not the child had been previously cared for full time by the relative. For placements made by mutual agreement the child was more likely to have been previously cared for full time by the relative, but this was not the case for placements instigated by relatives or by Social Services.

It is possible that, in cases where the placement was instigated by Social Services, there was some degree of reservation on the part of the relative and this could have manifested itself in tension with the child or lack of closeness in the relationship.

Factors not associated with relationship quality

Despite not reaching significance, there was a trend in the association between relationship quality and whether the relative had previously cared for the child full time. In 36 per cent of placements where there were no problems with relationship quality, the child had experienced previous full-time care by the relative, compared to 15 per cent of placements where there were problems with relationship quality.

These remaining factors were not significantly independently related to placement stability and no trends were identified:

- child's gender or ethnicity; level of adversity experienced prior to placement;
- the carer's age; relationship to the child; which parent they were related to;
- whether the child had siblings in the same placement; whether there were other children or adults in the household;
- length of Social Services involvement prior to proceedings; type of order;
- whether the carer was assessed prior to placement; the type of assessment; whether the child went straight from home to kinship care; whether the child was in placement prior to proceedings;

---

[45] X2 = 10.86, df = 2, p = 0.004

- concerns expressed about placement during proceedings; parenting capacity as assessed during the proceedings; conflict/disagreement during proceedings;
- which local authority the case was from; whether the placement was within or outside of the authority boundary;
- level of support for the placement from Social Services while the case was open.

Outcome measure 4: Child well-being

This outcome measure is a continuous variable ranging from zero to a maximum of five. As reported in Chapter 3, 52 children (46%) had no difficulties in any domain of well-being, while 18 (16%) had difficulties in one domain, 20 children (18%) in two, 14 children (12%) in three, five children (4%) in four, and two children (2%) in five.

Factors associated with child well-being

Only two factors proved to be significantly associated with child well-being: the child's age at the end of the proceedings and the child's difficulties prior to placement. Regression analysis indicates that a combination of these variables explains 24 per cent of variance in child well-being, with both retaining significance.

Child's age at the end of proceedings

There is a significant positive correlation between the child's age at the end of proceedings and the level of the child's difficulties in placement:[46] the older the child, the more difficulties they presented in placement. As we have found before, the child's age is significantly related to a number of factors which might help to explain this. However, the only one of these factors which is *independently* predictive of the level of the child's problems in placement is the child's level of difficulties pre-placement.

---

[46] $r = 0.424$, $p < 0.001$

Child's difficulties prior to placement

The level of the child's difficulties pre-placement was significantly positively correlated with the level of the child's difficulties *in* placement.[47] Higher levels of difficulty pre-placement were associated with higher levels of difficulty in placement. Although this variable was also significantly correlated with the child's age at the end of proceedings, even when this factor is taken into account it remains significant.

Alfie, aged seven, was described on file prior to placement as *'restless and demanding'* and displaying 'unsocial and aggressive behaviour at school'. In placement, his difficulties worsened with a diagnosis of ADHD and attachment disorder, challenging and disruptive behaviour at school, refusal to take medication, and rudeness.

Factors not associated with child well-being[48]

The following factors were not significantly independently related to child well-being and no trends were identified:

- child's gender or ethnicity; level of adversity prior to placement;
- the carer's age; relationship to child; which parent they were related to; whether there were one or two carers; previously cared for child full time;
- whether the child had siblings in the same placement; whether there were other children or adults in the household;
- length of Social Services involvement prior to proceedings; who instigated the placement; type of order;
- whether the carer was assessed prior to placement; the type of assessment; whether the child went straight from home to kinship care; whether the child was in placement prior to proceedings;
- concerns expressed about placement during proceedings; parenting capacity as assessed during the proceedings; conflict/disagreement during proceedings;
- which local authority the case was from; whether the placement was within or outside of the authority boundary;

---

[47] $r = 0.432$, $p < 0.001$

[48] Farmer and Moyers (2008) report on child well-being but do not analyse the factors relating to better or poorer outcomes.

- level of support for the placement from Social Services while the case was open.

Overall rating of placement outcome

At the end of Chapter 3 we tabulated how well the children fared on each of the four outcome measures. To investigate what factors might be related to an overall outcome measure, we then divided the placements into three groups: those that achieved positive ratings on all four of the outcome measures; those that achieved positive ratings on between one and three of the outcome measures; and those that did not achieve positive ratings on any of the outcome measures.

Factors associated with overall rating of placement outcome

Child's age at the end of proceedings
As discovered for three out of the four outcome measures above, the child's age at the end of proceedings is a significant factor in explaining differences in our overall rating of placement outcome.[49] Children in placements with positive ratings on all of the outcome measures tended to be younger at the end of proceedings (mean = 2.5 years) than children with positive ratings on only some of the outcome measures (mean = 4.9 years). Older still were children in placements where there were no positive ratings on any of the outcome measures (mean = 9.3 years).

Whether the carer was assessed prior to the placement
There is a significant relationship between the overall placement outcome rating and whether the carer was assessed prior to placement.[50] Only nine per cent of placements where the carer was assessed had no positive ratings on any of the outcome measures, compared to 21 per cent of placements where the carer had not been assessed prior to placement. Thirty-five per cent of variance in overall outcome was explained by these two factors.

---

[49] $F = 21.4$, df = 2, $p < 0.001$
[50] $X2 = 7.49$, df = 2, $p = 0.024$

Factors not associated with overall placement outcome

There was a trend but not a significant relationship between the overall placement outcome rating and whether the child was cared for by a lone carer or a couple. Seven per cent of placements with single carers had no positive ratings on the four outcome measures, compared to 22 per cent of placements with couple carers.

There was also a trend between whether there was disagreement or conflict during the proceedings and overall placement outcome. Eight per cent of placements where there was disagreement had no positive ratings on the four outcome measures, compared to 32 per cent where there was no disagreement.

The remaining factors appeared to have no bearing on overall outcome:

- child's gender or ethnicity; level of adversity prior to placement;
- the carer's age; relationship to child; which parent they were related to; previously cared for child full time;
- whether the child had siblings in the same placement; whether there were other children or adults in the household;
- length of Social Services involvement prior to proceedings; who instigated the placement; type of order;
- the type of assessment; whether the child went straight from home to kinship care; whether the child was in placement prior to proceedings;
- concerns expressed about placement during proceedings; parenting capacity as assessed during the proceedings;
- which local authority the case was from; whether the placement was within or outside of the authority boundary;
- level of support for the placement from Social Services while the case was open.

Factors associated with better outcomes

The foregoing analysis identified 11 variables which had a statistically significant association with at least one of our outcome measures (Table 4.3).

It is striking that of these the only one which has explanatory value across more than one domain is the child's age at the end of the proceedings. As we have noted, this factor is also significantly associated with other variables which, while they appear to have no explanatory power on their own, may help to explain why age is such a potent factor. In particular, older children were significantly more likely to have experienced pre-placement adversities. These differences are also reflected in the fact that older children had had lengthier periods of Social Services involvement prior to placement.

Table 4.3
Factors associated with better outcomes

	Outcome measure	
Protective factors	*Statistically significant relationship*	*Trend*
Younger children	Placement stability	
	Relationship quality	
	Child well-being	
	Overall outcome	
Placement with a grandparent	Placement stability	
Previous full time care by index carer	Placement stability	Relationship quality
Child's acceptance of care	Placement stability	
No non-sibling children in household	Placement quality	
Carer assessment pre-placement	Placement quality	
	Overall outcome	
Favourable assessment of parenting capacity at time of proceedings	Placement quality	
Disagreement or conflict about the placement during proceedings	Placement quality	Overall outcome
Single carer placement	Relationship quality	Overall outcome
Carer instigator of placement	Relationship quality	Placement stability Placement quality
Fewer difficulties prior to placement	Child well-being	

* At end of proceedings

87

Not all cases, however, followed this pattern. For instance, there were four cases of older children (aged 10–14 years at the end of proceedings) where the placement was continuing and stable or had ended but lasted as long as was needed. When we looked closely at these, the most notable feature was the much greater level of involvement the kinship carer had previously had with the child in the successful placements. All the carers in these cases had had very frequent or intensive contact with these children and, as demonstrated above, this factor has predictive power over and above its relationship with the child's age at the end of proceedings. One child had had frequent respite stays and two had previously lived with the carers for quite substantial periods. This contrasted markedly with the unsuccessful group where four of the five children had only had occasional prior contact with the index carer, the other having had frequent but not staying contact. Thus, in cases where older children were placed successfully, they already knew their carers well and probably had an existing emotional bond (and maybe, importantly, the carer knew them well and what they were taking on).

One uncle who had previously cared for one child for an extended period with a residence order commented:

I'd known him all his life and had him for five years before so there wasn't really much they could tell me about him!

Similarly, there were five young children (aged under five at the end of the proceedings) whose placements did not last as long as needed, despite the generally better outcomes for this group. All these placements terminated prematurely within 12 months. It is harder to see a common thread here. In two cases, there seems to have been some ambivalence to the commitment/lifestyle changes needed to parent a young child, either on the part of the primary carer or a partner. Failure to acknowledge risk to the child resulted in one further placement ending. One placement ended because of the child's behaviour and conflict with another child in the household. Another child was moved to improve her emotional well-being because it was considered she was being swamped in a large household. It may also be relevant that two of these failed placements were made out of the local authority area, where it was more difficult to supervise and the level of support may therefore have been reduced. (We look further at this issue in Chapter 7.)

It is also important to note the factors which did not prove to have a statistically significant association with any of our outcome measures, viz:

- child's gender or ethnicity; the type of prior adversity suffered, i.e. parental circumstances, environmental factors, instability, bereavement, abuse/child protections concerns;
- the carer's age; which parent they were related to;
- whether the child had siblings in the same placement; whether there were other adults in the household;
- length of Social Services involvement prior to proceedings; type of order.
- the type of assessment; whether the child went straight from home to kinship care; whether the child was in placement prior to proceedings;
- concerns expressed about the placement during proceedings.

Of these, perhaps the most surprising is the apparent lack of relevance of being placed with siblings, which some (Berridge and Cleaver, 1987; Quinton *et al*, 1998), if not all (Holloway, 1997; Rushton *et al*, 2001), foster care research has suggested tends to be associated with better outcomes. Farmer and Moyers (2008) also found that both kinship and non-kin placements were more likely to be continuing if the child was placed with siblings. The children we interviewed who were placed with at least one sibling also highlighted how important this was to them (see Chapter 8). We are unable to account for this finding. It does not appear to be a function of age since, while children with siblings in the same proceedings tended to be older than those without, it was the younger sibling groups which tended to be placed together.[51]

Another point worth highlighting is the unimportance of the carer's

---

[51] Our data do not enable us to fully explore the effect of a sibling split as we only have details of splits that occurred as a result of proceedings. There may have been many more occurrences of siblings being split that are not detailed in our data because they happened outside of the care proceedings.

age, which did not even show up as a non-significant trend. Indeed, as we have seen, placements with grandparents, who on the whole are likely to be older than other related carers, were more likely to be stable but no more likely to raise concerns on any of the other outcome measures. If "ageism", as some writers argue (Stogdon, 2001), does underlie the perceived reluctance of some social workers to place with grandparents, it cannot find any legitimacy in the findings of this study. What we do not know, of course, is whether those carers where there were either genuine grounds for concern or simply prejudice, were screened out.

The findings reported in previous chapters suggested that the identity of the local authority might be important in explaining outcomes. Although this proved statistically significant in relation to only one outcome measure (relationship quality), Authority A, which had poorer outcomes on this measure, also had poorer outcomes in terms of placement stability, placement quality and overall. The only outcome on which Authority B came out worse, and then only marginally, was in how the children were functioning in placement and this was not statistically significant. However, once included alongside other variables in the regression models, the identity of the local authority lacked any explanatory power. It therefore seems likely that the reasons for the differences lie with the cases themselves.

Children with poor outcomes

As reported at the end of Chapter 3, 19 placements in the sample had particularly poor outcomes, not scoring positively on a single one of our four outcome dimensions. At follow-up, there were pronounced problems in many of these placements with attachment, bonding and meeting the children's emotional needs, compared with the children whose outcome was middling or good (see Table 4.4). Sixty-seven per cent of the poor outcome children had behavioural or emotional difficulties (compared with 22 per cent of the middling outcome group and none of the good outcomes group).

Table 4.4

Relationship issues

	Poor		Middling		Good	
	No.	%	No	%	No	%
Child's limited attachment to carer	13	72*	4	6	0	0
Carer ever requested removal	12	63**	7	10	0	0
Child's emotional needs unmet	8	47***	5	8	0	0
Not close to at least one carer	5	36****	3	5	0	0
(N=)	(14–18)		(65)		(25)	

*n=18 **n= 19 ***n=17 ****n= 14

In most instances, these poor outcomes had not been anticipated: 14 (74%) placements had worked out less well than anticipated (compared with 14 (21%) of the middling outcomes and none of the good outcomes groups) and perhaps most surprisingly, only three of the 19 carers had been assessed as of marginal parenting capacity at the care proceedings stage.

As might be expected from the analysis in the earlier part of this chapter, children with all-poor outcomes tended to be older (9.5 years on average at the end of the proceedings compared to 4.9 years for those in the middling group and 2.5 years for those with all good outcomes). Nearly two-thirds (12) were between 10 and 14, with only four 5–9 and three under five.

The children also differed markedly from those with better outcomes in some aspects of their history. Over half (56%), for instance, were already manifesting emotional and behavioural difficulties prior to placement (Table 4.5), compared to only 13 per cent of the middling and none of the good outcomes children. They were more likely to have lived in households with large numbers of children or children close in age; and to have experienced instability, neglect and parental rejection.

In summary, the poor outcomes children were already very damaged, with complex needs, and would probably have struggled in most substitute care placements.

Table 4.5

Children's outcomes by previous adversities

	Poor outcomes		Middling outcomes		Good outcomes	
Adversity	No.	%	No.	%	No.	%
EBD before placement	10	56*	9	13	0	0
EBD after placement	2	11	6	9	0	0
Household 3+ children	16	84	31	46	8	33***
Many changes in household	13	68	25	37	8	32
Neglect by parent	18	95	49	73	16	64
Rejected by parent	10	53	22	33	3	12
Children close in age in previous household	8	42	17	25	4	17***
Child learning difficulties	7	37	13	19	0	0
Understimulated	7	39*	14	22**	4	17***
Domestic violence	14	78*	42	63	16	67***
(N=)	(19)		(67)		(25)	

* n=18. **n=64 ***n=24

That three placements of under-fives had poor outcomes was concerning. One of these placements was holding, while two (both children aged one) had ended.

The "holding" placement had continuing problems in respect of both child difficulties and the carer's capacity to manage these:

Hannah, aged four at the end of proceedings, had been exposed to parental drug addiction (probably starting pre-natally) and chronic neglect. The carers were neighbours with children of their own, aged 9 and 5. For the first months the placement went well but Hannah had attachment difficulties which appeared to become more pronounced with the passage of time. There were confrontations with the carer and quite negative interactions were recorded. Sometimes the carers considered giving up but have continued for six years.

The placement breakdowns of the two very young children appeared to be wholly attributable to kinship carer factors. The first breakdown involved a boy, Zac, who after a period in foster care and a failed rehabilitation, joined a sibling already placed with a seemingly committed paternal aunt and husband:

> After Zac had been placed for eight months his aunt said they could not keep the children: their marriage was under threat because her partner was no longer committed to taking on two small children. The carers refused to act as a bridging placement until adopters could be identified and both children were moved to short-term foster care.

The second placement breakdown was a child who was one of two siblings split between maternal and paternal grandparents, where there were significant inter-family disputes. The grandmother of this child developed a serious alcohol problem and concerns arose about the child's welfare. Care proceedings were commenced and the child was removed. This child, and Hannah above, were the only two children in the under-five group where emotional and behavioural development (EBD) problems were identified *after* placement.

In respect of the older children in the poor outcomes group, the pattern emerging in many cases was of very difficult children, damaged by extensive exposure to various adversities, placed with well meaning and often fairly competent kinship carers who nevertheless struggled to handle the child's difficulties. Often they became exasperated in their handling of the child and this could result in a negative spiral and usually eventual breakdown of the placement. Some carers – as in Aidan's case below – persevered despite great problems, while Scott's carers (an aunt and uncle) requested that he be moved.

> Aidan, aged seven, was removed with his siblings from his mother's care after years of neglect, exposure to domestic violence and parental drug addiction. Already with serious behaviour problems and learning difficulties, he moved alone to his paternal grandparents. He continued to have significant difficulties and ADHD was diagnosed. The grandfather became disabled by dementia and the grandmother struggled to cope, at one point hitting Aidan with a belt. When 14, he was moved by agreement to residential care but his behaviour became more risky resulting in a return to the grandparents after further

assessment with a support package in place. The placement is very fragile.

Scott, aged 12 at the end of proceedings, was probably subject to severe chastisement and assaults by his parents over many years and was placed with his maternal aunt and husband who were able to offer him a permanent home where he would be the only child. The kinship carers were in receipt of invalidity benefit because of health problems and finances were tight. An initial honeymoon period followed placement with the child relishing the individual attention. He developed a real love of fishing with the aunt's husband. Misdemeanours were dealt with effectively with the removal of privileges. However, there then followed a deterioration in his behaviour and he began lying and stealing. Eventually the carers felt they could no longer cope with his behaviour and he was accommodated by the local authority.

It was not unusual for children with poor outcomes to have siblings in placement with them who fared better, emphasising that both children and carers can vary in their resilience. Nine of the children with poor outcomes had siblings with middling outcomes:[52]

Dexter was aged 12 at end of proceedings. His parents had severe drink problems and had subjected him and his older sister to emotional abuse. After the children had gone to stay with their paternal grandparents for a while, they refused to return home. Care proceedings were instituted, in the course of which the father died. Dexter remained in the placement for less than two years after the care proceedings ended; he had problems in school and needed bereavement counselling; his sister was bossy and controlling of him. He resented the strict boundaries set by the grandparents and returned to his mother after two years (although this placement did not work out and he moved to foster care). His older sister managed better and remained in placement until she moved to independence. She fell in the "middling outcomes" group.

---

[52] A further five poor outcomes children also had six siblings in other kinship placements with a better outcome.

Some placements appeared considerably disadvantaged from the outset:

Sammie, 11 years, moved (in accordance with her wishes) to her adult half-sister, aged 22, at the end of proceedings. There were concerns about whether the sister had the insight and emotional qualities necessary to meet Sammie's needs, and she had to share a bedroom with her sister's toddler. There were problems from the start with house rules and boundaries, with the kinship carer being very negative. The placement lasted nearly two years. Sammie then spent nearly three years in foster care before returning again, aged 16, to the sister. This second placement lasted nine months until, after a series of confrontations with her sister's partner, Sammie moved temporarily to her maternal grandmother.

Jake, aged 10, was the eldest of a set of six half and full siblings, all placed with relatives. The children had a history of long-term severe neglect. On placement with the maternal grandmother, Jake became very delinquent. A psychiatric report stated that, although the kinship carer cared for him deeply, he was a profoundly damaged child and a specialist therapeutic placement was recommended. Before this could be investigated, the placement broke down as the grandmother found Jake's behaviour just too difficult to cope with.

It is important to emphasise how the carers of the four children (three placements) who were in fragile but continuing placements were struggling on and showing great commitment to very difficult behaviour, as the case of the Mills children below emphasises. In this case Kester and Jay fell into our poor outcomes group while Blake was in the middling group:

Kester, Jay and Blake Mills were aged 14, 12 and 7 at the end of proceedings. In their parents' care there had been concerns over many years including exposure to domestic violence, physical abuse, difficult behaviour, poor school attendance, inappropriate sexual boundaries, and parental mental health problems. As a result of the care proceedings, the three boys were placed together (after much professional debate) with their maternal grandparents. The grandparents were very committed and co-operated with Social Services to ensure a good standard of care. Unfortunately, Kester and Jay were profoundly damaged by their early experiences and had attachment disorders; Kester became a persistent offender and later was drawn into substance abuse, while Jay also had severe problems. Nevertheless, the kinship carers persevered. Blake showed a marked improvement in his behaviour on placement with the grandparents and alone was able to sustain this.

Kinship carers can therefore show a great level of commitment to children who continue to pose severe problems. The case of Ed and Julie (both with middling outcomes) illustrate that carers can even stick with, and achieve a degree of success with, children who have exhausted the capacity of non-related carers who have rejected them.

Ed and Julie (7 and 2) had been with their grandparents throughout proceedings but professionals would not agree to them becoming long-term carers because of age and serious health issues. The grandparents withdrew their residence order application and agreed to keep the children while an adoptive home was found. In the event the grandparents cared for the children for nine months before the care orders were made and then for a further 11 months until the children moved to adoption. The children then suffered two adoption breakdowns due to the boy's disruptive behaviour and the ill-health of one adoptive carer. The children both returned to live with their now widowed grandfather and the placement has worked out satisfactorily.

It is important to bear in mind how difficult it is for any carer to repair a child's early adverse experiences, particularly where they are being asked to care for children who have been exposed to poor attachment, neglect and drugs or alcohol *in utero*. A high level of care and understanding is needed on the part of carers if the child is going to have an opportunity to become secure. Most of the 19 children in our poor outcome group would struggle in any care situation and, if in non-kin care, would probably have accompanying support packages. This emphasises how pivotal support and training for kinship carers may be. This is considered in Chapter 7.

Children with all good outcomes

Twenty-five (22%) of the kinship placements worked particularly well, scoring positively on all our measures. As noted earlier, siblings placed together did not necessarily have the same outcomes – while our all-good outcomes group included two pairs of siblings placed together, it also included five children with a sibling in the same placement with middling outcomes. This highlights the role played by exposure to previous adversity and the resilience of individual children.

The importance of age is also reflected in the fact that not only were most of these good outcome children (20; 80%) under five at the end of proceedings but over half were under two (14; 56%). The other five children were aged between five and seven. **There was not a single child in the all-good outcomes group who was more than seven years old at the end of the proceedings**.

The all-good outcome placements had also, typically, gone smoothly from the start. In contrast to the post-placement histories of the poor outcomes group, the good outcomes children appeared to have rather ordinary, secure stories. There was only one case where the child had had difficulties at the point of placement.

Rosie, who was aged five at the end of proceedings, had experienced physical abuse at the hands of her stepfather. She had a very poor bond with her mother who wanted her to be adopted. Rosie went into non-kin foster care. The social worker traced her father's family and she moved to her paternal grandmother and her partner. At the start of the placement Rosie needed much reassurance, had temper tantrums, could be jealous of visiting grandchildren and was over-affectionate to adults. Over the next four years, however, she thrived, her behaviour settled and she made a lot of progress. The care order was changed to a residence order.

In contrast to the poor outcomes group, where we typically found there had been little disagreement about the kinship placement during the care proceedings, the good outcomes group had been highly contentious, with disagreement in 76 per cent of cases. This may well have been because in addition to parents wanting another chance with young children, the local authority may have taken the view that these children were eminently adoptable and this would be a less risky option than placing with kin. (Overall, there was disagreement about placement in 75 per cent of cases where the children were under five, compared to only 30 per cent where they were over 10.)

> Kes (5) and Zara (4) were part of a sibling group of six children who had all been neglected and suffered exposure to domestic violence and their parents' unstable lifestyle. The parents dropped out of the proceedings. The issue was then whether Kes and Zara should be placed for adoption, in line with the local authority's care plan, or go to their aunt, who knew them well and had applied for a residence order. The local authority objected to the placement as the aunt was young, single, without any children of her own, one of the children was exhibiting some difficult behaviour and parental contact was potentially difficult. The court made a residence order. The children adjusted happily to the move and are doing well. The aunt now has a partner and two biological children. She acts as the "co-ordinator" for contact with the four other siblings, two of whom are fostered and two adopted. Only the birth mother has occasional contact and this has proved unproblematic.

When the under-fives group is compared with our non-kin sample, slightly more kin children fell in the all good outcomes group than non-kin-placed children (37% of kin compared with 33% of non-kin).

Summary

Factors independently statistically associated with *placement stability* included: younger children, placement with a grandparent, previous care by the index carer and the child not having asked to live elsewhere at any point. These four factors together explained 50 per cent of the variance in this outcome measure.

Factors independently statistically associated with *placement quality* included: no other children in the household apart from siblings, assessment of carer prior to placement of the child, favourable assessment of the kinship carer's parenting capacity during the proceedings and some disagreement about the placement during proceedings. These four factors together explained 45 per cent of the variance in this outcome measure.

Factors independently statistically associated with *relationship quality* included: the child being younger at the end of proceedings, placement with single carers, and placement being instigated by the relatives or by mutual agreement rather than by the local authority. These three factors together explained 45 per cent of the variance in this outcome measure. There was also an indication of some association between the carer having previously cared for the child and a better quality relationship.

Factors independently statistically associated with *child well-being* included: children who were younger at the end of proceedings and lower levels of child difficulty pre-placement. These two factors together explained only 24 per cent of the variance in this outcome measure.

Factors independently statistically associated with our *overall outcome measure* included: children who were younger at the end of proceedings and where their placement had followed an assessment of their carer. There was also some indication that children fared better with single carers and in placements where there was some disagreement about the placement during proceedings.

Only the age of the child at the end of the proceedings had an explanatory value across more than one outcome. Older child age itself was significantly associated with other variables which had no explanatory power on their own. These associations included: high level of pre-placement adversity exposure, pre-existing emotional/behavioural difficulties and lengthy Social Services involvement prior to placement.

Cases that bucked the trend highlighted the importance of intense contact pre-placement with the kinship carer: children doing well had substantial staying experience with their kinship carer while children in unsuccessful placements usually did not know their carer well.

From the above, 11 variables could be described as protective factors in kinship placements:

- younger children;
- previous full-time care by the index carer;
- grandparent care;
- single carer;

- pre-placement assessment;
- positive assessment of parenting capacity;
- child's acceptance of care;
- no other children in the household apart from siblings;
- disagreement about placement during proceedings;
- placement instigated by carer;
- low level of child difficulties pre-placement.

No statistical link was found between the following factors and any outcome: child's gender or ethnicity; carer age; which parent the carer was related to; siblings in placement; other adults in the household; length of Social Services involvement prior to proceedings; order type; assessment type; whether the child went straight from home to the kinship carer; whether the child was in placement prior to proceedings; and whether concerns were expressed about the placement during proceedings.

Many of the poor outcomes children were very damaged with complex needs; 56 per cent had emotional or behavioural difficulties prior to placement, a far greater proportion than either the middling or good group (13% and 0% respectively).

In respect of the older children with poor outcomes, the pattern emerging in many cases was of very difficult children, damaged by extensive exposure to various adversities, placed with well meaning and often fairly competent kinship carers who nevertheless struggled to handle the child's difficulties. Often they became exasperated in their handling of the child and this could result in a negative spiral and usually eventual breakdown of the placement.

It was not unusual for children with poor outcomes to have siblings in placement with them who fared better, emphasising that both children and carers can vary in their resilience.

It is difficult for any carer to repair a child's early adverse experiences, particularly if these include poor attachment, neglect and drugs or alcohol exposure *in utero*. A high level of care and understanding is needed on the part of carers if the child is going to have an opportunity to become secure. The majority of our poor outcome children would struggle in any care situation.

In contrast, the children who had good outcomes on all measures would probably have done well in any type of placement, being typically young and presenting few problems from the start. A comparison of children aged under five at the end of proceedings, however, showed that those placed with kin were slightly more likely to have all-good outcomes than those placed with non-kin.

5 Making decisions about kinship care

The Children Act 1989 prioritised the use of kinship placements when children are unable to live with their birth parents (s23 (6)). Yet while there has been a slow growth in the use of kinship foster care nationally (DH, 1991, 1999; DfES, 2005a), there appears to be considerable local variation (Waterhouse, 1997, 1999; Hall, 1999; Hunt and Macleod, 1999; Jackson and Thomas, 1999; Mansfield, 1999; Broad, 2001; Sykes *et al*, 2002; Harwin *et al*, 2003; Morgan, 2003; Sinclair *et al*, 2007; Farmer and Moyers, 2008). Sinclair, for example, reports that the proportion of foster placements made with kin in the authorities in his study varied between six and 32 per cent, and suggests that councils with low rates of kinship placements could, to advantage, aim to increase their usage.

Are some local authorities failing to make appropriate use of kinship care and if so, why? Is it because some social workers are reluctant to use it? Are the reasons structural, to do with the way decisions are made often in an emergency, by workers who do not know the family (Waterhouse 2001)? Or is it that, from the beginning of their contact with a family, social workers focus too narrowly on the parents and are blind to the positive contribution the extended family could make (Stogdon, 2001)? Although our study was not designed primarily to address these questions, it may shed light on some of them. This chapter considers these issues by examining decision-making by the local authority, kinship carers and the courts.

Local authority decision-making

Could more children have been placed in kinship care?
Overall, 281 children in our four-year cohort went into non-kin substitute care. This represented 79 per cent of all the children unable to return to a parent, the remaining 21 per cent being in kinship care (proportions identical for our two local authorities). Our non-kin sample of 31 children

aged under five years at the end of proceedings was drawn from the first three years of this group and enabled us to look at whether kinship care had ever been explored as an option for those children and why it had been rejected.

Farmer and Moyers (2008) found evidence that a kinship placement had been considered in only 43 per cent of their study placements with *non-kin* carers. Our findings are more positive – surprisingly so, bearing in mind that our data related to care proceedings between 1995 and 1998 when kinship care had a somewhat lower profile. There was evidence that the kinship option had been considered at some time for 77 per cent of the 24 children placed in non-kin care (with very similar proportions for each of the two authorities [Appendix Table F1]). However, in a striking echo of earlier research on care proceedings (Hunt and Macleod, 1999), such consideration had *not* usually occurred *before* proceedings were initiated: only for six (25%) of our non-kin sample children was there evidence that relatives were considered at this earlier stage. Authority B had twice as many cases where file data indicated that relatives were considered at this point, although the numbers are obviously very small. Moreover, even where kinship care was considered at any stage, only 31 relatives, mainly maternal,[53] were noted, a rather low figure given that the children potentially would have had 48 sets of grandparents and maybe as many aunts and uncles.[54]

This rather limited exploration of kin is surprising in that the extended family had been by no means marginal in the lives of a substantial minority of the children in the non-kin sample. Six (20%) children had actually been in the previous full-time care of relatives (either informally (3) or as looked after children (3)). In two further cases, relatives had offered substantial care to older siblings of the index child (still on-going in one case). Additionally, 23 per cent of the non-kin sample children had

---

[53] 74 per cent maternal, 26 per cent paternal compared with 66 per cent and 34 per cent for index carers in the kinship cohort.

[54] The parents in the non-kin sample were significantly older at the end of proceedings than the parents in the kinship under-five group (see Appendix C), so there may have been a demographic component in ability to care, i.e. the possible relative carers in the non-kin group could be older and therefore less inclined to commit to taking on a child. We do not have the data to explore this further.

lived with their mothers in a relative's home at some point (almost always a grandparent) – slightly under half the rate reported for the kin-placed under-fives (47%), but nonetheless not an insignificant proportion. In a further two cases, relatives were involved enough to report concerns about the child to the local authority.

It is arguable that these findings of limited exploration of kin provide grounds for concern in that, for over three-quarters of the children, insufficiently wide-ranging enquiries were made, while for the remaining 23 per cent of the children there appeared no obvious record of any enquiries at all. It may be that either the parent was reluctant to identify extended family members (although in our kinship group there was evidence in only one case that the birth parent refused to allow relatives to be approached to take the child) or the local authority did not properly identify the child's own network of relatives, at least in a way that was formally recorded on the child's file.

When we looked at the reasons why kinship placements were not made in the 24 cases where relatives *were* considered, we found that the relatives were more than twice as likely to decline to take the child (12 cases) than the local authority was to refuse to place (5 cases).[55] Typical examples of reluctance by relatives to take on a child are illustrated in the two cases below.

Darren's paternal aunt already had residence orders for two of his older siblings and initially expressed a wish to care for Darren as well. She later withdrew as she felt unable to give him the individual attention he needed.

The maternal grandparents and an aunt had both been involved with Ellie's family. All, however, were concerned about her mother's capacity to disrupt a placement because of her psychiatric problems. The aunt, moreover, was pregnant and the grandparents thought they were too old. They wanted Ellie to be placed for adoption with her sibling, who was already in an adoptive placement, and to maintain letterbox links. The aunt had completed a life story book for the older sibling and agreed to do the same for Ellie.

---

[55] In the remaining seven cases it was not clear who was responsible for the matter not being pursued.

Of the five cases where it was clear that Social Services had refused to place with willing relatives, only two (both from Authority A) were rejected because of concerns over the relative's parenting capacity (one following a preliminary assessment, the other after a fuller investigation). Since, as we reported in Chapter 4, assessed parenting capacity was predictive of later placement quality, these decisions would not appear *prima facie* unreasonable.

Jamie's grandparents applied for a residence order one month into care proceedings. Social Services' preliminary assessment concluded they were unsuitable – all their children were school refusers, the parent had been the subject of a supervision order for non-school attendance; there had been poor co-operation with Social Services in the past. The grandparents did not agree with the assessment but withdrew their application. At the final hearing they were said to be considering their position and might still pursue their application but in the event did not do so.

Two other cases involved concerns about the child's safety because Social Services judged that the relative did not perceive the parent to be a risk, even though in one case it had been the relative who alerted them to the problems. In the fifth case, it was considered that the child 'needed a confidential placement to avoid family difficulties'. We wondered whether social workers were being unduly cautious in these cases, given, as we report later in this chapter, the general inaccuracy of their predictions about future problems. However, it should be noted that there was no evidence that guardians had opposed any of these decisions, four of which had involved applications for residence orders.

Curiously, we had two children in the study who were first cousins, going through proceedings a couple of years apart. One, Natasha, was placed with non-kin for adoption, although her maternal grandparents had applied to become carers. Two years later, when Bradley's case was brought, the same relatives applied to care and this time were successful. These cases illustrate some of the dilemmas in decision-making within care proceedings where the age of the child, existing bonds, the perceived parenting capacity of the kinship carer and local authority aspirations for a child all play a part in how a case is resolved and its subsequent outcome:

> Natasha, a dual heritage child, had suffered non-accidental injury by her mother's partner; other parenting concerns had also been reported by the relatives. After her mother failed a residential assessment, Natasha moved to foster care. Her maternal grandparents made a residence order application but were not supported by Social Services because of concerns that they did not recognise the risk posed by the mother and their relationship with her was difficult. It was also not considered an ethnically appropriate match as the grandparents were white British. The application was withdrawn. Natasha was aged one when the court agreed a care plan of adoption. An ethnically appropriate adoptive family was unsuccessfully sought for her and Natasha was subsequently adopted by her white short-term foster carers.

> Bradley's early care had caused concern because of lack of bonding with his depressed mother. Social Services took no further action as the maternal grandparents took over his care for much of the first two years of his life (during which time Natasha's case was going through the courts). Bradley returned to his mother but was removed after serious non-accidental injury (caused by mother's boyfriend). He was placed with foster carers as the mother refused permission for the grandparents to be informed. When they became aware of what had happened, the grandparents came forward and requested that they be assessed as carers and despite some reservations Bradley, now aged four, was placed with them at the end of proceedings. A recent discharge application was unsuccessful and Bradley remains monitored on a care order because of reservations about the placement.

Generally, the findings from our non-kin sample do not suggest that a negative stance by the local authority towards kinship placements was the *primary* explanation for children going to permanence in non-kin care, although it is possible that there was a degree of over-caution. There was some evidence that social workers could be more pro-active in exploring the potential for care within the extended family (see also below). However, it is also important to recognise that for some children there may be only limited options or even none at all. This suggests that expanding the use of kinship care may largely depend on the local authorities' commitment to supporting and enabling those relatives who have an existing relationship with a child, and actively wish to put themselves forward, to care.

Who took the initiative in exploring the kinship option?

Our kinship sample data regarding who instigated the placement also suggested there was scope for social workers to be more pro-active in exploring the resources of the extended family.

Farmer and Moyers (2008) report that 86 per cent of the placements in their study were instigated by the relatives themselves, 10 per cent by children or parents and only four per cent by social workers. Our data suggested a rather more active role for Social Services, who appeared to have been the prime mover in 33 per cent of cases (36 of the 109 where information was available), while in a further 17 per cent, the placement was initiated by a process of mutual agreement involving Social Services. The carers, however, did seem to have been the primary agents (47; 43%), with children and parents playing a minor role (6%).

This pro-activeness of the index carers was borne out in the carer interviews. Almost half the carers (18; 49%) said it was their idea that the children came to live with them:

I even wrote a letter to Social Services particularly stating I didn't want Lauren to go into foster care if for some reason her mother could not look after her – I was quite prepared to look after her.

Only 10 (27%) said that the initiative came from the local authority.

Where the placement was expected to be long term from the beginning, carers were even more likely to cite themselves as initiating the idea (65% long term cf 21% short term). In contrast, Social Services was said to be the initiator in more cases where the placement was originally envisaged as short term (42%) rather than long term (17%).

It seems essential, then, that at the very least, at an early stage in care proceedings social workers should undertake a mapping exercise with the child's parents and other available relatives to ensure that a clear picture of the child's extended family is built up, including practical information regarding the location and contact details of relatives, so that all possible options for the child can be fully explored. Indeed, we would argue that such mapping should be routinely undertaken as part of social work with families of children at risk of care so that, if and when a crisis arrives, there is knowledge of potential resources.

The White Paper, *Care Matters: Time for Change* (DfES, 2007), published after our report was completed, outlines a 'gateway approach to family and friends care, to make sure that it is considered as a option at the first and every subsequent stage of decision-making' (para 2.38). The new procedures for care proceedings (the Public Law Outline, Ministry of Justice, 2008) also require that the extended family be considered as carers and information on this included as part of the care plan, which must be filed at the initiation of care proceedings.

Our findings would support these proposals. There is one slight caveat. In Chapter 4 we noted that the pro-activeness of relatives was significantly associated with a good bond with the child, i.e. there were more likely to be relationship difficulties in placements initiated by the Social Services compared with those initiated by the relative or by mutual agreement. However, we do not think it would be justifiable to conclude that this statistical link means social workers should not be more active in seeking out relatives, since there were successful placements which did not follow this pattern. Identifying all possible carers has to be the first step; assessing their suitability is a separate process.

We were surprised that only one kinship carer identified the guardian ad litem as taking the initiative, since other research (Hunt *et al*, 2003) suggests a more significant role. However, the file data did indicate that in some cases the guardian did play an active part 'behind the scenes' in terms of locating, supporting or encouraging the carer to make the approach, as the case study below indicates:

> Evan and his mother moved into the area when he was 18 months old. At the age of four Evan was made subject of an emergency protection order after sustaining non-accidental injuries. The guardian approached the estranged father, who had remained in the family's home area and had had no contact for three years. He and his mother discussed the situation and put forward a plan that Evan should move

to his paternal grandmother and her partner on a care order and, if the father gained confidence, Evan could move to his full-time care. The guardian supported them in this plan.

It is also not inconceivable that the presence of the guardian in a case will have affected the approach of the local authority. As can be seen later in this chapter, the guardian has an active and important role later in the proceedings. If it is known that guardians and courts will be vigilant in ensuring that adequate mapping of the extended family has taken place, that relatives are approached and that any offer to care for the child is properly assessed, then local authority solicitors are likely to advise social workers that this needs to have been at least started before the case comes to court.

Could the children have been placed earlier?

Sixty-three per cent (71) of the kin sample children went to relatives without an intervening period in other forms of substitute care,[56] with little difference between our two authorities. Most (59), moreover, went straight to the index carers, only nine spending a period of time with other relatives.

Forty of the remaining 42 children[57] moved into kinship care having spent between one night and 28 months[58] in non-kin foster care, with peaks for moving at one month post placement and six to 12 months (mean 6 months). Sixty per cent of those needing foster care spent three months or more in non-kin foster care (not necessarily the same foster home) with 19 per cent (8) not moving for a year or more.[59]

---

[56] This figure includes two children who had a period in hospital due to the injuries and one child who went to live with his estranged father before moving into the index placement four months later.

[57] During proceedings, two children moved back to their parent from non-kin foster care for an unsuccessful attempt at rehabilitation. When this failed they both moved directly to kinship care from the parent. These are excluded from the counts that follow.

[58] The longest stay (28 months) was a child who was eventually placed abroad.

[59] There was little difference between our two local authorities in the time children spent in non-kin foster care (38% in Authority A being there for six months or more, compared to 43% in Authority B).

Five of these 40 children had actually been moved to non-kin foster care from relatives. In two different cases, this was because the child was considered at risk of sexual abuse because of the associations of their respective grandmothers.[60] A sibling group of three was also temporarily moved – at the request of the index carer – because of the disruptive behaviour of an alcoholic father.

An examination of the remaining 35 cases suggests that there were generally cogent reasons why these children moved to non-kin foster care rather than directly to their kinship carer:

- Six children (all Authority A) had already been accommodated in non-kin foster care for some time when proceedings started. In four of these cases, the eventual kinship carer was not obviously on the scene either at the point of accommodation or when proceedings started. These children had the longest stays in non-kin foster care – 83 per cent having spent over six months and 50 per cent over a year, with a mean of 13 months.

- All 20 children[61] removed from home to non-kin foster care at the start of proceedings were moved in an emergency situation, with over half (12) subject to either police protection or emergency protection orders. This would have given little, if any, time to identify relatives who were not already known to Social Services[62] (although since all the cases were already known, perhaps this should have been anticipated by the local authority, with a search being made for possible

---

[60] One of these returned to their kinship carer, the other was placed with another family member.

[61] 3 Authority A, 17 Authority B.

[62] Children subject to emergency orders were less likely to be placed directly with the index carer. Of children subject to police protection/emergency protection orders (PP/EPO), 36 per cent were placed with the index carer compared with 57 per cent of agreed emergency removals. Social workers appeared, nevertheless, active in pursuing the wider kinship option as these figures rise to 57 per cent (PP/EPOs) and 62 per cent (agreed emergency removal) of children in kinship placements when non-index relative placements are included. However, it could also be that an emergency order was less likely to be needed if the child was going to a relative precisely because they were a relative and parents were more amenable to this (as opposed to non-kin foster care) and therefore the child did not require legal protection.

carers in the kinship network). In most instances, the eventual kinship carers were not easily accessible at the point of crisis: for example, in 12 cases the child had a distant genetic relationship with the index carer (e.g. grandfather's sister), leading to a delay in identification, while in 10 cases there were cross-county or even cross-country features.

- Eight children[63] were moved from their parents to non-kin foster care during the course of proceedings, by which time, it is arguable, there could have been contingency plans in place to ensure they moved to their index placements. However, four of these instances were accounted for by a sibling group placed overnight in an emergency "out of authority" foster placement in the town where they had been living with their mother, before rapidly moving on to their index placement in the study authority. In a fifth case, the potential kinship carer lived abroad and the child could therefore not be placed until the end of proceedings – that child already had had several respite periods with their non-kin foster carer. In the remaining three cases, however, one of which involved a failed residential parenting assessment, we did wonder why a direct move to the index carer could not have been achieved, particularly since in at least two, relatives were obviously in the picture by this point.

- The remaining case involved a baby removed at birth because of serious mental health concerns about the parents. This child went to non-kin foster carers because of allegations made by the mother against the eventual index carer (these were subsequently disproved).

In only three cases[64] were children moved to non-kin foster care in preference to kinship care because of concerns about the relative's capacity as a substitute carer.[65] An equal number of placements were made because of a difficult relationship between the parent and the eventual

---

[63] Out of a total of 20 moving from parents during proceedings.

[64] Excluding the two cases of children removed from their grandmothers referred to above.

[65] One case each: grandparent had criminal convictions; father alleging own childhood ill-treatment; parent alleging own sexual abuse as a child.

kinship carer,[66] including the only case we were aware of where the parent refused to let relatives be contacted at the point the child needed care. Overall, there were only eight cases where the failure to place with kin was not clearly explained in the file data and it could conceivably have been possible to achieve a direct move to the index carer.

As soon as Kirsty was born, the local authority applied for a care order and plans were made to assess the mother's parenting ability. Mother and baby were placed with first one maternal great-aunt and then another before moving into a residential assessment unit. When the assessment failed, however, Kirsty was removed into non-kin foster care where she remained for three months before moving back to the second maternal aunt who had asked to be assessed as a carer. It is not clear why Kirsty had not been placed direct from the residential placement.

Immediate placement with kin is obviously potentially advantageous to children not only because they are more likely to be moving to people they know but because it reduces the risk of serial moves. Of the 42 children who were with the index carer by the start of proceedings, only three (7%) had even one move during proceedings.[67] Even where children were placed with other relatives in the first instance, it was unusual (3 of 9) for them to have more than one move.

In contrast, 10 (32%)[68] of the kinship index children placed in non-kin foster care had two or more changes of foster placement during the care proceedings, while in our non-kin sample, 20 per cent had at least two foster placements during proceedings (including one child who had three changes).

Early placement with a kinship carer, however, carries its own risks in that it can preclude a thorough assessment before the child arrives. As

---

[66] Mother implacably hostile to her parents being approached; grandfather unwilling to take the child without a legal order as he was worried the child would be removed by the mother; mother's resentment towards the maternal aunt.

[67] Two of these driven by the local authority because of their reservations about the kinship placement, in the other the reason was unclear.

[68] 3 Authority A, 7 Authority B.

stated earlier, in Chapter 4, we found a relationship between whether the carer was assessed prior to the placement being made and placement quality, i.e. where an assessment was carried out prior to placement the placement was of better quality, so we would not necessarily wish to advocate early kinship placement at the expense of assessment. The use of early viability assessments that focus primarily on parenting capacity may help to resolve this tension. This is discussed later in the chapter.

Another potential problem with early placement is that it may also deny the child the opportunity to be placed with an estranged parent. There were two cases in the study where "lost" single fathers, possibly well able to care with their own family support, came forward in the proceedings but after the child had moved to a maternal kinship placement. Both sets of kinship carers considered the children had settled well with them and were resistant to the child being moved. By the end of proceedings the "status quo" of the child's placement was agreed by all the parties, albeit with some reluctance by at least one of the fathers. This emphasises that it is important for "family mapping" to include separated birth fathers as well as other relatives.

What do social workers think about kinship care?

Previous research

A potential influence on the decision whether or not to place with kin is likely to be the attitudes of social workers. Both UK and US research have shown that workers are generally positive in their views about the value of kinship placements (Beeman and Boisen, 1999; Berrick *et al*, 1999; Doolan *et al*, 2004; Sinclair *et al*, 2007; Farmer and Moyers, 2008). A UK study by Doolan *et al* (2004) found that all those interviewed supported kin placements, with a large majority seeing it as the best option and first choice for children. Indeed, 77 per cent of US social workers interviewed by Beeman and Boisen agreed that children were better off in kinship care than non-kin foster care.

Kinship care is valued by social workers as enhancing children's identity and sense of belonging and preserving family ties (Beeman and Boisen, 1999; Doolan *et al*, 2004; Peters, 2005; Farmer and Moyers, 2008). It can also lessen the stigma for a child (Doolan *et al*, 2004; Peters, 2005).

There appear to be mixed views as to the quality of care that kinship placements afford. Social workers in Peters' study (2005) considered that children do better in growth and development when placed with kin, while many of those in the study by Sinclair *et al* (2007) saw placements as offering poorer care. Research also suggests that social workers can simultaneously hold positive and negative views on kinship care and that some still subscribe to the ideas expressed in the phrase 'the apple does not fall far from the tree' (Peters, 2005; Farmer and Moyers, 2008), i.e. the problems the parents have experienced in caring for their children is attributable in large part to the care they received from their parents.

Kinship placements can be experienced as more time consuming and difficult to supervise because of role confusion (Beeman and Boisen, 1999; Berrick *et al*, 1999; Doolan *et al*, 2004) and more complex family dynamics (Berrick *et al*, 1999; Farmer and Moyers, 2008). Co-operation can be a problem (although 58 per cent of social workers interviewed by Beeman and Boisen thought most kinship carers were co-operative with agencies). Concerns have also been voiced about safety, collusion, divided loyalties and lack of objectivity about parents (Beeman and Boisen, 1999; Berrick *et al*, 1999; Chipman *et al*, 2002; Doolan *et al*, 2004; Farmer and Moyers, 2008). Social workers in the recent study by Sinclair *et al* (2007), while described as generally positive about kinship care, also emphasised that many carers required a great deal of support.

Findings from this study

Since the placements in our study were made several years ago it was usually not feasible to interview the placing social workers.[69] What we have to say is based on 24 interviews with the social work professionals involved in our active cases, where, in addition to questions about the specific case, we explored their general attitudes to kinship care. It is also important to note that, whereas our placements were made in the mid to late 1990s, the social workers we interviewed were giving a contemporary perspective on attitudes to kinship care.

The social workers identified many advantages for **children** of being

---

[69] We interviewed two team managers and two social workers who had been involved at the time of placement.

placed with kin. Echoing the research cited above, they considered it was less stigmatising; gave them a sense of belonging; provided more stability and continuity, facilitated contact, and enabled children to develop their identity within a context of a known history, particularly important where a placement needed to be culturally and religiously appropriate.

A huge advantage is that the kinship carer has knowledge of the birth parents and the children's situation and can report that to the children.

(Children can feel) this is part of your family, you are within your family.

They stay in the family, they can often stay in their community, continuities in their education, they can know who they are.

Children are subject to less uncertainty in kinship care (and have) less worry about being moved.

Interviewees also commented on the good relationships children enjoyed with their carers and reported that kinship carers 'seem more dedicated to the children' and were willing to 'cope with children staying longer into independence'.

When asked whether social workers had more anxieties about placing children in kinship care than non-kin care, a substantial proportion (11 of 24) said they did not, and most (8) said they only had marginally more worries. Indeed, one social worker even commented, 'No, it's the other way around. I wish I could place *all* children in families'. Generally, it seemed that social workers had concerns for children in both types of placement but the worries were different.

We did detect some ambivalence in the group about the merits of kinship care. While one told us that 'the results [of kinship care compared with non-kin care] can be much better', others voiced concern regarding less favourable outcomes, saying, for example, 'other children I work with do better'. Three reiterated 'the apple never falls far from the tree' idea: 'you can end up putting the child through similar childhood experiences to their parents'.

Some commented that the presumed benefits of kinship care might not always materialise: 'Not all children have that strong a bond with kinship carers and it can be as difficult for a child to make the bond with the kinship carer as with non-kin'. Contact was a double-edged sword, with more social workers stressing the potential difficulties than the advantages. Children might be adversely affected by the complexity of feelings the situation generates in their carers: '[grandparent placements] might not work so well . . . because of the intensity of relationships – they feel differently towards the child. An aunt and uncle may not carry the guilt that a grandparent does'. Children might be left longer in poor placements with kin than they would have been with non-kin and when a placement failed it could have a greater impact on the child than the breakdown of a non-kin placement.

What predominantly emerges from the interviews, however, is the challenge that kinship care can present to **workers** more accustomed to dealing with non-kin foster carers. It was notable that only a quarter of those interviewed had received specific training on kinship care, while 54 per cent said they would like such training.[70]

Almost all the interviewed social workers thought working with kinship placements was different from working with non-kin foster carers. Non-kin foster care was seen as a professional, detached task where boundaries were clear, support would be usually welcome and expectations were higher.

It is their choice to do it, they have training and are approved, they understand you have to be professional and not cross boundaries, they also get link worker support.

In kinship care, however, as one social worker put it:

It is different. You take on the whole family. It's a package with kinship care, you need to be in tune with who's who in the family and what their role is because of the carer's emotional response to parents. In non-kin foster care it's treated like a job.

---

[70] Training topics: some social workers were vague and said 'anything'. More specific training needs included responsibilities for separate support for child/carer; research evidence; joint training with kinship team to understand different viewpoints.

Interviewees stressed the need to take a more global and sensitive approach in kinship care:

You have to work with more than just the child.

The social worker needs to be more aware of the sense of loyalty, attachment, personal investment. Kin need to feel respected, you need to be tactful.

You need to be more sensitive to the reasons for placement, for example where grandparents have to adjust to a child being injured by the mother and her partner. Non-kin foster parents don't have those feelings.

They also repeatedly mentioned the need for clear boundaries, especially over parental contact. Nine of the social workers interviewed referred to the potential for conflict or collusion between kinship carers and birth parents over contact, which could be 'hard to manage', with carers being 'torn by limits imposed by Social Services':

The level of control is difficult, they tend to do what they want, they don't adhere to statutory requirements.

With kinship care, we're more lenient when we shouldn't be. Kinship carers can manipulate re: contact. We wouldn't tolerate foster carers behaving in this way.

Interestingly, however, only one social worker mentioned concerns over compliance with any other requirements:

They think the children are their own. Shared parental responsibility can be difficult – kinship carers wanting to make decisions without parents' consent.

Indeed, one social worker said that kinship carers were less likely to be resistant than non-kin carers:

Some foster carers are very good but some are not. [They can have] a real sense of power – don't tell me how to do this. You don't get that with kinship carers.

The fact that working with kinship care presents different challenges does not necessarily mean that relationships with carers are difficult. Fifty-six per cent of the social workers interviewed by Beeman and Boisen (1999) said they enjoyed working with kinship carers despite the difficulties of agency co-operation and complex family relationships. Indeed, one of the social workers in our study commented that she had found working with a kinship placement 'nicer, I enjoyed it as I had a lot of discussions about the past, and understood the child's difficulties'. However, three social workers did say they found such placements more problematic: '[it is] more difficult dealing with families who see Social Services as the baddies'. There was a need for mutual trust and for 'kinship carers to be honest with social workers . . . if there is a positive relationship between social worker and kinship carer it can work very well'.

Kinship carers were also seen to vary in their need for, and willingness to accept support. One worker felt that kinship carers were more dependent on social workers and another told us:

I love the idea of children in their families but anecdotally you hear of placements needing social work support to the end. Non-kin placements are an attractive alternative to years of social work support to keep things going.

In contrast, others saw kinship carers as, on the positive side, being more willing to sort things out for themselves, without involving the social worker, or more negatively, as being resistant to support:

You don't need to be so involved, as kinship carers are very willing to address concerns before getting the social worker to support them, compared with non-kin foster carers who would want a response from the start.

Non-kin foster carers are not committed to dealing with day-to-day issues, they will pass it out to social workers. Kinship carers try to resolve these issues. They don't see it as a job but as trying to keep the family together.

Foster carers are open to support and welcome it when it's in the child's best interests; kinship carers don't always see it that way.

Carer decision-making

Why do kinship carers take on this huge commitment? How well informed do they feel about what they are taking on? Do they have second thoughts afterwards? Why do some relatives decide they cannot offer to care?

The decision to care

He's our grandchild and we would never have stood by and let him go into care. We'd had him every weekend from when he was tiny so there was no question that he wouldn't come to us.

There has been surprisingly little academic interest, even in the broader sociological literature on kinship, in why relatives decide to care (Hunt, 2006). This is a complex question which we can do no more than touch on here.

There is no requirement in UK law for relatives to care for kin. However, a sense of family obligation clearly underpins many carers' decision to take on care (Geen, 2003). A recent survey of social attitudes in the general population in Scotland (Wasoff and Martin, 2005) found that 85 per cent of respondents thought that, where children could not live with their birth parents, grandparents should care if they were able to. This sense of 'felt obligation' (Pryor, 2006) was evidenced in our study in comments such as: 'they are my family and they needed help', 'you never turn your own family away' and 'someone has to look after them and if the family can't, who can?'

For many carers, however, obligation is likely to be interwoven with affectional bonds with the child (Broad, 2001; Geen, 2003). Most of the carers in our study had had a high level of involvement with the child prior to placement, with almost two-thirds of the children (65%; 72 of the 111 where this was known) having had at least weekend or respite stays, of whom almost a half (35) had cared full-time for a period.[71] Others had

---

[71] 35 children had previously been in the full-time care of their index kinship carer; 12 had lived with their mother with the kinship carer (always the grandparent); 25 children had had weekend and respite stays.

provided regular day care or babysitting or seen the child on a frequent basis. While this cannot be an essential pre-requisite, since in 16 cases in our study the carers had little or no prior acquaintance with the child,[72] it was notable that the majority of the carers interviewed explained their decision to care in terms of their pre-existing bonds with the child:

> *I was definitely emotionally involved with these kids. Was it because they were related to my eldest son? I don't know. They were just lovely, lovely kids.*

> *It was getting involved with him in the first place. If you're not involved you don't know them do you? If I didn't know him I don't think I would have done it . . . what you don't know you don't miss, what you've never had . . . you know what I mean. It would have been easier [to let him go if not attached], we wouldn't have known each other . . . been like strangers.*

Indeed, some carers told us that they were deliberately not getting involved with siblings more recently born to the child's parents because they knew that if anything went wrong they would feel they had to take these children in as well when they could not do it:

> *We have very little contact with Euan [the mother's third child] because we don't want to get involved and were frightened of making those relationships. We made it very clear from the beginning there's no way. If we had that in the beginning with the boys we wouldn't have found it so hard to let them go.*

One carer also told us that she had felt able to let the child's sibling go to another relative because she did not have a relationship with this child, a young baby: 'I wasn't attached to the baby and I wasn't going to [get attached]'.

Some carers also explained their decision with reference to the likely impact on a parent:

---

[72] 11 carers had seen the child occasionally; one had only met the child once; one had never met the child and three children were placed shortly after birth.

It was an opportunity to keep Ryan here for his Dad so that he could keep contact with him.

I had to do it for my daughter's sake. I would have had a dead daughter on my hands if I hadn't – she almost committed suicide over what had happened.

However, there were remarkably few examples of this, possibly because of the circumstances in which relatives were taking on care and the often poor relationships with parents by this point (Chapter 9).

Most of the carers interviewed told us that if they had not taken on the care of the child, then there was nobody else in the family who could do so and thus prevent the child being exposed to what they saw as the uncertainties of the care system (see also Broad, 2001; Spence, 2004).

He would have gone from foster carer to foster carer, from home to home and I feel he may have gone down the wrong road, would have got in with the wrong people.

If they had been adopted, they would have had to move from stranger to stranger and it would have been very difficult for them to feel trust and feel settled.

I knew that it would be foster care or homes and it wouldn't be anywhere settled for him.

It is interesting to speculate whether, if the carer system was better/perceived as better, fewer relatives would step forward. Certainly a small number of our interviews with kinship carers suggested this was possible:

We didn't want them to be shunted around from foster carer to foster carer. If we could have got a cast iron guarantee that these two would have gone to a good adoptive home then we would have said yeah – do that.

They said he'd go to a white family as there were no Asian families. They tried to seek out an Asian family on a couple of occasions. Initially at the beginning I thought he would move on. If they had found an Asian family that would have been OK.

We suspect, however, that for many carers it is not the quality of the care system which is the key issue but the mere fact of the child going out of the family. Sometimes this was expressed by our interviewees in terms of what the child would lose, including some interesting comments about remaining with their family being a child's 'birthright' and the injustice of an innocent child being deprived of that:

It was not fair for him to be away from his family. He could visit his mother and brothers and sisters if he was with us.

I felt it was unfair to put her out of the family when she hadn't done anything wrong.

Others referred to their own need to keep in touch with the children or, more broadly, to the desire to keep the family together and ensure its continuity:

She was our granddaughter. She belongs to us. Family should stay together.

We just felt somebody's got to do it, otherwise she would be lost to the family.

The common thread in the responses, however, was a sense that carers felt they had no real choice, they had to act as they did. Carers were also adamant that this did not result from external pressure (only one carer reported feeling under some slight pressure from Social Services and no one referred to any overt pressure from their families). Rather, carers were driven by their own sense of what was "right", with one commenting, 'It wasn't pressure, it was something I had to do'.

Sometimes this was expressed very positively, as something that the carers wanted to do, in other cases it seemed more that they could not bring themselves to act otherwise.

I couldn't have lived with myself . . . I went through so many different things. I remember thinking what if I say no, I can't have you. I know that if I'd made that decision it would have been something that I would have come through and would have stuck by it but it would have been really, really hard to say I can't do this.

We didn't really feel under pressure just that we had no choice; there was nowhere else for Ryan to go apart from foster carers or adoption. Nobody else came forward to offer him a home. It would have been hard for us to accept he'd gone somewhere else.

How carefully do carers consider their decision?

As will be evident from the preceding section, one or two carers had clearly agonised over what they should do:

What was the alternative after they had lived on and off with us for years? They come back to us from rehab, then to say to us you decide whether you want to keep them or put them into foster care and when they were already very anxious boys. We couldn't see the wood for the trees to make that decision. It's the only bit of stability they've seen.

A few others reported giving it very careful consideration:

Mother wanted me to take Ashley from when she was one month old. But I had a lot of thinking to do, it was a big decision for me to take her and to start all over again. My own children were nearly grown up. That's why Ashley didn't come until she was 10 months old. Social Services contacted me to ask if I would be willing to have her. I said I couldn't say positively, I'd have to think about it and look at all the information and make a decision.

However, the dominant theme to emerge from our interviews was that many did not conceptualise their decision as a choice, or something to be pondered over, variously stating: 'it wasn't a big decision', 'it seemed the natural thing to do' and 'she's my granddaughter, how could I not?'. Sometimes this instant decision-making may have been because there really was no time – 14 of the 37 carers interviewed had children placed in a crisis:

A social worker rang out of the blue asking if I would have him, she said if you don't have him he'll have to go to a foster home. I said I'll have him – no foster home for my grandson.

Even where this was not the case, several carers referred to things being 'sudden', 'out of the blue' or 'not much time to think, all a bit of a shock'.

However, typically, carers also said that they did not need time to think; they just knew immediately, instinctively, that they were going to take on the child: 'I didn't stop to think about it'; 'there wasn't much to think about'; 'you act first and think later'. This bears out the findings of one US study, in which social workers reported it was difficult to get potential carers to look carefully at the implications of what they are taking on:

A lot of relatives don't really look at the factors that impact their taking care of the children. They operate on their 'gut' – it's blood – it's family, it's blood, we can't let the children live in the foster care system. (Geen, 2003, p 45)

It is possible, of course, that those who do take on care, particularly when reporting several years later, may see their actions as more spontaneous than they in fact were. US research suggests that, for some potential carers, decision-making may be affected by such factors as the child's age and severity of problems; the nature of the parents' problems and their likely impact on the kinship family; the carers' circumstances and resources; and the availability of services (Geen, 2003). It is also salutary to remember that in our non-kin sample of children placed with non-kin carers there were 12 cases (of the 24 where kinship care was considered) where relatives felt they were not able to care. The reasons reported on file include: the potential carer's age or health (5); commitments to their own children (4); work (2) or elderly relatives (1); concern over the likely behaviour of the parent (2) or, unusually (2), a simple reluctance to take on the responsibility.

Moreover, just because carers report that their decision was made spontaneously, it does not mean that it was not also thought about or discussed. When asked what the rest of their family thought about them taking on care, for instance, very few mentioned any opposition. However, several said that family members or friends had asked them to think very carefully, even saying, 'you're an idiot' and 'you're mad'.

They supported us when we'd decided what we were doing but they said, do you really know what you're doing? It's not easy bringing up teenage children.

They backed us 100 per cent. They did say, are you sure you know what you're doing? They were a bit concerned we might be taking on a bit too much.

Our friends warned us, you don't take on a 13-year-old girl, life's different now.

Over a third of the carers interviewed (37%; 13 of 35 responding) also admitted to having had some qualms about taking on care. Specific issues mentioned ranged from practical worries about finance and housing (4 cases) to concerns about the impact on their own children (3); the possible disruptive behaviour of parents (3); the child's behaviour (2) and their own capacity to cope and meet the child's needs (4):

I was petrified! I wondered where the boundaries would be because David was a bit older, a bit wiser, a bit more mischievous and he was clever. The concern was that he would just turn and do what he wanted to do and no matter what I said he might just open the door and say 'F you' and go off.

Billions. Especially in the early days. All sorts of stuff like what I was doing to my own family. I've got this thing about not being a good mother and even though mother had given the kids up I always felt like I was messing them up as well.

Would she be satisfied, get enough from me, one old grandparent – not a real family. I know my extended family is enormous but it's not the same thing. I'd rather she be with a mother and father figure.

Nonetheless, many carers seemed to have gone into this without any great concerns, either because they genuinely did not anticipate any problems or because they had decided to take things as they came: 'We just agreed to do it and we'll cross that bridge when we come to it'.

Act in haste, repent at leisure?

Despite what we have said about the "instinctive" nature of much carer decision-making, and the lack of time for measured consideration before the child actually arrived, almost all the carers we interviewed (31/37) said that, knowing what they now knew, they would do it again. Indeed, 11 of them emphasised this with words such as 'absolutely'; 'definitely' and 'without a doubt'. Moreover, only one carer said categorically that she would not do it again, while five were uncertain. What is also interesting is that there is no obvious relationship between the answer to this question and whether the placement lasted. Indeed, in all the cases where none of the children were still in placement, the carers said they would do it again. In comparison, of the 27 cases where all the children were still there, five expressed some doubts (or in one case, said no). Furthermore, when asked what advice they would give to potential carers, 15 carers said they would say to go ahead and only one said they would advise against it.

Were carers sufficiently well informed to make a decision?

Many carers also emphasised, however, the need to 'think very carefully about what you're doing'. Carers counselled not only thinking through the possible problems and the impact on their lives but looking into themselves to make sure it was what they really wanted to do.

You have to be honest within your heart that you want to look after the child.

If they have a chance to think about things to think it out seriously. And think very, very hard; especially if they're older grandparents. Be aware that it's a big lifestyle change, a complete change in lifestyle. I don't think we really comprehended the amount of change it would make to our lives.

Think it through very carefully, it's all very happy and nice at the start but if you have a child that comes with problems, be prepared for more problems later on in life.

These recommendations, given what we have said about the predominance of emotion in carer decision-making, might suggest that carers might have welcomed more opportunity to discuss these issues. A few carers did suggest this. As one put it succinctly, 'They should highlight the things that families don't think about before they do it and the child comes'. Most carers, however, were satisfied that their discussions with professionals at the time covered all the things they thought now were the important issues and those who did not were generally talking about the need for practical information on such matters as finance.

Nonetheless, it is our view that consideration should be given as to how best potential carers might be enabled to think through the implications of what they are taking on. Since some may be reluctant to discuss this with social workers, we wonder whether involving another person who does not have a decision-making role – such as someone with experience of kinship care – might be a useful strategy. The provision of written material such as that developed by Family Rights Group and the Grandparents' Association, or perhaps producing a leaflet using a frequently-asked-questions format, might also be helpful. This could also cover the implications of the various legal arrangements, since, as we report later, it was evident that some carers did not fully understand the differences and what say they had in the choice of order.

It has to be acknowledged, however, that some carers may not be very receptive to any form of communication at this point. One of our interviewees, who had gone on to foster and adopt non-kin children, when asked what advice she would give to a potential carer responded:

That's a hard one. Think. They would have to look within themselves very hard first. Because once they've made the commitment they wouldn't be able to back out. Look within yourself. When that child is having a tantrum and you would rather be with your mates down the pub, could you cope when the child is screaming and shouting about something at school that you have no control of? Could you deal with things like that? How long could you deal with it for; a lifetime? Because that's what you're committing yourself to.

Interviewer: *If someone had said that to you?*

I don't think I would have listened; I had already made my mind up. For me the first six months it was 'anybody can say anything, I already know what I want'.

Carer involvement in formal decision-making processes

As noted earlier, most of the carers in our study were already very involved with the child prior to their placement. Moreover, in almost half the cases (46%), someone in the child's network had been active in bringing their concerns about the child's care to the attention of the authorities, overcoming the traditional 'norm of non-interference' by the extended family in the upbringing of children, which is well documented in the literature in relation to grandparents and grandchildren (Dench *et al*, 1999; Dench and Ogg, 2002). Indeed, far from covering up parental shortcomings, some carers were critical of what they perceived to be an inadequate or tardy response from Social Services:

> *I don't think Social Services were very helpful while Lee was still with his mum and dad. He was left there far, far too long. I felt really angry, they should have acted a lot, lot sooner. They did have the information. It was dreadful, they were drunk all the time and them candles, I was afraid they'd fall asleep in a stupor and I used to ring Social Services and get 'we can't do that without evidence'. I said go there now but they would not do it. I used to ring up and ring up and my daughter used to do it as well. They wouldn't do anything until finally . . . they rung me at work and said there'd been an incident . . . months and months it went on and no one seemed to do anything until the very end.*

The extended families of the children, therefore, had often demonstrated their readiness to put the child's welfare before their loyalty to a parent even though this action might potentially put them in conflict with that parent. Moreover, this appears to be an important element in the decision to place early in kinship care: in 18 of the 31 cases (58%) in which children were placed with relatives without an intervening period in non-kin care, a relative had raised concerns, compared to only 35 per cent of the 20 other cases.

Given this evidence that, in a good proportion of cases, relatives were both in the picture and had indicated their readiness to put the child's welfare before their loyalty to a parent, we were surprised to find little evidence that carers had been involved in the formal decision-making process within the local authority, such as case conferences or reviews. There appear to have family group conferences in only 11 cases, a mere six being convened prior to proceedings. (It should be noted, however, that none at all were held in our comparison group of children placed in non-kin care.) Since neither of our two local authorities had imbedded family group conferences into their decision-making processes at this time, their paucity is not unexpected.

Family group conferences are advanced as a positive way of involving families in decision-making and, by harnessing the resources of the extended family, increasing the use of kinship care (Nixon, 2001). It is known from current practice in our local authorities that procedurally they can be difficult to convene quickly and so may not be sufficiently geared to crisis-response. If, however, Social Services were to become more *au fait* with extended families through the process of family mapping that we have suggested, then this may be less of an issue.

As academics, we consider that family group conferences have a useful part to play in the development of kinship care and in decision-making in individual cases. We therefore welcome the government's proposals (DfES, 2006a) to promote their use through a programme of national events and training. It has to be said, however, that the carers we interviewed were distinctly lukewarm about the idea with only five considering that it might have been helpful in their case and most indicating that had such a meeting been offered they would have been wary because of the potential for inter-family conflict/difficulties:

I don't think it would have benefited (us). It would have hampered the situation. We would have been on one side of the room and all the others on the other side of the room.

Moreover, none of the four carers who recalled attending anything like a family group meeting said that it had been helpful, and for some it had clearly been really awkward:

The mum was quite abrupt, quite rude and nasty. I had to say the truth which I didn't want to really. It put me in quite an embarrassing situation really.

(Was it helpful?) Not really. I ended up leaving, other people were unhappy at me being there. I had my say then I left. I thought, well we're not going to get anywhere.

The court process seems to afford carers more opportunity for involvement in decision-making. Although in just over half the sample cases carers were not parties to the proceedings (56 of 105; 53%), only two of our interviewees in this position said they would have liked to have been more involved.

We would have liked to have been present at the hearings but it was implied that it would be against the best interests of keeping him here to appear to be fighting.

All but two of the interviewed carers with party status were legally represented, typically separately from either parent (in the sample as a whole, 67 per cent [33] of those with party status were known to have legal representation). Other carers had sought legal advice. There were only two cases where carers reported being directly involved in the proceedings without either legal advice or representation.

Funding, however, could be an issue: while 11 carers had had some assistance from either legal aid (three in full, four in part) or Social Services (three full; one part), five had had to make some contribution and six had had no help at all. The sums involved ranged from relatively small contributions (the lowest being £200) to several thousands (largest £7,500). Seven carers reported spending £1,000 or more. Some other carers reported spending large sums of money on legal advice although they had not become further involved in the proceedings.

Apart from the practical difficulties occasioned to carers who may not be in a comfortable financial position, this did raise questions in our minds regarding the legitimacy of expecting potential carers to stump up such considerable sums of money when they are, in most instances, providing homes for children whom the state would otherwise have to accommodate. As one carer put it:

I paid so much (of the cost) myself . . . about £200. Luckily I could afford to pay. It wasn't that much, not a lot . . . if I couldn't afford to pay it would have been a bit upsetting along with everything that was going on. You don't want to be worrying about money as well. If you are doing it out of the goodness of your heart you don't want to be penalised . . . doing them a favour at the end of the day, wasn't I?

Assessment

The importance of good assessment is stressed by many writers on kinship care (Sinclair *et al*, 2000; Shlonsky and Berrick, 2001; Aldgate and McIntosh, 2006). It is recognised, however, as a complex area of practice which is likely to be more time-consuming than that for non-kin foster carers and uncomfortable for both the worker and the family (Waldman and Wheal, 1999; O'Brien, 2000; Laws, 2001; Doolan *et al*, 2004). Pitcher (1999) cautions that:

> Well done, an assessment is helpful to the person being assessed, gives confidence and helps the family discover its strengths and resources. Badly done, an assessment can be intrusive, alienating to the potential carers and gives the department a false sense that the child's needs are being met. (p 10)

Where the child being cared for is "looked after" by the local authority, carers have to be assessed as foster carers. Should they have to meet the same standards as non-kin carers? If not, as some argue (Flynn, 2002), what flexibility should there be? Should the process be the same? Current government guidance states merely that all standards are relevant but there should be recognition of the particular relationship and position of kinship foster carers and that mechanisms for assessing and approving should be designed in a way that encourages their consideration.

Practitioners and carers alike seem to be calling for an assessment format tailored to this form of care. Talbot and Calder (2006) suggest a model for assessment of "Evolving Networks of Relative Care" (ENORC) that feature family group conferences, rapid assessment, explicit care plans and supervision/support. Calder (1995) speaks of a need to balance partnership and paternalism; Talbot and Calder (2006) advise that professionals should avoid problematising a situation which may have many strengths, while Waterhouse (2001) proposes a shift away from an approving to an enabling basis.

When children are not looked after, the position is different, but even if the intention is for children to be placed on residence orders, then the courts, in care proceedings at least, are likely to require some form of assessment to be conducted. Also, of course, in many cases, children will have been subject to interim care orders during the proceedings (this applied to all but eleven children in our study).

One of the complicating elements in kinship assessments is that many children are likely to be with their carers while the assessment is taking place. Farmer and Moyers (2008) report that only 36 per cent of carers were assessed before the children moved in. In our study, only a tiny minority of children (10) were placed after a full fostering assessment and a further 18 after an interim assessment. The vast majority of children appear to have been placed with only either other forms of assessment or basic checks having been completed. It is of interest, however, that since Social Services were already involved with the families at the point the placement was made, they were not being faced with *de facto* arrangements.

By the end of proceedings, the carers of 61 per cent of the children subject to care orders had been approved following a full fostering assessment (Table 5.1). Most of the remainder had temporary approval. One assessment, where the child was not yet in placement, was yet to begin. Finally, in one bizarre, and probably illegal case, the carer had been assessed but approval as a foster placement could not be given because her partner had been convicted many years ago of a Schedule 1 offence and he refused to take part in the assessment. It was agreed that he should not have care of the child and should never be left with her unsupervised. The child remained with the carer on a care order for several months until rehabilitated, as planned, to her mother.

The assessments and approval of carers where children were eventually subject to residence orders were very varied, ranging from interim (14) or even full (10) fostering approval, to other forms of assessment (15) or, in a few cases (5), there being no record of any formal assessment at all. This probably reflects the different points in the case at which the decision about a residence order was made rather than necessarily differences in practice about the extent of the assessment needed in such cases.

Table 5.1
Assessment by end of proceedings by final order

(N=)	Full fostering approval		Interim fostering assessment		Other assessment only		No formal assessment recorded	
	No.	%	No.	%	No.	%	No.	%
Care order (67)	41	61	24	36	1	2	1	2
Residence order (44)	10	23	14	32	15	34	5	11
All cases (111)	51	45	38	34	16	14	6	5

Like Farmer and Moyers (2008), we found that the carers we interviewed gave very different accounts of the assessments they had gone through, from what appeared to be quite brief or basic checks to in-depth and sometimes very formal or lengthy processes.

Police checks. I can't remember much about it. They just asked a few questions. Medical checks. (Interim fostering assessment)

[It was an] integrated programme set out over five or six weeks. We worked on different things, different scenarios. They wouldn't allow our kids in the room. (Full fostering assessment).

Typically, as one would expect, the more detailed accounts were given by carers who had been through full fostering assessments, who remembered medicals, references, lots of interviews and forms, as well as the police checks which carers tended to mention irrespective of the kind of assessment they had had. However, some of those assessed as foster carers had little detailed recollection of the process while some subject only to other forms of assessment described what seemed to be quite a thorough investigation.

Social Services did police checks. Social Services were out (here) all the time anyway. I can't remember anything formal. (Full assessment)

They went right back to my childhood, I've got so much paperwork about it. (Interim assessment)

Where children were to move to live with a relative in another country, the investigation seemed to be remembered as particularly thorough. For example:

We had someone from [this country] here first, medical records, police checks. A children's aide. Social Services from the UK were here for five days. The guardian ad litem from the UK was here. So many questions from so many people. I met so many people in the five times I was back and forth (to the UK). I only wish I had kept a daily journal. I did not think that there was going to be so much involved.

Do kinship carers accept the need for assessment?

The vast majority of carers interviewed (26 of 31) accepted that some form of assessment was necessary, even though they were related to the child.

I felt they needed to do this as I might have been a terrible person. I knew I wasn't but they didn't, did they?

Of course you must be assessed, you can't place a child without checks. Social Services wouldn't have been doing their job.

Typically, as can be seen, this was justified in terms of child protection concerns, although one carer also expressed it in terms of helping her to think about what she was proposing to do:

It was right because you don't know what you're taking on. She asked me questions which forced me to ask them myself.

Only five interviewees objected as a matter of principle:

No, I think it was wrong. They should have just trusted that we were the grandparents and left it at that.

Demeaning, it was almost as if you felt you were not a good parent . . .
We thought it was a bit wrong that we should be assessed, especially

as we had brought three children up without any problems . . . made to feel substandard.

Could the process be improved?

Well over half the carers interviewed made no adverse comments about the way the assessment was done, typically saying it did not bother them. Others, while expressing some discomfort with certain aspects of the process, particularly the intrusion into their personal lives, nonetheless seem to have accepted this as understandable:

They grilled me but I remember being impressed too. God you really care about these kids, you're not just plonking them with anybody. They were making me accountable in a way.

This comment was particularly interesting because the carer found much of the process really uncomfortable:

I had to have medicals, which was humiliating. I remember being really upset about that. I had to have the dentist. I had to have my home checked. I had to talk about so much of my past. It was quite interesting too because I think sometimes I quite like talking and it was quite therapeutic, you can learn quite a bit about yourself. But the medical side was horrible and they interviewed my Mum, I had to have references and I remember thinking look you've left them here, you want to now assess me, it's a bit late for that!

Some carers were bewildered, upset or angry at some of the questions they were asked, suggesting the need for more explanation or more sensitivity:

It was right to check our home out but not right to go into our personal lives so much.

A load of rubbish. It was stupid, they wanted the ins and outs of everything. They wanted to know if you walked in front of your father as a child in your knickers. I said of course I did. We didn't have a bathroom, we bathed in front of the fire. I thought it was just stupid.

Going into our past when they assessed us wasn't very helpful. It brought up a lot of issues we had to discuss with our children which we didn't really want to revisit.

Other complaints included assessments being too rushed or alternatively too drawn out, too many people being involved, the fear of saying the wrong thing; being misunderstood; anxiety about losing the child and the sheer stress of being investigated:

I appreciate that some people aren't the right people to have their grandchildren but they had no reason to question me. I don't think I should have been put through so much stress. I was angry and I showed I was angry and they used that against me as if to say I was an angry person. I wasn't, I was just angry with them.

I think the stress was the worst. They've really got to look at how much they're distressing family because I felt like I was under question all the time. I know they've got to look into people because there are terrible cases of abuse but if they've got no reason to suspect you . . . Social Services should understand that when they're dealing with families they will be stressed. They should understand that perhaps they're not as nice as they normally are. They shouldn't automatically assume that there's something wrong with this person . . . it is quite natural to be upset in that situation.

For one carer, the assessment experience still rankled, and formed a key element in our interview. This lengthy quote encapsulates many of the key issued raised by other carers:

I understood why they were doing it but there were too many people involved. And you feared some of them, like the guardian. You realise how much power they have. And actually having to open up most of your life and let them into a helluva lot of information that you really don't even let your best friend into was quite hard going. I did feel at times, my god, go away and leave us alone. I never said it. They should never have gone into my past the way they did. I understand why they did it but I think there's a better way.

Interviewer: *How could they have done it better?*

That's the hardest thing. But maybe some of the questions need to be re-looked at. Maybe right at the beginning they should be saying, 'There's nothing to feel guilty about'. They should be looking at you positively. They have to work on that in the first two or three visits, to make you feel comfortable. You have form after form . . . In the first questionnaire you should be able to tell whether you need to pry. And then you need to tell them that you're going to do that and why.

Interviewer: *Did they ever explain why they were doing it?*

I think the guardian went through that . . . we have to look at every aspect of your life to ensure Vicki will be . . . I think they sort of said it but not in a way that I fully understood at the time. I just knew they were judging me. And because my fear was that I wouldn't be able to have her and then she would end up in foster care. The fear of losing her...in my head I was 'never looked after children, single, living in a one bedroom flat – I do not fit the criteria they are looking for'. It was a bit of a nightmare really. Until I knew how it all worked. That was the most frightening bit for me. I must admit I had quite a few sleepless nights.

We did wonder if carers who had been through a full fostering assessment might feel more negative about the process than those who had only gone through interim or other forms of assessment. If anything, however, the reverse was the case. Perhaps this is because relatives who are seeking to become long-term foster carers see the role of the local authority differently and accept their "right" to carry out a thorough enquiry, while those who see the arrangement as more of a private, in-family affair, are more questioning of its legitimacy.

Conflict and consensus in decision-making

Reaching decisions about placement

The majority of care cases are resolved by the parties rather than determined by the court (Hunt and Macleod, 1999) and such consensus seems even more likely in cases ending in kinship placements. Only 14 (13%) of our kinship cases went to a contested final hearing over the placement plan. In contrast, 22 per cent of our non-kin sample did so (compared with 15 per cent of the under-five kin-placed children). Moreover, some of these contests in the kinship sample primarily involved parents arguing for rehabilitation of the child to their care. There were only eight cases where the dispute was about whether the child should be placed with the index carers.[73]

However, as is again typical of care proceedings, this does not mean that the remainder were all consensual throughout (Hunt and Macleod, 1999). In total, there was evidence of some disagreement about the child's placement with the index carers in 22 cases. These disagreements (30 in all) involved the local authority in 14 cases (3 going to a contested final hearing); the parents in 14 cases (5 contested final hearings); and the guardian in two cases (none remaining contested to the final hearing). We look at the attitudes of each of those involved in the cases below.

Parental attitudes

It is unfortunate that our efforts to interview parents in this research proved largely unsuccessful.[74] We were therefore primarily dependent on information from file data and carer interviews in considering parental attitudes. These sources suggest a wide spectrum of parental attitudes about placement, from those who were positive to those who were actively opposed, with the rest passively accepting or being described as 'not bothered'. Indeed, parents in the same case might take different attitudes, perhaps not surprisingly, since many of them were separated by the end of the proceedings. In all, 11 of the 37 interviewed carers considered the parents viewed the kinship placement positively, with carers saying things like 'she completely backed us', 'she thought it was great', and 'they were happy' and in a further eight there was at least no active hostility. Of course this does not imply that the parents would not have preferred to have the children with them – although in one or two cases carers said parents knew they could not cope. Rather, it was that, if the children had to live elsewhere, parents preferred that they lived with a member of the family. Carers sometimes explained this in terms of parents thinking they

---

[73] Three cases (two families) involved local authority objections; five parental objections.
[74] Two interviews achieved.

would be more likely to be able to see the children than if they went into non-kin care or adoption:

> *Mother was pleased because . . . she knew that somebody in the family would have Charlie and she would have more contact and she wasn't going to lose her.*

> *They didn't mind. They could see Carl with me. It was either me having him or them not having him at all. At least they could see him when he was with me rather than not at all.*

Even where there was not to be any contact, however, some parents were nonetheless said to be positive about the placement merely because it meant the child would not go to non-kin carers:

> *Mother was really pleased. I think it was a real relief for her. She knew me so she could picture in her mind where her kids were.*

> *Mother said she was pleased with it and not to let Jade forget her. Jade still has a picture of mother in her room.*

One of the parents we interviewed commented in similar vein:

> *I knew Kiera would be safe there. I loved my auntie. As a child I used to go round there on Thursday for dinner.*

Over half (18) the interviewed kinship carers, however, described a degree of hostility from one or both parents at some stage during the case, which in some cases abated but in others (9) persisted throughout the proceedings:

> *Mother, initially, she was very upset. She was confused. The father had been telling her 'your mother is trying to take the baby away' and it looked a lot to her like I'd done that.*

> *They didn't like Dale coming to us even at the end. They said they were innocent and that he should return to them.*

In some instances, allegations against the potential carers led to delay in placement:

> Both parents had a long history of severe mental health problems and

drug misuse. Imogen was removed at birth on an emergency protection order. The index carers were already caring for two older siblings and were willing to care for Imogen. However, one parent made allegations of sexual abuse of herself, her older children and Imogen by one of the kinship carers. This issue was not resolved until the final hearing when the judge dismissed the allegations. Imogen went to live with the kinship carers a few days later.

This animosity between parents and the index carers is probably at least partly explained by the fact that several had reported concerns about the children to Social Services, as illustrated below:

Adam, a very young baby, suffered serious injuries, which were reported to Social Services by the relative. The local authority left Adam with her and brought proceedings. After a month, the kinship carer was concerned about the aggressive attitude of parents and was anxious about going out of the house in case of confrontation. The father blamed her for reporting concerns and for losing Adam. The baby was moved the next day by Social Services without consultation with the carer but apparently with the parents' approval. After rehabilitation to the parents was discounted, an independent assessment of the kinship carer and partner took place and they were successful in achieving Adam's return under a residence order but only after he had spent 16 months in foster care.

In over a third (13) of the 37 cases where the carers were interviewed, they spoke of the difficulties that followed their reporting of concerns:

When Ben was in hospital we had to face the parents on a daily basis. We were under police protection at the hospital because we had reported the injury and my brother was angry.

The attitude of Social Services to the proposed placement

Don't treat family the same as strangers. We felt we were fighting the system, the system wasn't helping us. We were made to feel like that all the time. It's a child's birthright to stay within their family. They should use all their resources to try and keep the child in the family, not use them to take her away. We seem to have gone full circle as a society because 100 years ago if anything happened to a child in the family the family just rallied round and did it; it was automatic. Now it seems to be if you do want to do it you have to fight for it, it's not your privilege. Grandparents have no more rights than people off the street.

In the majority of cases, Social Services seem to have been in complete agreement with placement with the index carers. This was reflected in our carer interviews in which almost three-quarters (27 of 37) said things like they were 'happy', 'fine', 'trusted us', 'supportive', and 'helpful in many ways'. However, as noted above, not all cases proceeded so smoothly. In all there was evidence of some local authority resistance to long-term placement with the index carers in 14 cases (four placements were with aunts and uncles, the remainder with grandparents). The extent of resistance varied from some initial hesitancy to outright opposition, including some cases where placements had been formally rejected by placement panels. Concerns included:

- Health (5 cases) or "advanced" age (1 case [carers were in their mid-50s with several additional concerns]);
- Carer's youth/inexperience (3 cases);
- Possible inability to control contact (3 cases);
- Criminal records of carer or partner (2 cases);
- "Unstable" life-style of kinship carer who had had sequential partners (1 case);
- Ability to protect (1 case [child suffered sexual abuse in the kinship placement and had actually been removed because of lack of protective behaviour]).

It was unusual for there to be professional resistance to the placement explicitly expressed in terms of the way the grandparents had brought up the child's parent, with only eight cases where this was clearly recorded as a placement concern. This was perhaps surprising given the context of parenting inadequacies which had led to the proceedings. However, we did wonder whether there was an element of this in four other cases where

Social Services was resisting care by maternal grandparents where the mothers themselves had either been in care or on the child protection register. We look later in this chapter at whether the concerns detailed above materialised.

It was rare for carers and Social Services still to be in opposition by the final hearing. Indeed, only one set of proceedings (two siblings) had to be settled by the court, with the guardian recommending the kinship placement against the local authority's plan for adoption. In another case, a senior manager from Social Services agreed on the final court date to the kinship placement which had previously been turned down by the placement panel. These children all remain in their placements.

It was not always possible to determine from the file data quite how disagreements had been resolved. In one case a new social worker taking over the case brought her own more positive view of kinship care. Sometimes an assessment by an independent professional or agency proved influential in the local authority changing its view. In others it was the position taken by the guardian.

Guardians

Undoubtedly a key factor in resolving disagreement was the approach of the guardian *ad litem* (now children's guardian). This could be indirectly, through bringing in other professionals or agencies to contribute expertise and take a fresh look at the case, or directly, through their recommendations to the court and more broadly the stance they took on the case. In most cases in our sample the guardian eventually supported the local authority care plan. However, in cases where the local authority was ambivalent or opposed to a kinship placement, the guardian's position could be pivotal to the eventual outcome.

Some disagreements between guardian and social worker related to a view (held by social workers in several cases) that, although the proposed kinship carers appeared of acceptable parenting capacity, the child should have a new start away from their family:

> Katie, a very young baby, had been very seriously injured by her mother and the local authority's plan was for non-kin adoption. An aunt and uncle had offered to care but had never been properly

assessed because the social worker felt Katie needed a fresh start. The guardian interviewed the relatives and thought they had good potential. She therefore advised the court that an independent home study should be carried out by an adoption/fostering agency; this concluded that the aunt and uncle had a good level of parenting capacity. The local authority did not oppose Katie going to them under a residence order. It recognised the loss of confidence the carers had in the Social Services and agreed to fund the independent agency supervising and supporting the placement for a year.

Aaron's parents suffered from serious mental health problems and were difficult personalities. Aaron was placed with his aunt at the age of two weeks and received excellent care. The social worker, however, was opposed to making this a long-term placement because she felt Aaron needed a placement away from the family. She also had concerns about family dynamics and the mother's capacity in the future to interfere with the placement. The guardian had made a more positive assessment of the kinship carers and additionally felt that, after a year with his aunt, Aaron was attached and should not be moved. Eventually the permanency panel approved the placement and the proceedings ended by agreement.

Had the guardian taken a different view in these cases and supported the local authority, the children concerned would in all likelihood have moved to non-kin adoption.

In the kinship carer interviews, there were seven cases (19%) where Social Services opposed or was significantly concerned about the placement but the guardian's stance was supportive. The carers recognised the importance of this in securing the child with them, whether because the guardian had actively backed their position, because s/he had pushed for further assessments, or because s/he had suggested more productive ways of dealing with the local authority:

Her backing was a godsend.

She thought we were a good choice and wanted us to be properly assessed.

> *She was constructive, she suggested we take more of a detached stance and stop being vocally supporting of the parents saying they didn't injure the child.*

However, in another case, the guardian appears to have been instrumental in dissuading grandparents from applying for a residence order to prevent the children being moved from their care on to adoption. Understandably, the carer we interviewed, who had resumed care of the children after two adoptive placements had broken down, was less appreciative of the guardian's contribution:

> *At the first court case she was the one who was against me and my wife having them, she said it's nothing personal. I said you can't say that, you're against me having them, that's very personal. She said it's in view of your age, you could be the best bloke in the world but it's your age (60 years old). The second time [following successful residence order application after the children had been returned] it was a different guardian and she was totally the opposite.*

Overall, in our kinship cases the guardian service provided the expected system of checks and balances with a fresh look at the extended family and generally (but not always) took a more liberal stance in enabling kinship placements to go ahead where there were local authority reservations. What we cannot know, of course, is what stance guardians took in the 281 cases in our sampling pool where children, unable to return to a parent, went into non-kin care. However, in our small non-kin sample, there was no evidence that any of the unsuccessful kinship applications had the support of the guardian, underlining the influence guardians have in decision-making.

The extended family

There were only a small number of cases in our study (11; 10%) where relatives other than the index carers had put themselves forward to look after the child/ren. Disputes about who should care were rare and certainly such disagreement was never an issue at any final hearing. While positive endorsement from the other side of the family was unusual, there was also only a little evidence of active hostility from other family members.

Indeed, as mentioned earlier, it seems that had the index carers not been prepared to take on the children, no one else in the family would have done so at that point. It was particularly noticeable that children often did not have relatives on both sides of their family who were actively involved in their lives:

> *They didn't want to know, they are all in bits and pieces anyway, in and out of mental hospitals and the grandparents were too poorly to care. They did compliment us at one meeting about the good job we'd been doing . . . that was the only help we got from them.*

> *They moved (away) and didn't want anything to do with him.*

There were six sibling groups in the study (17 children) who were retained in kinship placements but divided between different family members.[75] Eleven children (one group of three, four sibling pairs) were placed alone with different relatives and a group of six children (some full siblings, some half) were split between their maternal and paternal/step-paternal grandparents. Splits happened for a number of reasons: the kinship carer might be related to only one of the sibling group (although this did not preclude some from taking on the child); children moved from their parents at different times during proceedings; a grandparent had an established link with only one child; a carer still had their own children at home and could not offer care to the whole group.

There was only one case where the decision to split the children was a matter of dispute within the family. However, the fact that the arrangements were agreed in the remaining cases did not necessarily mean that relationships within the family were amicable. Indeed, in most (14), there was reference in the files to tension or volatile relationships, which in some cases persisted, creating difficulties in placement (see Chapter 9). Anticipated extended family problems could also lead to the court making

---

[75] In the kinship cohort as a whole, siblings were more often split than placed together as a consequence of the proceedings (44% of the children with siblings in the same proceedings were placed altogether, 26% placed with some siblings, 31% placed with none). Within our under-fives sample, kin-placed children were less likely to be placed all together than were the siblings in our non-kin sample, although the numbers (7) in the latter group are small.

a supervision order alongside a residence order, or even care orders (see below).

Reaching decisions about the appropriate legal order

The vast majority of the sample cases (85%) ended with the local authority retaining a substantial role in the form of a care or supervision order. Only 15 per cent of cases ended with a residence order alone. There were disagreements over what final order to make in 35 cases (32% of 111), 22 of which persisted until the final hearing. However, in most instances these reflected disputes over placement and particularly parental opposition to the child being removed from their own care. There were only eight cases where the kinship placement was agreed but there was disagreement over the appropriate order. In four cases, stronger orders were made than at least one party was seeking, while in four cases the converse was the case:

- two carers of three children withdrew their respective applications for residence orders and accepted care orders;
- the local authority, which had been reluctant to approve the carers as foster carers, agreed to accept a care order;
- a residence order with supervision order was made in one case where the guardian had been seeking a care order; in another case where the guardian had wanted a supervision order a residence order alone was made;
- residence orders with supervision orders were made in two cases where the local authority had wanted care orders.

Local authority differences

As can be seen in Table 5.2, the pattern of orders differed between our two authorities, with cases in Authority A being made subject to a higher level of control (fewer residence orders and more care orders) than Authority B. This difference was not statistically significant, only a trend, with Authority A having 71 per cent of cases ending in care orders compared to 50 per cent in B. Indeed, Authority A was more likely to have care orders made for all our age ranges of children. Nor did Authority B appear to be compensating by having many more supervision orders attached to residence orders since the difference was very slight (10 of the 17 residence order cases in Authority A – 59%; 17 of the 27 in Authority B – 63%).

This use of care orders is an interesting difference only partly explained by the presence of two large siblings groups all on care orders in Authority A. This might suggest a different approach by each local authority or the courts within Authority A erring more on the side of caution.

Table 5.2
Final orders

	Care order		Residence and supervision orders		Residence order only		
	No.	*%*	*No.*	*%*	*No.*	*%*	*(N=)*
Authority A	42	71	10	17	7	12	(59)
Authority B	27	50	17	32	10	19	(54)
All cases	69	61	27	24	17	15	(113)

There were no statistically significant differences between the local authorities in terms of the level of pre-placement adversities, so it was not simply that Authority A clearly had more difficult children. However, there were some trends which might help to explain these differences: Authority A had more overcrowded kinship households, more under 18-year-olds present in the households in addition to the kinship children, and more placements instigated by the local authority. These factors could be associated with greater support needs, which might translate into a higher rate of care orders. Analysis of the reasons for making care orders in the two authorities (see Table 5.3) indicates that Authority B was more likely to seek such an order because of anticipated difficulties with parents, while Authority A more commonly cited support needs.

Interestingly, at follow-up, in respect of those placements concluded with care orders, 41 per cent of Authority A's placements did not last as long as needed, compared with 26 per cent of Authority B's (15% difference with A having more care order breakdowns). In contrast, only one (5%) of Authority A's residence order cases did not last, compared with 6 (24%) of Authority B's (19% difference with B having more residence order breakdowns). These figures appear to cancel out any difference between the authorities in care order use referred to above.

This suggests that Authority A may have recognised more vulnerable placements and accordingly opted for care orders while Authority B was more "risk taking" in pursuing residence orders for "borderline" cases. However, even a care order did not seem to protect vulnerable placements from breaking down as there was no statistically significant difference between the two authorities in terms of placement stability (although Authority A did have a slightly higher rate of placements that did not last).

At follow-up, the two authorities had a similar rate of care order retention for continuing kinship placements (26 per cent for A's continuing kinship placements, and 22 per cent for B). This suggests that there are a "hard core" of about a quarter of kinship placements which continue on care orders. This seems quite a high retention rate particularly in terms of whether the children were able to develop a sense of permanency about their placement. It could indicate the need of such placements for support because of the difficulties posed by the child, as much as deficits in the kinship carer, or may simply mean that, once made, care orders are difficult to discharge.

Reasons for making particular orders
Care orders

As can be seen from Table 5.3, the main reasons care orders were made appeared to relate to anticipated parental difficulties (both in terms of adult relationships and child contact) and perceived need for support for the carers with this. Overall, for 38 per cent of children on care orders, a major reason for making this order related to potential parental or extended family difficulties.

Table 5.3

Reasons for care order

	No. of mentions		
	Authority A	Authority B	Total
Relationship with parents difficult or parental contact concerns*	7	12	19
Extra support provided by full CO	11	5	16
Child's situation needs extra protection/risk monitoring	4	5	9
Rehabilitation still possible	4	4	8
KCs not seeking RO, want LA to have responsibility	3	4	7
Long-term feasibility of placement unclear	1	6	7
Potential for extended family difficulties (one sibling group)	6	1	7
Concerns about KC's settled lifestyle, quality of care, coping ability	1	2	3
KC not yet approved as long-term carer or child not yet placed	3	0	3
Carer's youth or age	2	1	3
Carer not blood relative	3	0	3
Eventual plan child to be adopted by KC	2	1	3
Child's needs complex	1	1	2
Eventual plan child to be adopted by strangers	2	0	2
Child to be placed outside UK	0	1	1
Concerns about KC's protectiveness	1	0	1
KC has training needs	1	0	1
Not clear	1	1	2

(69 cases) *10 mothers, seven fathers, two both parents

CO = care order; KC = kinship carer; LA = local authority; RO = residence order

Daniella, aged five when proceedings ended, had been removed from her heroin-addicted mother following neglect and exposure to her violent lifestyle. She was placed with her maternal grandfather after an interim care order was obtained to prevent mother removing her from this placement. It was argued that a full care order was needed because grandfather needed support and advice in managing Daniella and wanted protection from harassment by mother. With a care order the local authority could take the lead in managing relationships with Daniella's mother who had the capacity to disrupt the placement.

An analysis of the factors associated with the different types of order (Tables 5.3 and 5.4) also indicates that care orders appeared to be more likely where the placement concerned an older child; where the case had come to court because of multiple concerns about abuse/neglect; where a parent was abusing drugs or alcohol; and where more than one child was being placed. Most cases where parents persisted in their attempts to have the child rehabilitated were also subject to care orders, as were cases where either the guardian or the parent had expressed concerns about the kinship placement.

Residence orders
Reasons for making residence orders seemed to fall into two groups. Such orders could be made as a positive choice – as much by the local authority as by the kinship carer – in that there were no concerns about the placement and no need for a stronger order (25 cases). The second group of cases (10) appeared to be driven more by the kinship carers' desire to ensure the local authority did not have control over decision-making, even if in some instances a care order might have afforded better legal protection. Where the local authority had had reservations about the placement, the relatives probably needed either the security of knowing that the child could not be removed without further court action or simply did not want Social Services continuing involvement.

Katie, a young baby, had been severely injured. The local authority initially opposed a kinship placement so her aunt made an application for a residence order. An assessment by an independent agency was positive about the aunt's parenting capacity and the local authority gave way. Since there were no significant protection issues to warrant a care order and the kinship carer now had little faith in the local authority, a residence order was made with post-placement support from the independent agency.

In a further three cases, it would have been difficult to approve the carer as a foster carer. Farmer and Moyers (2008) also found that carers could be steered towards residence orders for this reason, irrespective of whether this was likely to provide the placement with enough legal protection.

Table 5.4
Reasons for making residence order

	Residence order only		Residence and supervision orders		All ROs
			Number of mentions		
	Authority A	*Authority B*	*Authority A*	*Authority B*	*All cases*
To give carers parental responsibility/permanence without LA presence	3	6	8	8	25
Kinship carer positively requesting PR/court would not endorse LA care plan or level of requested control	3	1	3	3	10
Mother consenting to order	2	2	0	0	4
Foster carer approval difficult	0	0	1	2	3
Because it is a kinship placement	0	2	0	0	2
Placement abroad planned	0	1	0	0	1
Less likely to antagonise mother	0	0	1	0	1
Child's views	0	0	0	1	1
Not clear	0	0	0	3	3

*N = 44

PR = parental responsibility; RO = residence order

Supervision orders

Supervision orders were made for 27 of the 44 children placed on residence orders (61% of all residence orders, 59% for all Authority A's residence orders, 63% for Authority B). Perhaps surprisingly, only one supervision order seemed to be made because of concerns about the quality of the placement. Most (15) were made because of issues relating to contact/relationship difficulties with the birth parents. Of the rest: two were made to assist contact with siblings placed elsewhere; four to ease potential difficulties where children were placed with different family members, and five to provide generalised support.

Twelve-year-old Sammy had been subject to severe physical punishment in his parents' care and was refusing to return. He was placed with an aunt, initially against his parents' wishes. A residence order was made principally because Sammy did not want to engage with social workers. His carers were reluctant to lose the support of a care order and were only persuaded because they were assured the residence order allowance would be at the same level they had been receiving as foster carers. A supervision order was made to allow the local authority to have a peacekeeping role because of conflicted relationships within the extended family.

Were carers sufficiently well-informed about the implications of the different orders?

The majority of carers interviewed (21; 64%) were confident that they knew enough about the different orders to know what would be best, several commenting on the role of the social worker, their solicitor or, particularly, the guardian, in explaining it all. It is somewhat disturbing, however, that seven said they definitely did not know enough about different orders to make a decision and a further five expressed some uncertainty. Interestingly, all of those who finished up with only a residence order seemed happy with their level of understanding. Perhaps, since carers in this position are essentially carrying total responsibility for the child, professionals take more care with their explanations to ensure that they know what they are committing themselves to, and the carers themselves may be clearer about the boundaries of responsibility.

In contrast, three of the six with supervision orders were unclear about the reasons for this; indeed, one carer seemed unaware that there had actually been one and another thought it was "mandatory" if there was a residence order. The others explained it either generally in terms of providing support or to assist in handling contact or the relationship with the parent.

Four of the 20 carers in cases where care orders were made expressed uncertainty and five said they had not been sufficiently well informed. One carer told us, 'I didn't know there were any other choices,' another, 'I can't remember a residence order ever being discussed,' and a third, 'I didn't know what a care order meant at the time'.

Nonetheless, most carers seemed to have grasped the essential differences between residence and care orders in terms of the different balance of power between themselves and the local authority and the on-going involvement of Social Services:

I wanted a residence order. If there was a care order they would have put her back into foster care. I just knew I didn't want Social Services involved.

I understood Social Services would always be involved (with a care order). I didn't want that. If Becky, for example, wanted to go to a sleep-over, I wanted to make it normal for her – she's gone through enough upset.

We didn't want to go for a residence order as we wanted Social Services as a buffer. We didn't want the mother to keep threatening to take him away.

Given the complexity of legal options, especially with the introduction of special guardianship orders, and the fact that many carers are not legally represented, there seems a strong case for ensuring that independent written information is given to kinship carers to explain the varying types of orders and their advantages/disadvantages.

Were the right orders made?

Although, as discussed above, not all the kinship carers we interviewed were as well informed about the legal options as they might have been, with hindsight almost all were satisfied that the right order had been made at the time. There were six exceptions. Two carers said they wished they had had a residence order rather than a care order because of the intrusion of having Social Services still involved and two thought it would have been better to go for adoption straightaway:

We would have preferred a residence order straight away. We didn't want a care order, we felt it was intrusive, we didn't want (the child) to feel different. We were told that if he lived with us for about two years on a care order then if we applied for a residence order it would be almost automatic but it didn't turn out that way.

It has been so unsettling for Chelsea over the years. All the court cases and aggravation. I would still have taken her but I would have made different stipulations, I would have adopted her . . . I don't think I would have taken her [again] on a residence order.

Finally, two carers wished that they had opted for care orders because of the financial and social work support which would have been available.

We would have been financially better off under a care order, the financial situation has been hard as we're on a pension. The costs are the same, it's because we were relatives they decided to go for the cheaper option. We asked which was best as we were on income support. They told us a residence order was the best option. When Harry came over with his foster carer recently [the placement having disrupted], she said you were on the wrong one, you could have got a lot more, but it is too late now.

At the time we were [happy] but as time goes on we wish we hadn't agreed to that and we had a permanent social worker. We would have preferred more social work support. It was [Social Services'] idea to go and get the residence order although it is of no advantage to us. The advantage of us staying foster parents is we would have had a social worker all the time.

Gazing into a crystal ball

How successful were professionals in identifying the placements which were least likely to succeed? We already know (Chapter 4) that the raising of concerns *per se* was not predictive of any of our four outcomes, or overall. A comparison with how things actually worked out indicates that, while in 60 per cent of cases (66 of 110) the placement had gone more or less as expected, 15 per cent had done better and 25 per cent worse. In-depth case analysis also shows that most of the specific concerns raised at the time of proceedings were not later identified in placement and most of the problems which did arise were not anticipated. We examine the various concerns expressed below.

Protection from abuse and/or neglect. There were 14 cases in which concerns were raised at the time of proceedings, of which problems materialised in only one.[76] (While theoretically this could be because preventive work had been done with carers, we only found evidence of this in two cases.) However, there were ten other cases where concerns about abuse and/or neglect had subsequently arisen during the placement which had not been predicted at the time of proceedings. These included one case of serious and persistent sexual abuse by the kinship carer where, regrettably with hindsight, no concerns were raised at placement about any potential risk in this arrangement although the proceedings had started due to sexual abuse by the child's father (brother of the kinship carer).[77]

---

[76] Care proceedings had been brought because of neglect and physical abuse of the child by the mother who allowed a Schedule 1 offender to visit the household. The index placement was made with the maternal grandmother in spite of concerns that the grandmother had failed to protect her daughter from childhood sexual abuse by a stepfather and two neighbours. Subsequently, the child was sexually abused in the kinship placement by a visitor to the household (the boyfriend of the great-grandmother with whom the carer and child were staying temporarily).

[77] With hindsight perhaps a possible way forward in this particular case at the care proceedings stage could have been a specialist risk assessment of the extended family or at least some consultancy with such an expert. It should be borne in mind that there were 12 other cases where there had been concerns about possible child sexual abuse by, most usually, a parent/parent figure at the care proceedings stage but all these children appear to have been subsequently kept safe by their kinship carer.

Carer age and health. In 22 cases concerns were raised about carer age and/or health. Problems only materialised in seven. Unanticipated problems, however, arose in six cases during placement and while some – such as various forms of cancer – could not have been predicted, it might be argued that the risk of others – such as stroke and dementia – do increase with age.

Financial hardship. This was noted as an issue in only two cases at the time of proceedings and remained a major concern in one. However, there were serious financial issues in a further eight cases during placement. In none of these cases had the family circumstances changed significantly, which raises the question of how thoroughly the finances of the placement had been looked at during proceedings.

Carer's criminal record. Though this was an issue in seven cases during proceedings, no subsequent concerns were noted in respect of the carers and there appeared no link with any subsequent offending behaviour by the index child.

Stability of carer's relationships. There were four cases where concerns were expressed at the time of proceedings about the stability of the carer's past or current relationships. Although none of these concerns were borne out, in six other placements (7% – probably a figure that compares well with the population as a whole) the child was exposed to the unanticipated breakdown of the carers' relationship. One child experienced the formation and breakdown of three of his carer's relationships during his placement, which lasted just over two years. There was nothing on the files to indicate that this issue was a feature of the carer's history. However, it is interesting to note that in this case the most detailed assessment that was carried out was a temporary fostering assessment.

Meeting the child's emotional needs. In three cases there were doubts about the carer's ability to meet the child's emotional needs. These were justified in only one case. However, there were a further 14 cases where concerns were later identified during placement. In one worrying case the carer was particularly negative towards the child about his skin colour and whether he belonged in the maternal or paternal family because of his dual heritage. This carer had had a temporary fostering assessment but it is not known how fully the issue of meeting the needs of a dual heritage child was explored. She was offered parenting skills courses during the placement but did not attend.

Carer coping capacity. Concerns were raised about the carer's general ability to cope with the placement in 11 cases. While we have no direct measure of how well these carers actually did cope, it was striking that six placements had lasted as long as needed or were continuing and stable. However, it is interesting that only one of these 11 placements proved to be problem-free in terms of placement quality, with three placements having major concerns.

Parental contact. There was little congruence between anticipated parental contact difficulties and the difficulties that occurred (Chapter 9). Concerns were raised about maternal and/or paternal contact in 48 cases; only 14 proved partly or wholly justified. However, contact difficulties emerged in a further 52 cases.

There was no difference between the two local authorities in their ability to predict problems that might arise in placement except for contact difficulties. Authority B was better at anticipating the presence or absence of problematic contact (prediction correct in 63% of cases cf. 38% in Authority A). This difference was a trend but not statistically significant.

Professional opposition to placement

In Chapter 4, we saw that placements where there had been any disagreement during the proceedings were actually more likely to be of better quality. A similarly somewhat paradoxical finding emerges from our analysis of the 16 cases where either the local authority or the guardian was opposed to the placement at any point (with three going to a contested hearing). Only one of these placements did not last as long as needed and three were continuing but vulnerable. Of the remaining 12 cases, three placements had all positive ratings on the overall outcome measure and the remainder fell into the middle category of between one and three positive ratings. Therefore, it seems again that professional disagreement is more likely to be associated with positive than negative outcomes.

Assessment of parenting capacity

In general, then, it appears that professionals were not particularly accurate in predicting which placements were likely to run into difficulty. However, there was one important exception to this: judgement of parenting capacity at the point of the proceedings, which proved to have a statistically significant association with perceived parenting capacity during placement.[78] Overall, in 71 per cent of the placements where evaluations could be identified (95), the carer's parenting capacity was rated good at the time of proceedings and also good during the placement. In 13 per cent of cases, parenting capacity rated as acceptable or marginal during the proceedings was also rated the same in the placement. In seven per cent of cases, parenting capacity had improved since the proceedings, while in nine per cent of cases it had deteriorated.

Additionally, as reported in Chapter 4, assessed parenting capacity at the time of proceedings was also predictive of later placement quality. Placements where the carer had not been assessed prior to the placement of the child were of poorer overall quality than placements where the carer had been assessed prior to the placement of the child.

However, as we highlighted earlier, there are benefits to children of early placement with kinship carers (avoiding a temporary move to non-kin foster care and possible multiple placements; limitation of the trauma of crisis by moving to a familiar carer) and there is undoubtedly a tension between these benefits and the need to assess.

This suggests that a key element in any early viability assessment should be a focus on the parenting capacity of the kinship carer as this is the area where professionals appear to be most accurate at predicting concerns that may arise in placement.

For some children, such an early viability assessment of the kinship carers, enabling more rapid placement of the child, followed by a subsequent exploration of the wider issues involved in the kinship placement with carers, may be a productive way forward. This would allow carers to make – with the social worker carrying out the assessment – what must be an emotional journey through the issues that surround the court proceedings and parental risk so they can arrive at a decision about what

---

[78] $X2 = 23.25$, df = 1, $p < 0.001$

is best for each individual child, when they already have the care of the child. There is an argument that carers may be more ready and able to engage constructively in looking at the implications of the kinship placement and making long-term, viable, safe plans for the child if the issue of their own competency as substitute parents has been accepted and the child is in their care.

Summary

This chapter first examined local authority decision-making about kinship placements. It found some evidence that social workers are insufficiently pro-active in exploring the potential for care in the extended family. Mapping the child's network at an early stage could allow more placements to be made and/or placements to be made earlier. It might also be necessary for the local authority to have the power, possibly even a duty, to approach identified family members in advance of legal action, if necessary without parental permission. Quicker and earlier viability assessments could also facilitate earlier placement.

A degree of ambivalence among social workers towards kinship care may help to explain why they are not always as proactive as they might be in identifying possible carers and making early placements. Kinship care presents significant challenges to social workers. Training which covers both attitudes and skills in working with kinship care families could both increase the proportion of placements made and give social workers more confidence in their work.

However wide the net may be cast, in many families there does not appear to be a "bottomless pit" of willing and available relatives to care. More positive encouragement for and support of those relatives who actively show a wish to care for the child may be the best way of improving the numbers of children who are able to stay within families.

We then looked at carer decision making and carers' involvement in formal decision-making processes. Carers typically had a high level of involvement with the children pre-proceedings and most were motivated by pre-existing affectional bonds as well as by a sense of felt obligation. The decision to care was often instinctive rather than carefully weighed up. Ways of helping potential carers to think through the implications of care for themselves and their family need to be devised. Few carers expressed any regret about their decision, even where placements had broken down.

Relatives appeared well able to put the welfare of the child before their loyalties to a parent. Those relatives reporting their concerns about the child to the local authority were more likely to have the child placed with them at an early stage in proceedings. However, there was little evidence of any contribution by the relatives to formal local authority decision-making and family group conferences were rare, although few carers seemed to think that such a meeting would have been useful. Carers were more likely to be involved in the court process with nearly a half being party to the proceedings. Where no legal aid was available, kinship carers had to raise substantial amounts to cover any legal representation.

The chapter then examined the tricky issue of assessment. It was rare for a full assessment to be made before children were placed. The majority of carers accepted the need for assessment but some criticised the way the assessment was done and/or reported finding the experience unduly stressful.

The next sections dealt with the extent to which decisions were made by consensus. There was disagreement from some quarter to making the kinship placement in 19 per cent of cases. Resistance was usually resolved in advance of the final hearing and no kinship placements were made without the support of the guardian. Analysis of our small sample of children under five placed with non-kin carers indicated that, in 20 per cent of cases, identified relatives were rejected by the local authority and in a further 25 per cent, such relatives are not pursued.

Cases were legally resolved primarily by the making of care orders justified by anticipated parental difficulties and support needs. Kinship carers may benefit from independent written information about the advantages and disadvantages of various orders so they can take an informed view.

Finally, we looked at how accurate professionals were in forecasting how a placement would go. In general, we found predictions were rarely accurate: most of the specific concerns identified in the care proceedings did not materialise and most of the issues which arose in placement had not been spotted. However, practitioners were more accurate at predicting the future parenting capacity of kinship carers. Assessments should therefore keep a clear focus on this core task.

It may be that better assessment could identify more accurately what problems will arise in cases, but it seems more likely that crystal-ball gazing just has a high margin of error. If the latter is the case, it is salutary to consider whether some of the decisions professionals make not to support placement with relatives might also contain similar levels of error. Early viability assessments coupled with subsequent exploration with the kinship carers about the wider characteristics and implications of kinship placements may enable children to be placed at an earlier stage with relatives.

6   Caring

You'll need the patience of a saint. You'll need a level head. You'll have to put yourself very much in the background – you have to put them first always. (Carer)

Since kinship care is a naturally occurring family form, it is easy to assume that it is also unproblematic. In fact, research indicates that it is likely to present unique challenges, over and above the "normal" demands of parenting (Hunt, 2003a). The children themselves have difficulties far in excess of those expected in the general population (Hunt, 2003a) and those placed by the state are in many ways very similar to those placed in non-kin foster care (Sinclair *et al*, 2007; Farmer and Moyers, 2008). Non-kin carers, however, make a deliberate decision to offer care and will have been assessed to ensure that they have the financial, material, physical and emotional resources to do so. They will usually have ample time to assess and adjust to the impact on their families and lifestyle before any child comes to live with them and are entitled to support throughout the placement by Social Services. Kinship carers, in contrast, are usually faced with a dramatic and unanticipated change in their lives, one which requires significant sacrifice and places demands on resources which may be already strained. There is no statutory requirement for Social Services to be involved unless there is a supervision or care order, and even where relatives are approved as foster carers, they may well receive lower levels of support than non-kin carers (Rowe *et al*, 1984; Farmer and Pollock, 1998; Flynn, 1999; Tan, 2000; Waterhouse, 2001; Farmer and Moyers, 2008). Given these circumstances, rather than being disappointed that a proportion of placements fail, we should perhaps be surprised that so many continue. This chapter explores the experience of caring from the carer's perspective. The next chapter looks at the issue of support.

Challenging children

As reported in Chapter 3, the children in our sample had experienced multiple adversities. Most had been abused or neglected; few had had stable care; many had lived in households marred by domestic violence, substance abuse or mental illness. By the time of placement, 58 per cent were already manifesting emotional and 48 per cent behavioural problems.

Almost three-quarters of the carers interviewed recalled having to cope with children who were either developmentally delayed or displaying some form of disturbed behaviour: head-banging; wetting or soiling; constant crying; aggression; abnormal fears; obsession with food; night-mares; insomnia; hyperactivity; inactivity; stealing; self-harm; difficulties with peers; excessive demands; and sexualised behaviour. For example:

He [child aged four] *wasn't potty trained. He wouldn't talk because I think he got hit if he talked. He used to go and sit in the corner and rock.*

Paul was quite a difficult boy, he would wind people up, he was rude to them. He used to thieve. He used to have real issues around food, he used to just gorge himself because he didn't know when the next food was coming. One day he just had a complete fit. He screamed and cried and lashed out and I didn't know what to do and my other kids didn't know what to do and I remember we were in that room and the only thing I could do was hold him. It was my instinct because he wanted to hurt somebody and he wanted to hurt himself but at the same time he had to go through it. His brother was more inward, he was quite subdued, he used to wet the bed. He was very quiet, I used to really worry about him.

Over time, problems generally tended to diminish in severity. However, a substantial number were still evident years later, others had got worse and occasionally new problems emerged. Some placements broke down under the strain:

Declan ran away from home when he was 12 years old, making allega-tions of physical abuse against his parents and siblings. He steadfastly refused to return home and maintained his allegations throughout the subsequent care proceedings. After two weeks of being cared for by one set of relatives, he was moved to his aunt and uncle, Mr and Mrs Stead, who struggled to cope with him for the next two-and-a-half years but eventually had to give up:

There was a honeymoon period initially for several months then he relaxed, found his feet. He played us off one against the other. He wanted someone's full attention, he'd never had that before at home. We just couldn't cope with him in the end. We needed specialist help; we weren't strong enough to cope. We didn't know what was coming up. He was getting so naughty towards the end we didn't know what he was going to do next. Fire-setting, he set fire to an old tree house, he was involved in setting fire to a caravan up the road, we didn't know anything about this until a policeman arrived on the doorstep and said haven't you told these people about it? We didn't know anything about it at all as we'd given him freedom which he'd never had at home. We didn't want him to go but we'd reached the point where it was so stressful because of his behaviour that we couldn't cope.

Other carers were continuing to cope with what could be very troubled children, as their scores on the Strengths and Difficulties Questionnaire (Goodman, 1997) indicate (Chapter 9).

Mr and Mrs Harvey have cared for their two grandchildren, Rea (now aged 7) and Joseph (6) for six years, on a residence order. A third sibling's placement broke down some years ago. Joseph has multiple problems: ADHD, autistic spectrum disorder, dyspraxia and a form of epilepsy. He also wets and soils. His behaviour is having an impact on his sister, who is now receiving counselling at school.

He's very intelligent but can't control his emotions. If someone upset him, he was always very aggressive; if he was happy, he was screaming and running. He never slept; it was nothing to be up with him five times a night. He likes to be in control; if you ask him to do something he won't do it; then 10 minutes later he will, because he has decided. If you try to turn the computer off he'll have a screaming fit. He's always right. If he decides it's night time, you'll say look, the sun is out, but he won't have it. He won't back down, he's got to be right. It takes us at least 20 minutes to get him to take his tablet. We used to have to lay him on the floor and pin him down. At one point I was having to carry him from here to school every day and back. It was just doing me in. It wasn't that he didn't want to go to school but he just would not walk.

Challenging circumstances

In addition to the stress of caring for Joseph and Rea, Mr and Mrs Harvey also have other family responsibilities: aging parents in poor health; a sister whose marriage has collapsed; and a son in serious financial and personal difficulties. They appear to be the people the rest of the family call on and for the past few years their lives have seemed to be one problem after another. They have financial problems because Mr Harvey had to reduce his working hours to support his wife and is now off work because of (an unrelated) illness. Both are on medication for depression. Their marital relationship is suffering – as Mr Harvey put it: *We don't have a relationship much at the moment; we're in the same room with each other but that's as far as it goes.*

This is probably one of the most extreme examples of carer strain in our sample because of the combination of pressures. It is also fair to say that, when asked about the impact of caring, a few carers came up with only positive responses, and some reported that the challenges of caring had only served to strengthen their relationship:

My daughter was happy to get some other children in the family because she was an only child.

Nothing. I'm fit and well and it keeps me young.

It's brought us closer together. We have to communicate all the time. The commitment of having him has meant we've had to make a commitment to each other to make it work.

Most of those interviewed, however, referred to some problems that had arisen because of their decision to care or which had an impact on their ability to care.

There were material difficulties occasioned by the additional demands on money and space. While, as reported in Chapter 2, the levels of financial difficulties experienced by the families in our study do not appear to be as great as those reported in other research, nonetheless the majority of the interviewed carers indicated that taking on care had put a strain on their finances, increasing outgoings and eroding savings (Chapter 7). Financial difficulties undoubtedly exacerbated the pressure on both the Steads and the Harveys, although the former were adamant that this was not the reason for the placement eventually breaking down.

Families had to move house, adapt their existing accommodation or simply squeeze in together until either their own or the kinship children left home. In one case, an elderly relative had to be moved into a nursing home:

I had the two boys in one bedroom; the two girls in with me, auntie had the other back bedroom and my husband slept on the sofa. It didn't get sorted out until auntie went into a home. I didn't have room for the children and her. It wasn't a nice mixture with the children and auntie together. Children make a lot of noise and she wanted peace and quiet. She wasn't all right about it, she blamed the kids. She used to pick on the kids, it's your fault I'm in here (the home). But they were very good, they used to go up and see her and run errands for her.

Having to share physical space could lead to tensions with other children in the household. Birth children could also resent the presence of the kin children or suffer from their difficult behaviour and the demands it made on the carer's attention. While we would not wish to over-emphasise the issue of conflict with birth children – most of the carers we interviewed who had had their own children at home indicated that relationships were fine, or at least were no more difficult than might be expected with siblings – in a few cases it was a major problem. Indeed, as mentioned in previous chapters, in one case, this was a contributory factor in placement breakdown, while in another, the carers had decided the only way to deal with the situation was for the kinship children to remain with one of them and for the other to move out with the remaining children.

It's difficult for us because we're in a pretty unique position that we've still got children. I think if all our children had left home it wouldn't have been so bad. The main problem we've had is friction between the boys and our children. We had worries but we never realised how bad it would be. We were hoping our kids would accept them and that we could work together but the more problems the boys developed the worse they became. My older son, he's moved out now but he lived with the boys for a long time and he used to retreat to his bedroom and couldn't cope with it all. My older daughter, she lived away on and off and she's here now but it's as much as she can do to keep her distance from them all. The younger one has been quite suicidal throughout it sometimes; well, she has attempted it a few times. The youngest has grown up with them so he's coped better. But he does get angry with them.

Kinship carers may also experience more difficult circumstances than non-kin foster carers in terms of their age or health. As we noted in a previous chapter, concerns were raised about these issues at the time of the care proceedings in 22 of the sample cases. Over a quarter of the main carers in our study (29 of 108; 27%) were over 50 by the end of the care proceedings and 10 were 60 or more. This would usually have precluded them from being accepted as non-kin foster carers. While this emphatically does not mean that they were not capable of providing good enough care, it is, nonetheless not what people normally expect to do at this stage in their lives and caring 24/7 for any child, let alone those with the difficulties presented by the sample children, might be expected to be a challenge. 'It's hard work, tiring' was a common theme in our carer interviews and at the risk of appearing "ageist", the older you are the harder it is to find the physical and emotional energy to do that work and to remain "young" for the child.

Mrs Evans is 76 and took on care of her grandson, Michael, who is now 11, when he was four. Michael is developmentally delayed and attends a special school. Mrs Evans is finding his behaviour increasingly hard to manage:

It is a lot to deal with – it wasn't what I was expecting to do at my age. Sometimes I think he's just too much for me to cope with. My friend said you shouldn't do it, you're too old, you'll wear yourself out, he'll be the death of you. I wasn't used to a child in the house, it was a bit of a nightmare when I first had him. [There have been] many points when I've felt . . . if only I hadn't got that child, he's just that bit too much for me.

Nonetheless, there was only one case in the sample where the carers decided (at the age of 73, having had the child, Josie, for six years) they could not continue to care because they were too old to cope with the behaviour of a challenging teenager. When Josie was younger they had largely managed to adjust their lifestyle to meet her needs, but had to call it a day when she was 15:

We weren't too old when Josie first came but we are now. I felt when she was smaller it was fine but they get to be their own person and you can't break into it. It got too much work for us. If she had been with younger people, who would take her out, it may have worked. We don't get out much. I have arthritis in the knees and that was difficult.

Other carers also experienced health problems which may have made it more difficult for them to care – diabetes, arthritis, stroke, cancer, seasonal affective disorder – or, where partners were affected, made additional demands on them (dementia, psychiatric illness, heart attacks, degenerative disease). Indeed, as noted in a previous chapter, where these were identified at the time of the proceedings, they could raise questions about the viability of the placement. However, there was only one case where the placement broke down because of ill-health; in general, as has been the theme throughout this chapter, carers just got on with it.

Finally, some of the very strengths of kinship placements, such as sibling placement and the facilitation of contact, may place greater demands on carers (Young and Smith, 2000). Relationships with the birth parents may already be strained and may worsen after placement (Portengen and Van Der Neut, 1999; Gordon *et al*, 2003), particularly since, as noted in a previous chapter, relatives will often have drawn the attention of the authorities to the parents' deficiencies in care. In this study we found that problematic contact was common, while in 44 per cent of cases there was conflict between the carer and at least one parent

(Chapter 9). As family, carers may struggle with a turmoil of feelings about the birth parents and the problems which led to the child having to be removed (Dannison and Smith, 2003; Osby, 1999; Farmer and Moyers, 2008). While grandparents may be particularly vulnerable in this respect, other relatives are not necessarily immune. One aunt, for example, told us:

The guilt is there. The shame about it being part of your family. I felt at the time I had to hide that away. Since life has gone on, I can stand up and say I'm not ashamed; I have dealt with it and I've come out the other end, but at the time I didn't.

Sacrifice and loss

You have to remember your life is never going to be the same and you have to really forget about what you want.

You have to think about what it entails, what aspects it's going to take out of your life.

I don't regret it but sometimes I think 'what would I be doing today?'

In addition to coping with the needs of distressed and difficult children in what are often less than ideal circumstances, carers are likely to have to make considerable sacrifices for the sake of their young relatives and adjust to a variety of losses and changes (Minkler and Roe, 1993; Young and Smith, 2000; Richards, 2001; Farmer and Moyers, 2008). Three main themes emerged from our carer interviews.

First, taking on care is a major disruption to carers' life plans and expectations. Indeed, one carer told us 'you put your life on hold'. Older people lose the prospect of a retirement without child-rearing responsibilities; those of working age may have to give up work or substantially reduce their working hours,[79] with consequent impact on their finances and pension rights; the youngest carers may find their careers and ability to establish themselves seriously impeded. One aunt, for example, with a good job in business, was enjoying her life as a young single woman, with

---

[79]   48 per cent of the carers interviewed who had been working before taking on care reported some impact on their employment position: giving up work completely or for lengthy periods or substantially reducing their working hours.

her own small flat. Taking on her six-year-old niece meant giving all that up. She now lives in a council property and has completely changed both her career plans and her lifestyle:

There are sacrifices you make. I'd been in the flat for 10 years, it was my home. I could have had a house by now. That was on my list. I will never have a pension. All my savings got used up right at the beginning because I had to make a home for her. Life changed overnight. I was a single person, going to work, going out, going to college, doing what single people do. I didn't have to cook at home at a certain time; I could eat at midnight or 3am, my role was just to look after me. That first six–eight months was possibly the hardest in terms of my own needs, my own changes. I don't resent it in any way but when I look back I think yeah, if I hadn't taken her on . . . But I'm quite happy here, and in a lot of ways it's far richer. In other ways . . .

The second theme was the loss of freedom to pursue outside interests and maintain peer group relationships (Jendrek, 1994; Minkler *et al*, 1994; Shore and Hayslip, 1994; Farmer and Moyers, 2008). 'I don't get out as much as I did,' we were told; 'I don't go out now in the evenings' and 'you have to give up your social life'. While carers who still have their own children living at home may be less affected, since at least some of their friends will probably still be at that stage of life, both older and younger carers may find it difficult to maintain relationships with peers in a very different position.

Third was the loss of the relationship they had, or might have expected to develop, with the child. Research typically comments on grandparents missing out on the pleasures of the usual grandparenting role – having all the fun but none of the responsibility; enjoying them but being able to send them back. Some of the grandparents in our study also raised this point:

You lose the grandparent role. I was looking forward to being a grandparent. You're a parent not a grandparent.

However, other relatives also expressed regret for the change in their relationship with the child:

They lost their fun auntie that never told them off, took them swimming, took them to the park, did all the fun things. They lost that person and they got auntie that doesn't let them stay up late. Now I've become the person that tells them to tidy their rooms and brush their teeth. I do think they lost that side of me. I felt it was a shame for them but I couldn't do both. I couldn't set the rules and be the fun character with no responsibility.

Carer stress

Given the various challenges detailed above, it is not surprising that kinship care has been found to be a psychologically stressful experience for a substantial proportion of carers (Burton 1992; Kelley, 1993; Emick and Hayslip, 1996; Fuller-Thomson *et al*, 1997; Grant *et al*, 1997; Cimmarusti, 1999; Giarrusso *et al*, 2000; Sands and Goldberg-Glen, 2000). Indeed, the stress experienced by kinship carers has been found to be higher than that associated with other forms of care (Strawbridge *et al*, 1997). Care-taking grandparents have been found to be almost twice as likely as those without care-giving responsibilities to be categorised as depressed (25%; Minkler *et al*, 1997) and some studies report that more than half their sample of carers were suffering from depressive symptoms (Minkler and Roe, 1993; Janicki *et al*, 2000). Relatives caring for children with disabilities or special needs are likely to be particularly vulnerable (Burnette, 2000; Janicki *et al*, 2000).

Many of the carers interviewed in this study tended to be fairly matter-of fact about the impact of caring on them. Nonetheless, it was clear that some were experiencing, or had experienced, substantial levels of stress.

It's been a nightmare. You can't say it's been easy as it wasn't then and it isn't now.

We have been under great stress and pressure. We felt very powerless.

I don't think we understood fully the total implications of it all and responsibilities of it all. It's a hell of a lot of responsibility for us and it's knocked us sideways.

In fact, analysis of scores on the General Health Questionnaire (Goldberg and Hillier, 1979) revealed that, in 45 per cent of households where placements were continuing, at least one carer was currently scoring above the normal range threshold (compared to well under 20 per cent for the general population). Over a quarter of carers in continuing placements (8; 27%) told us they had felt like giving up at some point; indeed some were feeling like this at the time of interview and others had recently gone through a bad patch:

On occasion [I have thought about giving up] but I know I can't. Quite often I think let Social Services sort it out, but it doesn't last. Up to the end of last year I was getting quite a few of those [thoughts].

Social support

Social support is one of the factors considered to buffer against stressful life experiences (Kelley *et al*, 2000). Although the findings in relation to kinship care are somewhat mixed (Hunt, 2003a), they suggest that carers cannot necessarily rely on helping networks. Several studies report carer isolation and loneliness (Kelley, 1993; Minkler and Roe, 1993; Dowdell, 1995; Kelley and Damato, 1995 [cited in Kelley *et al*, 2000]; Osby, 1999; Farmer and Moyers, 2008). Even where carers report being part of social networks these may be tenuous (Burnette, 2000). Perhaps most significantly, help may not be forthcoming from other family members (Burton, 1992; Worrall, 1996; Osby, 1999). Worrall (1996) writes of the "myth" of the New Zealand legislation that the extended family will be collectively responsible. In reality, she argues, care by the extended family just means care by one of the related nuclear families.

The findings of our study are rather more optimistic. A few carers, it is true, seemed to be pretty much coping on their own:

I've been left to get on with it. I've had no help at all from family members, no respite or day care.

Carer 1: *No family members have been supportive or realised what we were going through. There hasn't been anyone that's appreciated it really.*

Carer 2: *We don't push it, we don't like to. It would be nice for one of our family to come and say we'll have them for a couple of days. We've never gone to our family and said would you do this, we'd be too embarrassed really.*

Most carers (30; 81%), however, said their family and friends were supportive of them caring for the child/ren. We did not get the impression of significant numbers of carers feeling socially isolated. Interestingly, although four of the children we interviewed described what seemed to us to be quite limited social networks, none of their carers reported feeling unsupported.[80] Moreover, most people (31 of 35; 89%) said that in a crisis there was someone they could rely on to look after the children temporarily.

In general, however, support was likely to be emotional and occasional rather then practical or regular. Over a third of carers (14) said they did not receive any practical help in caring from their family or friends: 'I've just been left to get on with it'. Others mentioned babysitting (10 carers), help with day-to-day care (9), and having the child overnight (8) but all on an occasional basis. Only one person mentioned receiving help from the other side of the child's family (having the child overnight occasionally). Twenty-seven percent of carers (9 of 34) said they would have liked some other form of help from their family and friends, the most commonly specified being respite care or babysitting:

[I would like] possibly more support in looking after her so I could have my independence to some degree. Because I had been going out, going on courses and all that stopped. I have one solid friend. I can tell her anything and I'm not judged by her. She gives me emotional support. She'll babysit if I'm desperate but really it's her I'd like to go out with. I don't go out to any great extent. I think my mother could do a bit more than she does. I get a bit niggled with that. There are always excuses.

---

[80] We did not interview any of the children living with carers who did not feel supported.

Continuing to care

The commitment carers show to the children is a consistent theme in the research literature (in the UK Malos and Bullard, 1991; Russell, 1995; Pitcher, 1999; Tan, 2000; Farmer and Moyers, 2008). Why do relatives continue to care despite the sacrifices it often entails for them, the difficult circumstances they may find themselves in and, above all, perhaps, the challenges presented by the children?

Our interviews with carers, particularly those who were having a difficult time, suggest that "doing the right thing" is an important factor, sometimes combined with sheer determination to see things through and perhaps hope that things will improve:

Just because it gets difficult you can't jack it in, it's children's lives. If you're fostering you could hand them back; you can't with family; they're your own flesh and blood.

You keep hoping things are going to change, get better. Maybe they will when they get older.

Just my upbringing I suppose, you make your bed and lie on it.

It would be wrong to give the impression that most carers were having to steel themselves to go on or that a sense of obligation implied dutiful but cold care-giving. On the contrary, many carers spoke of the love they felt for the child, who was now an integral part of the family, whom they could no more think of giving up than a birth child:

We love her, we all love her. Love is the main thing.

We love them all dearly. That's the trouble.

We just treat him as one of our own.

Another common theme was the rewards which caring brought: watching the child develop; seeing them make progress; and the satisfaction of giving the child a secure and loving home and contributing to their welfare:

When she comes home with brilliant school reports. When other people tell me what a lovely kid she is. Her confidence has got a lot better.

Watching her develop basically. She's a changed child. And it's not just me saying that, it's the school, my mother, my friends, anyone who is associated with the past and the present. That's really good.

Seeing him get on well at school, seeing how popular he is.

I get enjoyment out of seeing them happy.

Carers also spoke of the sheer pleasure they had in the children (Hatmaker, 1999; Pitcher, 1999; Gordon *et al*, 2003):

He's a loveable little boy. It doesn't matter how naughty he is, he's still loveable.

She's mischievous, funny. She brings a smile to your face in the morning.

She is a very lovely little girl and such a beautiful person. I am very proud of her and I know she loves us deeply.

She's an absolute delight.

Indeed, for some fortunate carers the experience had been entirely positive – one carer, for instance, told us that she had 'enjoyed every minute'. For one widowed grandfather, taking on his two grandchildren had been rejuvenating, and while appreciating the occasional respite weekend offered by other family members, he was delighted to see the children again:

Some weekends [another relative] has them and I'm glad, but they only have to be gone a night and I miss them then. I enjoy it and I just want to see them get to 16, 18 and get good at school. They are both nice children, everyone says that.

More commonly, however, the experience was more mixed and it was the rewards of care and/or the commitment to the child which enabled carers to cope with the challenges and the stress. As one hard-pressed carer put it:

It's very rewarding despite the ups and downs. It has been hard. Then he'll come in from school and he'll just look at you and all those thoughts go away.

In the next chapter we look at what professional support carers received and what might have helped them to cope more effectively and/or at less cost to themselves.

Summary

The interviews with the 37 kinship carers provided our data on the experience of caring. The children had experienced multiple adversities and most (75%) had emotional, behavioural or learning difficulties on arrival. Although these problems diminished over time, a substantial number of children presented problems years later.

Notwithstanding various concerns flagged up by professionals in cases at the care proceedings stage, only one case in our interview sample broke down because the carers decided that they could not continue – they thought they were too old to cope with a challenging teenager – and only one case broke down because of carer ill health. Despite this low figure, in 27 per cent of continuing placements, carers had felt like giving up caring at some point. Tensions and strains were evident and 45 per cent of continuing households had at least one carer scoring above the normal range threshold on the General Health Questionnaire. Finance issues and overcrowding (particularly where the carers had birth children living in the household) caused notable stress.

The interviewed carers highlighted how taking on care affected them in many dimensions, including life plans and expectations, freedom to pursue outside interests/maintain peer group relationships, and loss of the expected "grandparent/aunt" relationship with the child. Most (81%) carers enjoyed some support from their family and friends (but more in an occasional or emotional way rather than in practical ways) and 89 per cent had someone they could rely on to temporarily care for the children in a crisis.

Overall, the rewards of caring, including genuine love for and enjoyment of a child integrated into the family, outweighed and compensated for the challenges and difficulties.

7 Sustaining kinship care

We would like acknowledgement that the people who are doing the caring are doing a full-time stressful job and that if they want them to carry on doing it and not the government taking on responsibility, then they do need looking after themselves.

I think the government should be aware of the situation of how many people do care for people within the family, and they need to think hard about some help for the carers.

It will be evident, from the material presented in Chapter 6, that caring for children who have been abused and neglected, even if they are related to you, presents significant challenges, and that carers who take on this challenge are likely to need support. Thus, while this form of care offers many advantages to children, and indeed to Social Services, it is not, as Sinclair puts it, a *'free lunch'* (Sinclair *et al*, 2007, p 150).

There is broad agreement in the literature on the kinds of help needed to support kinship care families (Hunt, 2006):

* adequate financial help;
* information, advice and sometimes advocacy to help navigate the complexities of the legal, benefits, education and social services systems (Russell, 1995; Pitcher, 1999; Bourne and Porter, 2001; Richards, 2001; Doolan *et al*, 2004).
* different forms of practical help including, for example, regular respite care and holiday clubs (Russell, 1995; Pitcher, 1999; Bourne and Porter, 2001; Richards, 2001);
* equipment (Doolan *et al*, 2004);
* transport (Pitcher, 2001);
* assistance in obtaining larger or more appropriate accommodation (Pitcher, 1999; Richards, 2001; Laws, 2001);
* signposting and ready access to services, whether broadly-based ones

such as Sure Start or more specialised ones such as therapy and counselling (Russell, 1995; Pitcher, 1999);

• assistance to kinship carers so they themselves can help the children with their school work – which will be very unfamiliar to many grandparents (Richards, 2001) – their feelings about their situation (Flynn, 2001) and above all, their behaviour (Flynn, 2001; Doolan *et al*, 2004; Farmer and Moyers, 2008);

• help for carers to deal with parents, including managing strained relationships and coping with contact (Russell, 1995; Laws, 2001; Richards, 2001; Doolan *et al*, 2004; Farmer and Moyers, 2008).

However, while what is needed to support kinship care may be clear, there is also much evidence that it is not always provided. Kinship placements tend to be given lower priority by Social Services departments than traditional foster placements (Rowe *et al*, 1984; Flynn, 1999; Tan, 2000; Waterhouse, 2001) and tend to receive inadequate levels of service (Farmer and Moyers, 1995; Tunnard and Thoburn, 1997; Hunt and Macleod, 1999; Laws and Broad, 2000; Richards, 2001). Social workers underestimate carers' needs and their desire for ongoing support (Rowe *et al*, 1984). Help may not be given sufficiently early (Laws, 2001) and/or tail off too soon (Laws, 2001; Harwin *et al*, 2003). The level of service provision may bear little relation to need (Farmer and Pollock, 1998; Hunt and Macleod, 1999). Carers report feeling 'isolated', 'taken for granted' and having to go 'cap in hand' for services (Pitcher, 1999).

Kinship foster carers are unlikely to be allocated a link worker (Hunt and Macleod, 1999; Tan, 2000; Farmer and Moyers, 2008). Some may not even have a social worker (Hunt and Macleod 1999; Farmer and Moyers, 2008) but, if they do, the focus is likely to be on the child, not the carer (Waldman and Wheal, 1999). Indeed, some carers report being told that the worker is not there for them (Hunt and Macleod, 1999) or that they are not entitled to help because the child is 'alright' (Richards, personal communication). Some complain that social workers vary in their responses, are difficult to contact and are not sufficiently knowledgeable (Pitcher, 1999). Kinship carers may be reluctant to press for help, sometimes for fear of being regarded as incompetent (Malos and Bullard,

1991; Russell, 1995; Bourne and Porter, 2001) and may not be aware of the mechanisms to address their concerns about poor service (Pitcher, 1999).

However, it is not just a question of specific services but of the way kinship carers are regarded and treated. An insistent message emerging from the research on carers is the desire to be valued, and to be shown respect and consideration (Bourne and Porter; 2001; Laws, 2001; Richards, 2001; Wheal, 2001).

All these themes are reflected in the data in our study.

Financial and material assistance

If carers didn't take on responsibility, then someone else would have to, so it's not too much to ask to have enough to live on. At the moment it seems they want things both ways. They want the family to care but they're not prepared to invest enough money so you can do it.

We were told we couldn't have anything as we were grandparents and we were expected to want to bring them up. But there is a difference between wanting to and being able to.

Whether and how kinship care should be publicly funded is a key policy issue, both here and internationally (Hunt, 2003a; Richards and Tapsfield, 2003; Blaiklock, 2005; Broad, 2004). There are problems with all the different ways in which kinship families can be currently financially supported (Masson and Lindley, 2006) and many studies have shown that finance is a serious issue (Russell, 1995; Flynn, 1999; Waldman and Wheal, 1999; Bourne and Porter, 2001; Laws, 2001; Richards, 2001; Blaiklock, 2005; Aldgate and McIntosh, 2006; Farmer and Moyers, 2008). The Family Rights Group is leading a well-supported campaign for the creation of a state benefit to meet the costs of care, either an unsupported child element in the tax credit or an extended guardian's allowance (Richards and Tapsfield, 2003).

Although in law it has been many years since grandparents were financially responsible for their grandchildren, the interchange of money, goods and services between close relatives is a recognised part of family life (Finch, 1989) and may even be regarded as in some sense an obligation. Thus, even carers in strained economic circumstances may feel uncomfortable about receiving, and particularly asking, for financial help (Farmer and Moyers, 2008). Social Services' attitudes to this question may be influenced by a variety of considerations: limited budgets; the fact that, unlike non-kin foster carers, kinship carers are not a general resource for the department and may be seen as providing lower standards of care; suspicion of the motivation of carers who ask for money (incidentally, a view which used to affect the financing of non-kin foster carers too). Hence kinship foster carers have been found to receive lower allowances than non-kin foster carers (Waterhouse and Brocklesby, 1999; Farmer and Moyers, 2008) while residence order allowances are likely to be even lower and, being discretionary, something of a lottery.

As noted in Chapter 2, only a minority of the carers in our study appeared to be experiencing financial hardship sufficiently severe to be impacting on the quality of care given to the child. We speculated that this probably had a great deal to do with the fact that all the study cases had been through the court process, where the issue of the adequacy of financial support should have been examined. And certainly there was evidence that some care orders were made to ensure that carers received the higher allowances payable to foster carers.

The dire poverty reported in many kinship households in the USA is, at least in part, due to the fact that a high proportion of carers are lone women, living on either benefits or a pension. The majority of children in our study, however, as in that of Farmer and Moyers (2008) were cared for by a couple (72% and 73% respectively). Moreover, in most instances (71%), at least one carer was in paid employment and in 27 per cent, both (although typically the main carer was only employed on a part-time basis (67%)). Although information was sparse, only two families were recorded as being in receipt of working family tax credit, or similar support, with 10 of the remaining 32 on income support.

Most families in our study (95; 88%) also received some form of on-going regular financial support from Social Services post-proceedings with a high proportion (63%) in receipt of fostering allowances either throughout the period for which we have data or until the order was converted into either an adoption or residence order.[81]

Nonetheless, finance was an issue for many carers. While financial difficulties were recorded on file in less than a third of the cases, our interviews with carers suggest that this is a gross underestimate. Only 14 of those interviewed (38%) said they were managing/had managed without difficulty. What was surprising about most of the remaining responses was how matter of fact and uncomplaining carers were about having to budget very carefully to cover the essentials and do without the "little extras" such as holidays and activities which most families would nowadays take for granted, let alone having money to spend on themselves or provide for their own futures:

I definitely have to watch what I spend. I tend to be tight about putting heating and electric on, I get them to put extra jumpers on. I tend not to buy myself as many clothes as I once did. I did go through a period of buying own brand foods but they wouldn't eat them. Holidays we don't seem to have; we've had one. And going out we tend to do short day trips. (Single female carer, part-time employment; child adopted)

---

[81]   We did try to obtain up-to-date allowance rates from our authorities for kinship carers with children on special guardianship, residence and care orders. However, such information proved extremely difficult to gather and to compare. Authority A provided some examples of payment levels under different order types. Grandparents on state benefit with a 15-year-old grandchild on a care order could receive £147.84 per week maintenance plus annual allowances of £591.36 if approved as foster carers (additional "skills" allowances appearing only to be available for non-kin foster carers). The same case on a residence order would qualify for a residence order allowance of £124.61 (plus child benefit of £17.45) thus lost income in changing to a residence order would be around £850 annually. SGO allowances were new but were thought to be similar in level to residence order allowances. Larger discrepancies in foster and residence allowances become apparent when a kinship carer was working, as both allowances are means tested. A couple with their own child and a mortgage of £100 per week and net weekly income of £220 could receive the full allowance for a kinship child aged 12 months of £89.50 less child benefit of £11.70 but a family earning £285 net with no mortgage caring for a child under 10 would get a reduced allowance of £46.80. Such an allowance would gradually diminish as income rose. Thus, it is true that the change from care to residence orders significantly reduces maintenance levels for a child, and a partial loss of maintenance offsets any financial advantage of a return to work by the carer.

They never go without. We're limited in what we can do but we manage. Some things we have to say no to. We can't afford a holiday. You haven't got the spare money for taking them swimming; taking them to the cinema. I know there are a lot of things you can do, without spending money but . . . It's a job to put it in words but really . . . It seems if you become a carer you've got to give up a certain quality of life. (Grandparent carers, on benefit, children on residence orders)

There were also surprisingly few examples of carers pressing for extra money.

Mr and Mrs Gardner are caring for their nephew, Dean, who was aged 12 at the end of the proceedings. Mr Gardner has chronic asthma which prevents him from working. Since Mrs Gardner does not work either their sole income was invalidity benefit. During proceedings Dean was on an interim care order, but since he did not wish social workers to remain involved, a residence order was made. Mr and Mrs Gardner had reluctantly agreed to this on the understanding that the allowance would be paid at the same rate as they had been receiving. When this proved not to be the case, they said they could not manage and Dean would have to go into non-kin foster care. The local authority agreed to restore the allowance to the previous rate.

Not unexpectedly, kinship carers in receipt of a residence order allowance were more likely to report a degree of financial strain than those receiving fostering allowances. Only four of the former (27%) said they had not had any difficulty, with 10 (67%) reporting finding it a struggle. The comparative figures for those on fostering allowances were 50 per cent and 14 per cent. (The fact that as many as half of those on fostering allowances reported some financial stress may reflect generally unrealistic rates or, as we know to be the case in a few instances, that the carers were not receiving the same amount as non-kin foster carers would have done.) One of the social workers we interviewed in a current case was highly critical of the fact that an enhanced allowance which had been paid to the carers because of the child's special needs was taken away because of budgetary constraints. The placement of our study children, of course, pre-dates the 2001 court decision known as the "Munby judgment" in which it was ruled illegal to pay kinship foster carers less than non-related foster carers simply because of their status.[82] Therefore, up until that decision, kinship foster carers were usually paid a reduced fostering allowance.

Several carers commented on the discrepancy between foster care and residence allowances, either in terms of the basic rate or the extras paid for foster children:

Even with the child benefit it [residence order allowance] isn't enough. It doesn't cover the cost of the upkeep of a child. The costs soon mount up. School dinners, shoes, uniform, Brownies, trips. Foster parents get an allowance for the actual child; the older they are they get more, the more problems they have they get more, plus they get extra to help with birthday and Christmas presents and clothing. We perform the same function as a foster parent only we're related. You cannot provide for children if you haven't got the finances. It's a very big part of it.

It could be particularly galling when, as happened in a few cases, siblings were split, with some going into non-kin care, and the carers were aware of the discrepancies in the allowances:

The boys' [foster] carers were given £140 and £120 a week. We didn't get anything like that. It was something like £60 . . . I can't remember exactly but it was about half what the other carers got.

The idea of a state allowance which could be paid to all kinship carers as of right, as suggested by Family Rights Group, was generally well received by our interviewees, although several people emphasised that it should not be means tested like the residence order allowance, nor taken into account in assessing eligibility for other benefits:

With an allowance then you know you're going to get the money. You should be told you're going to get the money if you are family carers.

People in our situation really do need more money and it shouldn't be means tested. Every time my husband got a rise they would take more

---

[82] R v Manchester Council [2001] EWHC.

off the allowance. It's [the child's], it shouldn't be affected by whether I work or not or whether you get a rise. It shouldn't be means tested, it should be the same amount for each child. If I wanted to work part time they would take some [money] off the allowance and you end up working for nothing.

Over half those interviewed thought any allowance should be on a par with the fostering rate, on the grounds that 'we are doing the same job'. It has to be said, however, that a substantial proportion were uncertain about whether they would want this and two carers actually said no:

Yes and no – you need the same amount of money but you are part of the family.

I suppose you have to be careful people aren't doing it just for the money. You may find people aren't so interested in the children as they are in the money and that's not a good thing, but as long as their background's been checked out . . .

Because your priority is your grandchild not fostering. The difference is we would go without, whereas strangers wouldn't.

In addition to (or, in a few cases, instead of) any regular financial support, around half the carers in the whole sample received other forms of material assistance such as help with start-up costs – bedding, clothing, furniture, etc – and other expenses such as child care, transport and nursery/school fees, or money to help with contact, for a limited period. Some of the carers interviewed, however, had apparently been unaware at the outset that such help might have been available and stressed that people should be told more about their entitlements and should not be left having to struggle or even get into debt:

I went out and got second-hand clothes for her because I didn't know what else to do. And toys. And it wasn't until 6–8 months later that I realised I could actually ask for these things. They were the kind of things I really needed knowledge about earlier rather than later. To run into charity shops and grab a whole load of clothes because you've suddenly stopped working and you've got bills to sort out, is quite a drastic . . .

Money should be paid right from the beginning. When the children first came here we had no money for six months, we got behind on rent and bills. That had a knock-on effect. We had to spend time catching up.

I didn't know if any money was coming, if I'd known I would have been happier. However much you love a child, if it's difficult to pay the bills you get worried about how you are going to manage.

Apart from regular adequate financial support and help with special expenses, carers may need other forms of material help. In 16 cases, for example, carers were assisted in obtaining more suitable accommodation. Indeed, in one case, the local authority made a grant of £50,000 to enable the carer to move to a larger house. Some others were not so fortunate and either had to somehow find the money themselves, or had to struggle on in overcrowded conditions. In one case, as reported earlier, this overcrowding appears to have contributed to placement breakdown. In another, according to the social worker, it soured relationships between the family and the department:

We could have helped them more with housing. The family part-bought a house in the end to make their circumstances easier. If we had been able to help with housing they would have seen us in a better light.

Other material forms of assistance which carers told us they would have welcomed included assistance to buy a bigger car and money towards a holiday. Our data do not enable us to say whether help of this nature was provided in any of the sample cases. Neither, however, seems an unreasonable request.

Social work input

Did Social Services remain involved long enough after the proceedings?

Some research (Laws, 2001; Harwin *et al*, 2003) has suggested that Social Services tend to close kinship cases too early, before carers feel comfortable on their own. We did not generally find this.

There were only 12 cases (11%; n = 110) where Social Services involvement was not expected to continue once the care proceedings were over (Appendix F Table F2). Most of these cases were formally closed very speedily, although three appear to have remained open for more than six months. In almost all the remaining cases (98), there was a legal requirement for continuing involvement in the form of either a care order (68; 69%) or a supervision order (26; 27%), although there were four cases where ongoing support was envisaged where only a residence order was made.

A further 41 cases (36% of 113) were closed while the placement was ongoing. The duration of continuous involvement in these cases ranged from six months or less (two cases) to more than five years (six cases). Only 11 cases closed within a year. As one might expect, these were typically cases where either a supervision order had been made (8) or only a residence order (2). Only one care order case, where the child remained in placement, was closed within a year, when a residence order was made. There was no evidence that any cases had been closed earlier than had been anticipated in the care proceedings.

Moreover, the majority of the 22 carers we interviewed, whose cases had closed while the placement was ongoing, seemed quite content that Social Services had backed out when they did; indeed, for some it could not come early enough:

> *They were required to be involved and we didn't want them to be involved. We just wanted to get on with it on our own.* (Case closed on expiry of supervision order)

> *I would have preferred it to have been earlier. I felt insecure with Social Services – 'are they going to take him anytime' was in the back of my mind.* (Case closed after 20 months when child was adopted by carers)

Only two carers said that at the time they had wished support could continue and one that, with hindsight, they wished their case had not been closed:

> *[I would have] preferred longer. We were a bit worried about the mother turning up on the doorstep. We wanted a bit more backup.* (Case closed on expiry of supervision order)

At the time we were. But as time goes on, we wish we hadn't agreed to that and we had a permanent social worker. (Case closed when residence order made four years after proceedings)

Once cases were closed they generally stayed closed, with only 12 (23%) known to have been reopened, again indicating that premature closure was unusual. It should be noted, moreover, that sometimes cases reopened merely because a social worker's report was required in court proceedings for adoption or residence. Only a few appear to have been prompted by problems in the placement. Most cases closed again fairly rapidly. However, two closed only after a rather longer period of involvement, two remained open and one appears to have been intermittently closed and reopened ever since the care proceedings. The researcher reading this last case file commented:

> The social work record is a catalogue of SOSs from the carers about the child's behaviour. There is also the clear message that the carers did not feel that Social Services had done enough to help in the care of the children.

This is one of the few examples of a reopened case where carers do seem to have needed a more sustained period of involvement. Another which gave us some cause for concern involved a carer who had been diagnosed with a terminal illness and was also having difficulties coping with the child's behaviour. Social Services did discuss contingency plans, referred the child to Young Carers and asked the school to monitor the situation. Ideally, a more active involvement was probably necessary. However, since there had been a very poor relationship with the carer who 'couldn't wait to get rid of them' after the proceedings, the decision to maintain a watching brief was probably not Social Services' sole responsibility.

None of the carers we interviewed who had renewed contact with Social Services reported experiencing any difficulty over this – although one carer commented on the length of time it took for a social worker to visit, and two expressed some dissatisfaction with the help they had then been offered.

We were getting bogged down [with the behaviour of the child, Alice]. We phoned [X] office; they said to contact [Y]. Everything seemed to take so long – Alice was up and down. By the time they came she was alright.

I got in touch last year. I was really down and was feeling I couldn't cope. They said there was nothing they could do – all I wanted was a play-scheme but they couldn't help.

Others, however, were very positive about the help they had received when they had gone back to Social Services. This carer, for instance, sought help when the behaviour of her granddaughter, Marie, who had lived with her since she was five, deteriorated badly when she started secondary school:

We got to a bad patch and didn't know which way was up. We thought we were totally failing her; she was stealing, shouting. The social worker put things into perspective; said we were doing it right. She gave us our confidence back. She put us in touch with the mental health people who said there was nothing fundamentally wrong with Marie, she was just affected by her past. They recommended family therapy but that hasn't happened yet.

It cannot be assumed, of course, that because carers did not re-contact Social Services things were going well. Where placements were continuing but Social Services were no longer involved, we asked carers whether they would be willing to get in touch if they had problems. Only five (of 15 responding to the question) said they would, and five said they would not know how to go about it. Those reluctant to seek help, not unexpectedly, tended to be carers who had had a poor relationship with Social Services; indeed, some of them felt they had had to fight to get the children, and they had been keen for their case to be closed. There was also a sense of people wanting to manage on their own. Most of these families did not seem to be experiencing any problems and perhaps their answers would have been different if they had been. However, three carers were having a degree of difficulty managing the child's behaviour but had not gone to Social Services for help.

One of these cases is of particular interest because the carers, who were under extreme stress dealing with their six-year-old grandson (who had ADHD, among other problems), were reluctant to contact Social Services even though their earlier experience with the department had been very positive:

Carer 1: *The trouble is you feel as if you should cope and you're frightened to ask for help; frightened of admitting that you're drained and you just can't do it.*

Carer 2: *You worry about Big Brother and the state; Social Services saying you can't cope, we'll look after them; we'll take the children.*

Carer 1: *If they see that we're stressed out they might think that we're going to start harming [the children].*

Carer 2: *You want the support but you don't want to lose . . .*

Carer 1: *The authority.*

Carer 2: *Yeah, the decisions are ours now, you don't want someone else taking decisions. It could be taken out of your hands again.*

Carer 2: *We really don't want any more stress in our lives. It would be nice if it was on our terms. We're shattered.*

These cases suggest there is probably a need for readily accessible **alternative** sources of help for kinship carers. This may be particularly important where carers have been at loggerheads during proceedings and would be understandably very reluctant to seek help. However, as can be seen from the case above, it might also be attractive to other carers. Furthermore, carers may find it easier to make later approaches for help if social workers or guardians, in their earlier contacts with families, emphasise that, given the prior experiences of these children, some difficulties are to be expected and will not be taken to reflect badly on carers.

How well was the placement supported while Social Services were involved?

Farmer and Moyers (2008) judged that, excluding considerations of financial help, 69 per cent of the kin placements in their study received little or no support from Social Services; compared to 47 per cent of non-kin foster placements. Our findings are more optimistic. While these ratings are, inevitably, subjective, all three of our data sources present broadly the same picture. Thus:

- In the researchers' judgement, based on the information available in the files (80 cases), 55 per cent of placements were well-supported post-proceedings for as long as Social Services were involved and 28 per cent had received some support. Only six per cent appeared to have received little support. Moreover, while in 11 per cent of cases levels of support fluctuated over time, there were only 14 per cent which were deemed to be receiving little or no support at any of our four time points.[83] Overall, 88 per cent had received at least some support throughout.

- Most of the carers we interviewed were also quite positive. When asked to give Social Services marks out of 10, the scores ranged across the entire scale. However, the average was 6.2, with only 10 of the 31 carers responding to the question (32%) giving marks of less than five, compared to 45 per cent awarding marks of eight or more.

- The social workers we interviewed were asked to rate the input from their department to the sample case on a 1 to 5 scale. The average rating was 3.8, with only nine (38%) giving a score of three or less compared to 58 per cent awarding four or more.

- Combining all three sources and, where they conflicted, taking the most *pessimistic* assessment, we judged that 34 per cent of placements had been well-supported, 46 per cent had had some support and 20 per cent had had little or no support *while Social Services remained involved*. Where a care order was in place throughout, only 12 per cent of families had little or no support; this rose to 27 per cent in cases where a residence order was made at the end of proceedings or a care order was discharged, with the least well supported being placements where children were adopted. At the other end of the spectrum, however, only 31 per cent of those with care orders received good support, compared to 38 per cent of other cases. This rather paradoxical

---

[83] Snapshot data were collected at four time points: 12 months; three years post-proceedings; five years; and the latest point for which data were available after five years.

finding is probably explained by the fact that support in care order cases was measured over a longer period, so there was more chance of deficiencies emerging.

- There was no difference between our two local authorities in terms of the proportion of cases judged to have had little or no support (20%), although Authority B had a higher proportion of placements which were judged to have received good support (45% compared to 26% for A). In terms of the different sources of data, Authority A was also given somewhat lower ratings by the researchers (19% of A's placements were judged to have received little or no support and only 41% consistently good support, compared to 8% and 71% respectively for B). Social worker ratings were also marginally lower (a mean of 3.5 for A compared to 3.9 for B). Interestingly, however, Authority A received rather higher ratings from carers (6.7 compared to 6.2).

It is worth noting that there were some surprising discrepancies in some of the evaluations. One might expect that carer ratings of the support received would be lower than those of either the researchers or social workers and, indeed, there were cases which fell into this category. However, there were also instances where the carer's rating was higher. In one such case, both the researchers and the social worker considered that the placement had had little support. The carer, however, gave the highest possible score, not because of any practical services which had been provided but because she always felt support was there in the background:

Just letting us know that they're there to talk to and reassuring us we're not on our own. The [current social worker] is easy to get hold of and I can discuss things with her.

In the following sections we look in detail at the various elements in Social Services involvement with the placements which help to flesh out this picture and identify any gaps in service provision.

How much contact did social workers have with the placement?

There was clear evidence of insufficient contact in just over half the cases while the case was still formally open. In 22 per cent of cases, there was known to be a period when no social worker was allocated.[84] In other cases, it was documented that either the carer or the social worker would have liked more frequent visiting. This appeared to be more of an issue in Authority A (60% compared to 44% in B), which we know had problems with high staff turnover for at least part of the research period:

If there was a change [of social worker] there was a gap before any contact. We had 10 social workers and three link workers. For one year [the child] had no social worker at all. One came and mumbled all the time and we couldn't understand him. Then he said, 'I don't think you need a social worker anymore' and no one came for a year even though she was on a care order. I kept saying she didn't have a social worker but nothing was done about it.

Table 7.1
Insufficient social worker contact

	No.	%	(N=)
Period when case not allocated	23	22	(103)
Social worker not able to visit as frequently as they wanted	25	32	(79)
Evidence carer would have liked more contact	13	17	(75)
Any of these	54	52	(103)

Farmer and Moyers (2008) report that the proportion of kinship carers who were visited regularly by the social worker was very similar in both kinship and non-kin foster placements (68% and 72%). However, the kinship placements tended to be visited less frequently, with 23 per cent

---

[84] Farmer and Moyers (2008) found that 13 per cent of kin-placed children were without a social worker for at least part of the study period, compared to eight per cent of children in non-kin placement.

seeing the social worker less than once in three months, compared to 16 per cent of non-kin placements.

In this study we noted from the files the *frequency* of social worker visiting over the previous six months at each of four time points: 12 months post-proceedings, three years, five years and the latest point for which data were available after five years. This was then categorised as either high, moderate or low frequency. As can be seen from Table 7.2, most cases which were still open at the 12-month point had been visited at least twice in the previous six months and 17 per cent were seeing the social worker once a month or more (maximum 12 visits). Only six per cent were being seen less than this.

As one would expect, visiting frequency diminished over time: even where cases were still open six years on, only one was being visited monthly or more and over half were being seen six-monthly or less. By this time social workers were unlikely to be visiting on a regular basis: only nine of the social workers interviewed (39%) said they were making regular visits, with ten describing their contact as only 'fairly regular' and four as 'sporadic'. However, it should be noted that none of the eight carers we interviewed in open cases were asking for more contact at this point; indeed, two would have preferred less.

Table 7.2
Frequency of social work visiting post-proceedings

Frequency	12 months		3 years		5 years		>5 years	
	No.	%	No.	%	No.	%	No.	%
Low	3	6	6	21	7	44	7	54
Moderate	31	65	17	61	7	44	5	39
High	14	29	5	18	2	13	1	8
	(48)		(28)		(16)		(13)	

*Low = 6 monthly or less; moderate = 6 weekly to 3 monthly; high = monthly or more.

What did carers think of social workers?

Twenty-two of the carers interviewed (63%) found something positive to say about social work involvement (Table 7.3). Indeed, a quarter (9; 26%) only made positive comments and a further four (11%) at least said nothing negative:

> *They are all good people in my opinion. They try and help and comfort even if they can't solve it. I've no criticisms at all. No one ever behaved in a way I didn't approve of.*

> *They were very nice. They were all honest. They did a thorough job.*

> *I've got on with them all. They've always been positive and good at listening to me.*

However, just over a third (37%) tempered their praise with some criticism and a quarter (9; 26%) had nothing positive to say at all.

> *Neither of us has been very impressed.*

> *I can't think of anything helpful they did.*

> *None of it was very helpful really. We just did it ourselves. Nothing they said helped. We were left high and dry by them. Ms [X] taking him out for the day to give us a break. That was the only thing. Others just came to drink tea and eat biscuits.*

Table 7.3
Kinship carers' views of social workers

	No.	%
Positive views only	9	26
Negative views only	9	26
Mixed	13	37
Neither	4	11
(N=)	(35)	

Some carers, of course, had experience of several changes of worker; a source of criticism in itself:

> *The most needy thing is consistency in a social worker applied to a*

family. That's a difficult one as they come and go and it's not what kids want. They had a lot of changes of social worker, a lot of different ones. Continuity is important. One would leave and you'd have another one. The same person all the way through would be good.

Social workers only stay long enough to get their feet on the ladder. As soon as you get one, they're there for a few months and then they're gone to be a manager at a different office. They're always moving on. We just got – friendly isn't the word – but with [X], she used to be very good; we could talk to her – she saw us through the court and then, as soon as that was done, she moved on. Then we had another one and he didn't really know the family, all he knew was what he'd read from the reports. We explained it to him and then he'd gone. So then there was another one and we had to go over it all again. Then that finished. There's no continuity. Most of these things, instead of being a help, they're just someone else to be involved. I can't blame the Social Services; it's all the cutbacks from the government. They're over-stretched. But it doesn't make our situation any easier.

It was interesting that where carers had had more than one social worker, many explicitly differentiated between different workers, indicating that it was not always simply a question of their general attitude to local authority involvement:

Mr [X] didn't come across officially, he came across as a real human being. The others came in very stiff, stern, we're in charge.

I did have a good social worker at the start, I must admit. She was very supportive, chatty and down to earth, some of them you have to work quite hard with. She made me feel quite relaxed. She was one of the exceptional ones I have worked with.

Ms [X] took Mark out every two months. She gave him little treats by taking him out but it wasn't solving anything, it wasn't helping his problem. Mr [Y] was nice but he was totally useless – when Mark burnt the caravan he said, 'Boys do those things at that age'. The last social worker, Mr [Z], was good, he was the one who got to Mark and

Mark knew it . . . He was good for Mark, he knew how his mind worked. He would listen carefully and you could talk to him.

On the other hand, it was clear that, for some kinship carers, Social Services' opposition to the placement – and in some cases their removal of the child from the carers in the first place – had compromised the chances of building a constructive working relationship. As one rather depressingly put it:

It was just really us caring for Joanne and Social Services were involved too. We didn't have the kind of relationship where they were supposed to be helping us out.

Moreover, these cases tended to be closed quite quickly after proceedings so there was little opportunity to test whether the damage was irrevocable or could have been repaired by skilful social work.

What did carers find helpful and unhelpful about the social work input post-proceedings?

There were three dominant themes. First, the specific help social workers had provided in terms of assisting with particular problems. One carer, for instance, was particularly grateful for the social worker's rapid and effective intervention which stopped the harassment she had been subject to from the children's father. Others appreciated advice on contact, and on tackling behavioural problems. Second, organising and in some cases advocating for various services and resources – making arrangements for the child's education, for instance, and dealing with difficulties which arose, including accompanying carers (who felt particularly intimidated) to meetings, and securing remedial help.

The third theme was less to do with the specifics of social work input than with the worker's perceived professional competence and approach. A carer's confidence in the social worker could be undermined where the worker was new to the job, lacking in life experience, perceived to be naive, or insufficiently focused on the child:

The girl who came to see me was very young. The same age as my youngest daughter. I thought, what do you expect to tell me about bringing up children?

There should be more medical advice for social workers dealing with alcoholics. You don't know where you are. You tell the social worker the truth about the alcoholic but they think you are trying to get at the alcoholic, they are lenient with alcoholics, they want to keep in with them.

We never 100 per cent felt that [the child's] social worker had his best interests at heart, he focused too much on the mother.

Overall, carers wanted social workers to be accessible, approachable, to listen to, and respect, their point of view, to keep them informed, to do what they promised to do and to be flexible and supportive. Unfortunately, as far as the carers were concerned, these expectations were not always met:

Some have good personal skills . . . but they sometimes talk down to you.

Some didn't do anything that you asked them to, even though they said yes they would.

I think sometimes they have to listen more to what the carer or child is saying rather than following the book like a bible. They have to listen to what you are saying and then not totally discount what you said. I think that does happen an awful lot.

With some things I've felt my opinion wasn't really taken into con-sideration. With the timing of [one child] moving, with telling the children about their father's death, with contact.

The use of link workers

Farmer and Moyers (2008) found that it was extremely unusual for kinship carers to be allocated a worker for themselves (only 6% compared to 96% of non-kin carers). In the light of this finding, it was surprising that separate workers were recorded in almost a third of the cases in our study at some point. In cases ending in care orders, the proportion rose to 48 per cent, with 59 per cent in Authority A. This may have compensated to some extent for the higher proportion of cases in this authority where there was evidence of insufficient social work contact.

It is possible, of course, that in cases where this information was supplied only by carers, there may have been a degree of confusion, with some interviewees including in their response family placement workers, for example, who conducted the assessment. However, since even the file data indicated separate workers being allocated in 15 per cent of cases, this is clearly not the whole explanation and there does appear to be some difference in experience between the carers in the two studies. This may be a question of different local authority approaches (there were differences even between our two local authorities). It could also be a difference between the two samples. Farmer and Moyers (2008) note that kin carers who had been allocated family placement workers appeared to be in particular need of extra support and it is possible that carers going through care proceedings may be, or may be perceived to be, more needy.

Are link workers a useful form of service in kinship care?

The responses to our question about whether carers had found it helpful to have a link worker were overwhelmingly positive:

Link workers do more than the social workers, they are there for us. The link worker was there to advise us and for us.

Invaluable. It was important to have someone to ourselves.

I had a really good link worker. I could tell her things I couldn't tell my husband about how I was feeling.

When asked whether they would have found such a worker useful, four carers said no, and seven felt unable to express an opinion. However, six were more enthusiastic about the idea, typically so they would have someone to 'listen to us':

Once we'd realised how [the abuse] had affected [the child] this would have been useful. Extra support for us and someone who'd understand the effect on our [biological] daughter.

One carer who had experienced both situations, having subsequently fostered non-related children, was quite clear about the value of having a separate worker:

I think you need the two bits: the social worker for the child so they can do that and a link worker for the carer. For them to lean on one person who's not asking all those questions.

Support groups and training

Non-kin foster carers will usually be required to attend some form of training and invited to attend a support group. Previous research has found that kin carers are rarely involved in either activity (Farmer and Moyers, 2008). This was certainly the case in relation to support groups in our study. As far as we could judge, such groups were offered in only seven cases and of the five carers we interviewed who had been invited to attend, none had actually gone. Twelve carers, however, said they would be interested.

In more than a fifth of cases (28) some training was offered, although this is unlikely to have been targeted at kinship carers. Ten of the interviewed carers said they could have attended training, of whom six had attended at least one session. A further six said they would have liked some training. Given the extent of the problems the children in our study posed in terms of emotional and behavioural difficulties (see Chapter 3), and the difficulties around contact arrangements (see Chapter 9), there must be strong arguments for providing training opportunities for kinship carers faced with such problems.

Respite care

One of the services to which non-kin foster carers have access is respite care (now called "short breaks"). Only 11 per cent of all the kin-placed children in our study, however, had had respite care since the proceedings ended (and only 15% at any point). This is only marginally higher than the proportion reported in Farmer and Moyers' study (8%; 2008). Nor were many families making their own arrangements: only eight of the carers interviewed (22%) said the children ever stayed overnight with other family members. In all, nine carers (24%) said they would have appreciated someone to take the children off their hands occasionally and, in at least four, this reflected a fairly desperate need for relief. Two of these placements broke down, the other two were vulnerable. Mr and Mrs Harvey, for instance, as we reported in Chapter 6, were under severe pressure, struggling to care for a child with multiple problems:

Mr Harvey: *They should organise more respite care for people like us. I think a lot of people in our situation would say the same.*

Mrs Harvey: *Just a day when you could forget about it and you're not at somebody's beck and call. What we really want is someone to say, 'We're here, we'll look after the children for the evening,' so we can out, have a drink in a pub or something.*

Mr Harvey: *We don't go out together. It's very rare we can get someone to look after the children so we can go out together. If there was somewhere like a holiday camp, someone else to take the children, so we could have a holiday too.*

Mrs Harvey: *Even if it was only for a long weekend so we could recharge our batteries. A lot of people suggest it but they don't say what you do. Who organises it. How do we do it. [X] at the Carer's Association said if I was your GP I would write you a prescription for a week's holiday. I go to the GP and he says you could do with a break. But he doesn't do anything about it.*

As can be seen from this quote, even carers who saw respite care as a potential lifeline were not asking for the earth: an occasional night off or a short break. So the demand on Social Services' resources is unlikely to be huge. Moreover, not all carers will need, want or be able to make use of such a service: one carer, for example, had turned down an offer of respite care and one child was reported to have refused to go. But for some it could offer much-needed relief and perhaps enable some placements to continue and/or provide a better quality of care because of the reduction in the stress experienced by the carer.

Post-placement support plans could consider whether it is possible to identify a member of the child's family or network who could be approved to offer such regular support, particularly where a child poses behaviour problems. Some foster care schemes encourage foster carers to identify such a "supporter" familiar with the child and provide a mechanism for payment so that such an arrangement is formalised. This model could well be applied to kinship care.

Specialist services for children

As detailed in Chapter 3, the well-being of 53 per cent of the children in this study was compromised in at least one respect. Universal services may have been sufficient for some – carers spoke warmly of the help received from family doctors and health visitors, for example. Other children were likely to need specialist intervention. In all, at least 40 children (36%) were known to have received some form of specialist help with physical, educational, or psycho-social problems, of which the most commonly recorded (17 children) was seeing a mental health professional (a counsellor, therapist, psychologist or psychiatrist).

These interventions were not always experienced as helpful by carers or children. Indeed, some children turned down offers of help and others stopped attending. Nonetheless, it was worrying to find evidence of un-met need in seven cases (including some where services set out in the care plan appear never to have materialised). One carer, who is looking after a child who was sexually abused and has learning difficulties, told us:

She did and she does need help with coping with the trauma of her abuse and I can't help her, I haven't got that sort of skill. The play therapist she had was aimed at that. But she needs counselling now and I keep saying this but they haven't got the sort of counselling she needs – it's accepting the past and moving on from it. The social worker is willing but unable to provide it. I don't have confidence in the GP to ask him to refer her.

Only eight of the interviewed carers reported the children having any kind of life story work. Nine of the others thought this might have been useful. None of the children in the sample are known to have attended any groups for children in foster care, let alone one for children cared for by relatives. Nine of the 37 carers interviewed thought that the children they were/had been looking after might have benefited from this. However, it should be noted that most of the children we interviewed were not over-eager for such work and, as we discuss in Chapter 8, it is possible that a life story book may not actually fit their needs as well as it does those of children placed with non-kin.

What services do carers want?

To recognise grandparents, or kinship carers, as carers that need the same support and financial help and the same rights as any other person. Without that you can't provide the care that is really needed to help a lot of these kids who have a lot of problems, let alone your own children!

We asked all the carers we interviewed whether they could think of any form of assistance, other than financial/material, which would have helped. Only 13 volunteered any suggestions. This might be taken to indicate that most carers were satisfied with what they had been offered and indeed, we did not find high levels of discontent. It has to be remembered, however, that since these placements had all been made many years ago, most carers would have learned to live with their situation and, where the placement was now going well, it could be hard to think back to what might have helped.

Moreover, as one carer pointed out, 'You can't say what you'd like as it's not until it's given you that you realise it was helpful'. As will be apparent from earlier sections of this chapter, however, we did ask interviewees specifically whether various forms of service available to non-kin foster carers might have been helpful. If we add in the responses to these questions, the number of interviewees identifying additional services they thought would have been helpful rises to 26 (70%). To summarise, therefore: top of the list comes a support group for carers (12) followed by: groups for children (9); respite care (9); services for children (7); training for carers (6); a worker specifically for the carer (6) who could help them access necessary services (1); and help in dealing with the child's behaviour (3) and their impact on the family (2). One carer, who had subsequently given birth to twins, would have appreciated someone to come in for a while and give some time to the kin-placed children. Another, who had experienced a traumatic placement breakdown, said how much the family would have welcomed some follow-up assistance in dealing with the experience. Instead, she said, 'We felt completely dropped. We had served our purpose.'

Out-of-authority placements

Sixteen children in our sample were placed with carers living outside the boundaries of the placing authority and another child subsequently moved away with his carers. In all but three cases, the placements were a significant distance away from the home authority; indeed, two children were placed abroad and a third spent a substantial period abroad before returning to this country.

Our interviews with nine of the out-of-authority carers indicate that such placements may be at particular risk of poor service provision, even where children are on care orders. Indeed, the fact that out-of-authority carers were over-represented in our interview sample (53% agreeing to be interviewed compared to 38% of other carers) probably reflects this fact. The following issues were noted from the interviews:

How to key into appropriate training

I can't go [to training] because they are so far away. I would like to go to training locally but the authority where I'm now living won't help me.

Courses were always up in [placing authority]. They never suggested [home authority] for us. Really it would have been good if we'd been linked in with training here for coping with problem children.

We did occasionally get a foster carer's letter from [the placing authority] but it wasn't feasible to go and we certainly didn't get any information from [home authority]. It would have been useful to go to a meeting where you could say this is what's happening and other people could say how they've dealt with it . . . sharing.

Isolation from support/advice

We were left high and dry by them. Max had to be placed somewhere quickly and they wanted to get him out of the county and away from his parents . . . they just didn't seem to bother [subsequently] with the problems we were having.

*All the Social Services departments should work together. When I have
a problem I have to wait for a social worker to come from [placing
authority]. I can't go locally to [home authority]. This has to
change . . . There were times when it would have been nice if they'd
rung up, I needed to talk to someone about Steven's behaviour. Being
so far away it was difficult to manage. Maybe I didn't tell them how
bad his behaviour was. Social workers would ring up and say, 'We're
Steven's social worker but we can't come and see you'. And I'm
saying, 'Can we have a conversation and can I ring you up? Can you
just give me your phone number so we know who you are?' They
expected you to answer questions on the telephone.*

Lack of statutory visiting of children on care orders
*If I'm honest, once Thomas was here the problem was solved for them
really. They would ring up, we could have done away with him really,
for all they knew. They did come but it wasn't every six weeks. [Home
authority] didn't know we had him as it was done through [placing
authority]. It was a long distance placement. I think it passed through
[home authority] without them knowing he was here.*

These data clearly indicate the need for co-ordination between the placing
and the home authorities and proactive efforts to link carers into whatever
support and training are available locally. Given the pressure on budgets
in all local authorities, it may be necessary for the placing authority to
spot purchase a support package.

Out-of-authority placements where children are on residence orders
are potentially most vulnerable to isolation, although interestingly, one of
the cases in which the carer felt well supported by the placing authority
was a residence order case. There were huge difficulties over contact, with
the mother making repeated court applications. Although no social worker
was allocated, and indeed the case seems to have been technically closed,
the original social worker, who still worked for the placing authority but
in a managerial position, continued to act as an unofficial point of contact
and support. The carer was quite satisfied with this and could not speak
of him highly enough:

It's been the right level of help. If I have to see them they come. They are very helpful, especially Mr [X] who deserves a special mention.

Most carers of children on residence orders, however, are unlikely to be able to rely on being able to access help in this serendipitous way. As noted earlier, it can be difficult enough for carers still living in the same authority to know who to contact for help. This is likely to be even more daunting for carers in authorities with whom they have never had any contact.

Placements abroad are potentially even more vulnerable and certainly in the case of the child who moved abroad for a period, there was evidence that he did not have the psychological help that had been recommended and which he clearly needed. However, in the remaining two cases, the placements were now receiving high levels of support, which may indicate readier access to specialist children's services in their receiving countries rather than, necessarily, better social services provision, since one was adopted and the other on a residence order. Both children, who had spent substantial periods in non-kin care, had emotional and behavioural problems and both had other special needs which, again, may explain the level of services they were currently receiving. One carer, however, did comment on the gap in service provision in the early days of placement, with the counselling and follow-up she had been promised by the placing authority not materialising.

The first year is the hardest, getting used to a new person and all the changes it implies . . . but I don't regret it . . . it is a lot better now than I thought it would be . . . it would have been easier with more support [from family or government agencies].

Again, better co-ordination between the placing authority and local services would seem to be required.

Would better service provision have improved outcomes?

Inevitably, our answer to this can only be speculative. There is some evidence from US research (Hunt, 2003a) that appropriate support can reduce placement breakdown in kin placements. However, the rather different social conditions in the US make it impossible to conclude definitively that the same results would obtain here. Clearly, what is needed is experimental research testing out various forms of support for kinship placements and evaluating outcomes against each other and no support conditions. However, our research does provide some grounds for thinking that improving service provision could lead to better outcomes.

Support and placement stability

The quantitative data does not indicate that those placements which did not last as long as needed received any poorer support, nor that Social Services involvement ended earlier than was the case for other placements. Indeed, the reverse seemed to be the case: in all but two of the premature terminations (94%), Social Services remained continuously involved throughout the duration of the placement, compared to 40 per cent of other placements. Further, while service deficits were noted in just over half the premature terminations (52%), this was less than was noted in other placements (70%).

What this suggests, therefore, is that, while Social Services had not abandoned the most obviously vulnerable families, the support they provided was insufficient to maintain the placement. In about half the cases where there was a care order throughout the placement, there was evidence of insufficient/inconsistent social worker input, in that there were either periods when there was no allocated social worker or the allocated worker was not able to visit as often as either s/he or the carer would have liked. In addition, placements did not receive the same range of support that non-kin foster carers could have accessed. Thus, only five placements had been supported through respite care, only five carers had had a link worker, and fewer had any training (3), attended a carer support group (3) or had domiciliary help (3).

In itself these data provide indirect evidence for the hypothesis that with better support at least some placements could have continued. Close analysis of the circumstances in which premature terminations occurred suggests that in 12 of the 31, although there may have been some service deficits, better provision would probably not have made a difference. Many of these cases involved children determined to return to a parent. Four placements were terminated by Social Services because of concerns about the quality of care offered to the child in circumstances where the issue of support would seem to be irrelevant.

However, we did identify 15 placements which did not last as long as needed which might conceivably have been sustained with different or more consistent support. Almost all of these cases involved children presenting very difficult behaviour, whose carers eventually found themselves unable to carry on. Similarly, of the six carers we interviewed where placements had not lasted (involving eight children), four thought that things might have worked out differently if they had had more support. While the forms of help identified varied – help with accommodation to reduce the pressure on other children in the family, respite care, a consistent social worker, therapy for the child – the common factor was help in dealing with the child's behaviour and/or managing its impact on the rest of the family.

Mattie's behaviour – most of the time she was here we had behaviour problems. It seemed to be more determined as she got older and be more of a problem. She'd try you out all the time, test you. She was bad tempered and wouldn't do as she was told. It went on for at least a year. I said we couldn't cope with her any more and she would have to go . . . Social workers never seemed to stay long enough. They did not have a lot of interest in her. We had a lot – about 10 different ones . . . It would have been good if we'd been linked in with training for problem children . . . It would have been helpful for her to have somewhere to go for a holiday, respite, somewhere to send them where there are activities . . . She would have liked a group. (Care order, placement lasted for five years but ended with the child, now aged 15, going into non-kin foster care)

In addition, of the 18 placements which were continuing but vulnerable, we consider there were nine in which better service provision might improve the chances of the placement lasting.

Providing an appropriate legal framework

As noted in Chapter 5, 69 children (61%) were made subject to a full care order. Forty-seven remained on these orders throughout their placement.

Of the remaining 22 children, eight were adopted[85] and 14 went on to residence orders (two with an initial supervision order). None of the children placed on residence orders at the end of the proceedings experienced a change in legal status although one carer had made an unsuccessful application for an adoption order.

Almost all the carers interviewed in ongoing placements were comfortable with the legal orders they currently had. Of the three who were not, two carers with residence orders would have preferred adoption in order to secure the placement and be able to exclude difficult parents, while a relative with a care order just wanted to be rid of Social Services.

Achieving legal permanence

Adoption

Is adoption an appropriate permanency option in kinship care? Indeed, do kin-placed children who have a sense of psychological permanency in their placement need legal permanency? Traditionally, in the UK relative adoption has tended to be officially discouraged because it is deemed to distort family relationships and therefore potentially create confusion for the child (DoH/Welsh Office, 1992). In the United States, in contrast, the low incidence of kinship adoption has been a cause for concern and some states have made strenuous efforts to increase its use. US research on social worker attitudes suggests that, while most consider adoption appropriate, many tend to assume that carers will be resistant and may not even discuss it with them. Research on carers' views, while not entirely consistent, does indicate a degree of reluctance, whether stemming from a reluctance to terminate parental rights, fear of the effect on the relationship with parents or unwillingness to become involved in court proceedings (see Hunt, 2003a).

There were eight children in our sample who had been adopted by their kinship carers. For six of these, adoption had been a possible long-term goal when the care orders were made. Indeed, in three instances, the permanency panel and, in one, the guardian had encouraged such legal security. In one of the two cases where adoption had not been envisaged,

---

[85] Adoption orders were made between 19 and 50 months after the end of proceedings.

the carer was keen both to give the child extra security and to exclude Social Services; in the other, the child (aged 7) appeared to be the prime mover. All the children were considered to be definitely attached to their carer (compared to 77 per cent in the rest of the sample) and all the placements were considered very stable and likely to continue. Half (4) of the adopted children fell into the all good outcomes group compared with 20 per cent for the rest of sample.

Although the adopters comprised three grandmothers as well as five aunts, they were all relatively young (32–44 years old at the end of the proceedings compared to an average of 44 for the rest of the sample, the oldest carer being 69). The children also tended to be very young, half being under two at the end of the proceedings (63 per cent of the adopted group were under five compared with 48 per cent for the rest of the sample). Four had lived with their adoptive parent virtually since birth. They also tended to be placed at some distance from their parents (including one child placed abroad) and to have poor or non-existent maternal contact – although paternal contact was somewhat better (12 months after proceedings only one mother was in regular contact, compared to three fathers). Parental opposition to the placement at the time of the proceedings was also more marked than in the rest of the sample.

We asked the 32 interviewed carers who had not adopted (and had not tried to do so) whether they had ever thought about it. Most said they had not and would not, for reasons that included their age, anticipated lack of Social Services help and, crucially, because of the continuing, positive role of the parent in the child's life and the risk of confusion:

We wouldn't do that because he's still in contact with his mum. If she wasn't around it might be different.

It would change our relationship. I can't bring her up as my daughter because she's not. She's almost got two mums really and she's lucky to have that.

Similarly, two carers who had considered this option said they did not see it would be of any benefit and could be harmful to the child:

Social Services did suggest it to me. The children have got a mother

209

and I didn't think it would be nice to confuse them. They know I'm not mum. I'm proud to be grandma, I don't want to take my title away.

However, there were five carers who thought that adoption might have been useful but had decided against because of potential difficulties with the parent and sometimes also financial considerations. In one such case the child, who had been subject to repeated court applications by her mother, was said to be desperate to have the security of adoption:

She has been very distressed, she wants her name changed. She wants to be adopted. [I have not pursued adoption as] the problems I have with the mother are too much and financially it would be extremely difficult.

It may be legally easier but it also could be expensive and a lot of paperwork. I'm not sure what my brother [the child's father] might think. We've never pursued it.

In the one case, where the carer had unsuccessfully sought adoption, the opposition appeared to come from the social worker completing the Schedule 2 report, who considered that adoption would confer no advantage on the child. The carer, who thought otherwise, intended to apply for special guardianship as soon as she could.

Special guardianship

Although special guardianship orders had not been introduced at the time we carried out our interviews, we took the opportunity to ask carers in continuing placements whether they might be interested. This usually necessitated some explanation since most interviewees had not been aware of this forthcoming change in the law although two (one with a residence order, one with a care order) were already planning to apply.

However, only four other carers (all with residence orders) expressed any interest. Most carers were happy with the status quo and did not seek any change, either because there was no need or because the application might adversely affect a parent:

The situation is settled and secure with current order.

There's no need for it and Mum wouldn't cope, she's poorly – mentally and physically.

Children still on care orders

Our latest information indicated that 18 children in continuing placements were still on care orders, many years after the original proceedings had concluded. At the point our research was carried out, the average age of these children was 14, with the youngest being only eight years old. Why had these children not achieved a greater degree of legal permanence? Did it matter?

Age would seem to be a relevant consideration. More than half (54%) of the care orders made on children under five at the end of proceedings were discharged, compared to just over a quarter (27%) of those aged between five and nine, and none of those older than this. These children may have been displaying greater difficulties. It is also possible that legal permanency may have been seen as less important for young people or that the services available for children maturing out of care may have provided a powerful disincentive. The financial benefits for children on care orders who wish to enter higher education are considerable, now being worth thousands of pounds to a family, and certainly at least one single carer was aware of what she had to lose if the care orders on her three teenage kin children were discharged.

We were only able to interview six of the carers where children were still on care orders. It was notable, however, that only one considered that a different order might make any difference to the child's current sense of security. While another was planning to seek discharge of the order by applying for special guardianship, this was because she no longer wished Social Services to be involved rather than concerns over the child's sense of permanency.

We did, however, interview all the social workers in cases where children were still on care orders. In most instances (12) the care order was still considered to be necessary, largely because extra support was needed by the carers. Social workers cited difficulties in relation to parental contact, the child's difficult behaviour, elderly carers or risk of placement breakdown. In nine of these cases, the possibility of applying for a residence order had been discussed but carers were said not to be keen because they did not want to lose the extra support and, in some cases, the certainty of a financial allowance.

The question of adequate financing was also a theme in the six cases where social workers felt it was not appropriate that the child should still be on a care order. Changing the child's legal status had been discussed in all these cases but although all the carers agreed that the care order was inappropriate, all were concerned about the drop in income this change would entail. Indeed, in one case, the carers were said to have declined to pursue a residence order application unless the local authority signed a legal contract saying their allowance would continue at the same rate. Since the local authority refused to do so, an impasse had been reached.

If the issue of financing kinship care was resolved, as discussed elsewhere in this chapter, it seems clear that more care orders could be discharged, with the consequent saving to the local authority in terms of the staffing resources needed to provide even a minimum level of servicing to these placements. Special guardianship could have a role here, since there is provision for providing support, including continued remuneration for up to three years, to assist foster carers with the transition to their new position.

However, it is questionable whether this would have a substantial effect on children's sense of security. Only one of the social workers interviewed thought a change of legal order would make the child feel more secure. Moreover, when asked to rate the child's current sense of security on a five-point scale (where $1 = $ high, $5 = $ low) the mean rating was 1.7, indicating that most children were believed to feel secure in their placement irrespective of legal status. All the 12 children interviewed felt safe and secure in their placement regardless of their legal orders.

That is not to say, of course, that legal security is not important for some children. As indicated earlier, some children very much wanted to be adopted and at least two children in the sample were relieved to be on residence orders. These siblings, who had originally been placed with their grandparents short term, had then suffered failed adoptions and were back with their grandfather. He considered that as long as they were on a care order they had a lingering fear that they would be removed again.

Conclusion

The findings of this research in relation to supporting kinship carers are not new; they merely reinforce what has been said in a number of other studies. Indeed, in some respects, the placements in our study, probably because they had been made in the context of care proceedings, were possibly better supported than those made in other circumstances. The issue, therefore, is not so much what needs to be done, but how policy-makers in central and local government can be galvanised into taking the action which is clearly necessary. We look at this further in our concluding chapter.

Summary

Finance was an issue for many carers, with only just over a third having managed without any difficulty and several suffering financial strain. Carers with children on residence orders were more vulnerable to difficulties. Carers had inconsistent experiences, with some receiving grants for start-up costs, extensions and special expenses.

In 47 per cent of cases, Social Services involvement ceased while the placement was still ongoing. Cases rarely re-opened and usually did so because of the need for a court report rather than because of problems in the placement. A few carers needed more sustained Social Services support and had mixed experiences when they did seek help. There is a need to identify readily accessible alternative sources of help for carers, who may be reluctant to contact Social Services.

While the case was open, 34 per cent of placements were judged to have been well-supported, 46 per cent to have had some support and 20 per cent little or no support. Social worker contact was considered inadequate in just over half the cases and in nearly a quarter of cases there were periods when no social worker was allocated. The frequency of social worker contact diminished over time.

Thirty-seven per cent of the interviewed carers made no negative comments about social workers but a quarter had nothing positive to say at all. The frequency with which social workers changed was a source of difficulty. A constructive relationship was more difficult where Social Services had opposed the kinship placement, again suggesting that alternative sources of help may need to be identified.

About a third of kinship carers had had an allocated link worker at some point and overwhelmingly those carers saw this as beneficial. Carers were rarely involved in support groups or training even where difficulties persisted with the child's behaviour or contact. Respite care was rarely provided by Social Services (11%) or by the extended family (22%). In about a quarter of cases, such help would have been welcome and in four cases, there appeared a desperate need for it at some point in the placement. All these issues should be more actively considered in post-placement support plans.

Over a third of children were receiving specialist help usually from mental health services in respect of EBD. There was evidence of unmet need in a few cases.

More attention needs to be paid to supporting out of authority placements.

The research provides some grounds for thinking that better service provision could lead to better outcomes. Placements that did not last as long as needed were more likely to remain open throughout their duration but support was insufficient to maintain the placement, care order children were unallocated or infrequently visited, and carers were not able to access the same range of services as non-kin foster carers. Fifteen of the 31 premature terminations and nine of the 18 vulnerable but continuing placements – all where the child's behaviour was a major stressor – may have had better outcomes with better support.

Most kinship carers were comfortable with the legal framework within which the child was placed. The eight adopted children – the majority very young when placed – were notably doing well. However, most (32) of the carers interviewed did not want to pursue such an order although five had been put off adoption either by the cost or the desire not to upset the parents. Most carers were not aware of the arrival of special guardianship orders and few were interested.

Eighteen children in continuing placements were still subject to care orders (average age 14). Young children were the most likely to have their care order discharged; no care orders were discharged on children who were aged over nine at the end of proceedings. Social workers considered that care orders appropriately continued where there were parental contact difficulties, the child had EBD, or the carers were elderly. In six cases, social workers considered that care orders continued largely because of the kinship carers' concerns about loss of financial remuneration. If adequate financial support was available to carers on residence or special guardianship orders, more care orders could probably be discharged.

8 Being cared for

This chapter is based on interviews with 12 children (aged between 11 and 18, mean age 13) still living with their kinship carers (in 8 households) and two young adults, both aged 20, who were living independently. The two young people differed from the children interviewed in that they had moved at a much older age to kinship care and their placements had been less stable, with disruptions. Full details of the methodology are set out in Appendix A. In constructing the interview schedule, we drew heavily on other research in this area and on children generally. We are particularly grateful to Jane Aldgate, Ian Sinclair and Danya Glaser for allowing us to access their questionnaires.

A number of other researchers on kinship care have interviewed children, usually as part of larger projects. In designing and reporting on this research, we considered the following studies in particular:

- Broad *et al* (2001): 22 young people aged 11–25 years.
- Doolan *et al* (2004): 11 children.
- Farmer and Moyers (2008): 16 children.
- Aldgate and McIntosh (2006): 30 children in long-term placements in Scotland.
- Altshuler (1999): six African-American children in the USA aged 10–15.
- Wilson and Conroy (1999): 100 children in kinship care in Illinois, USA.
- Smith *et al* (1999): 10 children in foster or kinship care in New Zealand.
- Messing (2005): focus groups with 40 children in California.

These studies have generally been encouraging in finding that the children themselves feel very positive about their placements with relatives. However, since the children interviewed in the above studies were in ongoing placements, they may present an overly optimistic view of the experience. The findings of our study are also likely to be positively slanted as not only were 12 of the interviewed children in ongoing placements but their outcomes were, on average, better than those of children who were not interviewed (Appendix F Table F3). Research focusing on children and young people whose placements have not worked out would help to correct this imbalance.

How were the children doing? The Strengths and Difficulties Questionnaire (SDQ)

The children (but not the young adults) completed the self-assessment version of the SDQ during the interview (for details see Appendix A). For all 12 children we also had SDQs completed by the carer, and for 10, by teachers.

Eleven of the 12 children scored themselves within the normal range for total difficulties. The twelfth child's score was borderline. None of the 12 children scored themselves in the abnormal category for either pro-social behaviour or behavioural symptoms, although one girl was borderline for emotional symptoms and one boy for pro-social behaviour. This latter child, who had ADHD and attended special school, was given abnormal scores by both his carer and teacher, and so appeared to take an optimistic view of his difficulties. The girl scoring herself as borderline had a normal score from her teacher but an abnormal score from her carer. Other research reporting on children's self-completed SDQs indicates a higher rate of abnormal scores: 21 per cent of the kin-placed children in Aldgate and McIntosh's study (2006) scored themselves abnormal for EBD although all were in the normal range for pro-social behaviour, while 36 per cent of children on care orders scored themselves in the abnormal or borderline category (Harwin et al, 2003).

Seven out of the 10 teacher SDQs coincided with the child's self-assessment. Two indicated more problems than the child's self-rating and one less. In general, teachers' ratings indicated the interviewed children were doing well, in that eight were within the normal range, almost the same proportion as would be expected in the general child population.

For eight children the carer's rating was also comparable with the child's. However, four children, three girls and one boy, were thought to have more problems. This possible underestimating by girls is interesting given the very positive picture they also gave in their responses to the

Table 8.1

The ecomap data: Mean number of persons in different circles and different segments of ecomap compared with Brannen et al, 2000 data (Brannen et al, columns marked *)

Column no.	1	2	3	4	5	6	7	8	9*	10*	11*	12*	13*
	KGP lone	KGP & ptr	All KGPs	K aunt sole	K aunt & ptr	All aunts	Other rel	All kin	Two parent	Lone parent	Step parent	Foster care	All chn
All persons in 3 circles	10.8	20.0	13.8	23.7	21.0	22.6	23.0	18.3	31.2	21.5	33.0	27.7	28.1
Persons in inner circle	8.5	8.0	8.3	10.0	14.5	11.8	15.0	10.4	23.7	12.9	22.2	19.3	19.3
Persons in middle circle	1.3	7.5	3.3	10.0	3.5	7.4	5.0	5.2	5.1	3.1	7.6	4.4	5.0
Persons in outer circle	1.0	4.5	2.2	3.7	3.0	3.4	3.0	2.8	2.4	4.4	3.4	3.8	3.5
Persons in household segment	1.5	2.5	1.8	3.3	6.0	4.6	3.0	3.1	4.7	3.2	4.3	4.5	4.1
Grandparents out of household) – 3 circles	0	0	0	1.0	1.0	1.0	0	0.4	1.5	1.3	2.2	0.7	1.4

Column no.	1	2	3	4	5	6	7	8	9*	10*	11*	12*	13*
	KGP lone	KGP & ptr	All KGPs	K aunt sole	K aunt & ptr	All aunts	Other rel	All kin	Two parent	Lone parent	Step parent	Foster care	All chn
Persons in other family segment including grandparents	5.5	9.0	6.7	8.7	8.5	8.6	12.0	7.9	10.1	10.0	16.6	12.3	12.1
Friends – 3 circles	2.8	7.0	4.2	11.0	3.5	8.0	4.0	5.8	12.7	6.8	9.5	7.5	9.0
Friends – inner circle	2.8	2.0	2.5	2.7	2.0	2.4	3.0	2.8	8.4	3.1	6.1	6.1	5.8
Formal others – all circles	1.0	1.5	1.2	0	3.0	1.2	4.0	1.4	4.2	1.8	2.5	3.2	2.9
Formal others – inner circle	0.5	0.5	0.5	0	2.0	0.8	3.0	0.8	2.4	1.3	1.6	2.0	1.8
(N=)	(4)	(2)	(6)	(3)	(2)	(5)	(1)	(12)	(15)	(17)	(15)	(15)	(63)

KGP = Kin grandparent
Kaunt = Kin aunt
Ptn = Partner

belonging and relationship questionnaires. This is covered later. Overall, carers' ratings put 67 per cent of the children in the normal range for EBD, 25 per cent in the abnormal range and eight per cent in the borderline range. Although, as pointed out earlier, these figures are lower than for the non-interviewed children, they are still higher than would be expected in the general child population.

Friends and relationships: the ecomap

Children were encouraged to complete an ecomap as a way of helping them to describe their network of relationships. We used it both as a tool to aid discussion as well as an attempt to measure closeness in relationships. The concept of ecomaps is well known to child care practitioners and has been used in recent research on kin-placed children by Aldgate and McIntosh (2006) and Farmer and Moyers (2008) and by Brannen *et al* (2000) on a broader child population.

Our ecomap (Appendix A) consisted of an A3 drawing of three concentric rings of closeness radiating out from the child. The circles are divided into quadrants assigned respectively to household, other relatives (including parents), friends and formal others. At various points during the interview, the child was invited to place significant people in their lives within the ecomap. People with whom the child considered they had a close relationship were placed near to them within the inner circle, those less close being placed increasingly further out from the centre.

Brannen *et al* (2000) used ecomaps to study the family relationships of 63 children in four different types of households – two-parent, lone parent, step-parent and foster care. This provides a useful comparison for our study. We have therefore based our analysis on theirs, counting the people included by the child in the various circles and quadrants on their ecomap.[86] Table 8.1 compares the findings from the two studies.[87]

---

[86] The counts are based on individual persons named by the child. In the couple of instances where children referred collectively to, for example, 'my cousins' or 'my class' we have counted the plural as two people.

[87] Farmer and Moyers (2008) and Aldgate and McIntosh (2006), although using the ecomap in their interviews, did not analyse the content in sufficient detail to allow a comparison with Brannen *et al* (2000).

The ecomap as a whole

As can be seen from Table 8.1, the mean number of persons in all three circles identified by our kinship children was 18.2 (range 7–34 persons). Girls placed far more people on the whole ecomap than boys (mean 21.3 compared to 12.0) and also identified more people in every ring and segment. However, when only the inner, most personal, ring was considered, the figures were not dissimilar (11.3 girls; 8.3 boys). Boys, on average, placed 69 per cent of people identified within the inner ring, compared to the girls' 53 per cent. This could reflect larger, less personal relationship patterns for girls but it could just be that the girls applied themselves with more thoroughness to the task.

Overall, the children in our study described much smaller networks than all of the types of household in Brannen's research (see columns 9–12 of Table 8.1). The figure for those living with lone grandparents (column 1, 10.8 persons) suggests that these children may have substantially lower levels of social activity (comparative figures are 20.0 for those placed with a grandparent and partner, 23.7 for those placed with a single aunt, 21.0 for those placed with an aunt and partner and 23 for those with other relatives). This may, in part, reflect a different age profile (aunts 38 years on average, grandparents 63), although those children placed with a grandparent and partner appeared to have larger networks. The social isolation of some kinship families was noted as a concern in Chapter 2 for four children, all placed with grandparents (including two lone carers).

Household quadrant

Seventeen per cent of the people children identified were placed in the household segment. This figure was similar for both boys and girls. As might be expected, children placed with lone grandparents identified the smallest number (mean 1.5 compared with 2.5 for couple grandparents; 3.0 for other relatives; 3.3 for a lone aunt and 6.0 for aunts and partners; the figure for aunts was high because of the presence of the carers' birth children).

It was notable that all but one of the children placed their kinship carer in the innermost zone of the ecomap. The child who did not (a teenager with close paternal contact) placed his carer in the middle circle. The four children in two-carer households all placed their relative's partner within the closest circle on the ecomap as well.

Where the interviewed child was living with a sibling, the child always placed them within the inner circle. Indeed, virtually all household members were placed in the circle closest to the child. The two exceptions to this were the teenage boy mentioned above who placed his aunt's daughter (along with his aunt) in the middle circle, and a teenage girl who placed the lodger in the middle circle.

"Other family" quadrant

In the "other family" quadrant of the circle, the children identified on average 7.9 people (compared with a figure of 12.1 people in Brannen's study, column 13). Forty-eight per cent of all the people identified by boys fell within this quadrant, compared with 42 per cent of those by girls. Children in the care of a lone grandparent again identified smaller numbers than children in any of the other types of kinship household (Table 8.2). The single aunt and distant relative appeared to have larger extended family networks.

Table 8.2
Number of people placed in "other family members" quadrant

Placement type	Mean number of people identified in segment
Single grandparent	5.5
Single aunt	8.7
Grandparent and partner	9.0
Aunt and partner	8.5
Distant relative	12.0
All placement types	7.9

Only two children, who were having little or no parental contact, placed neither of their parents on the ecomap. In contrast to the children interviewed by Aldgate and McIntosh (2006) – who cited mothers more often than fathers – the children in our study made equal reference. Four children put both parents on their ecomap, three placing their mother closer and the other making them equidistant. Three placed only their father and three only their mother. In reality, there was virtually no contact for any of these children with their second parent.

Five of the 12 children (42%) placed one parent (two fathers, three mothers) within the same circle as their kinship carer (Farmer and Moyers' [2008] figure is 60%). Four (33%) placed the carer closer (within the inner circle), the parent being in the middle or outer circle (Farmer and Moyers: 40%). As mentioned earlier, one boy placed his parent closer than his carer.

Only four children (three of whom were siblings), all living with aunts, placed any non-household grandparents (all grandmothers) on the map. Although there were potentially more grandparents who could have been included, it should be remembered that six of the children were now living with grandparents, probably those to whom they would have been closest. The lack of reference to other grandparents probably reflects the loss of contact with one side of the extended family (see Chapter 9). Children were more likely to mention aunts, uncles and cousins. Nine children placed numerous cousins and 11 aunts/uncles on the maps.

In addition to the "in-household" siblings, six children identified 23 full or half-siblings living elsewhere. Not all of the siblings known to reside outside the household were mentioned. Thirteen of those who were, were placed in the inner circle, eight in the middle and two in the outer circle. Fifteen of these children were with the interviewees' respective mothers, four had been adopted and four were in foster care. In three cases, the children placed their mother and those siblings living with her in the circle closest to them.

"Friends" quadrant

Overall, the children placed 5.8 persons in the friends' quadrant, with half placed in the inner circle. Although girls identified more friends in total (6.8 compared to 3.8 boys), the numbers placed in the inner circle was not dissimilar (2.3 boys, 3.0 girls, all children 2.8), boys tending to rate a higher proportion of friends as close (60%; 44% girls).

A positive finding is that all the children placed at least one friend in the inner circle. Six placed all their friends there, while the others spread them out, usually over all three rings. As indicated above, the girls were more likely to spread their friends over more than one circle, probably reflecting a broader gender pattern regarding both actual and perceived friendships. However, it appears that kinship children, whoever they are placed with, may have smaller networks of both close and distant friends than other children. The children in our study and that of Aldgate and McIntosh (2006) placed, on average, between five and six friends on their ecomaps. This is lower than the children in any of the household groups, including those in foster care, in Brannen's sample (mean 9.0; range 6.8–12.7 – see columns 9–13 of Table 8.1). The children in that study also placed, on average, 5.8 friends in the closest circle, compared to 2.8 of our kinship children. This difference may reflect patterns of socialising when living with older carers, emotional caution by the children because of their different histories, or even a degree of isolation.

The three children in our study with the smallest number of close friends (two each) were all boys – one with ADHD at a special school, one wishing to return to the care of his mother and spending much time in that household, and one with a history of past instability and unsettled behaviour.

In interviews, the children mostly related comfortable and easy relationships with friends. This was reflected in their self-completed SDQ scores in respect of peer relationships, where only one child scored herself in the abnormal range, and two borderline. They spoke of significant friendships, for most including sleepovers:

My best friend is 13. She lives just across the road from me so I can easily go and see her. We go to each other's houses a lot. (14-year-old girl)

I've got loads of college friends . . . they're really nice people to hang around with and that. They're always there for you, any problems or in trouble or anything, they help me out. (18-year-old girl)

One dual heritage girl appeared more ambivalent. On a positive note she spoke of one good friendship: 'She's really nice . . . yeah I've gone to her Mum's and her Dad's and she's come over here before and we go shopping together'. However, relationships in her primary school appeared less easy and she recounted a long history of bullying, which she attributed to her racial background:

I wasn't getting on well because children were bullying me and making racial comments about me . . . I've been bullied since reception.

The accounts of the children interviewed are not dissimilar to those of Farmer and Moyers (2008), echoed by Aldgate and McIntosh (2006), where the children spoke of having plenty of friends although a few seemed isolated, a number reported bullying and some attributed this to their kinship situation.

"Formal others" quadrant

Interestingly for children whom one might suppose had had a high level of agency involvement, half placed no one in this quadrant. The remaining six children named 17 people between them. Aldgate and McIntosh (2006) similarly note the absence of youth workers, social workers and other key adults on their children's ecomaps, with only two of 30 mentioning social workers. Our figures for social workers were somewhat higher (2 of 12 children) but it was noteworthy that only one of the three children still on care orders put a social worker on their map. Teachers featured more frequently (but only mentioned by girls) and though the overall proportion was lower than that reported by Aldgate and McIntosh (five of 12, compared to 20 of 30), half were placed in the inner circle.

Again, the data for this quadrant suggests that the kin-placed children saw fewer formal others being of significance to them than Brannen's sample (mean 1.4 compared with 2.9).

Key points from the ecomap analysis

- All except one child appeared close to the kinship carer and, where present, their partner.
- All but two children included at least one parent on the ecomap, with half of these indicating a close relationship with one parent.
- Where the child had contact with siblings either living in the household or elsewhere, their positioning on the ecomap indicated positive, close relationships.

- The children all identified networks of relatives and friends to whom they considered themselves close.
- The girls were more likely to identify teachers to whom they were close. Other key adults such as social workers were seldom placed on the ecomaps.
- The networks of the kinship children appeared smaller than those of children in other types of households (Brannen *et al*, 2000). Those children placed with sole grandparent carers appeared to have the smallest networks.

How much do children understand about their histories?

The children were asked to tell the researcher their "story" about how they came to be living with the relative. We allowed them to give their accounts as they wished, and avoided pressurising in any way about sensitive family history.

Eight children were aged five years or less at the end of proceedings. Most, therefore, were too young to have any clear memory of the events leading to their move to the carer and their accounts reflected what they had been told or "picked up" from others to explain their circumstances. The three children with interrupted placements had particularly complicated histories, which tended to obscure their stories of their original move.

Clarity and confusion

All the children were able to give some sort of explanation of how they had come to be living in their placements. However, this did not always reflect the information we had from the files or carer interviews. Of the nine children who had been with their carers continuously since proceedings, three gave accounts which well matched the known facts, two versions vaguely matched the known facts, while four children gave seemingly inaccurate accounts.

Despite the fact that the children were all in kinship care because of child protection concerns, only five clearly alluded to risk in terms of abuse, neglect or rejection by a parent. For instance:

I know what actually happened . . . my mum was living with a bad man and she thought he was hitting me. (Child with non-accidental bruising)

It was basically that my Mum and Dad, they don't get on and my Dad has a drink problem . . . they used to just like fight and stuff and that was when we were put into care because it got too much and then my aunt took us in. (Volatile parental relationship and alcohol problems)

Other children either vaguely alluded to risk or referred only to the move from a previous placement:
Because my real mother couldn't take care of me so that's why I came here.

The last foster parent I was living with, she couldn't have us for the whole of our life and we had to move.

Like Altshuler (1999), we found that children who had experienced physical abuse tended to have a clearer understanding of the reasons for placement, with others showing more variation.

All the children in the study had been subject to at least one set of court proceedings. However, only five referred to some sort of court involvement in their placement. Moreover, in the children's minds, the court case appeared to be associated with the relative winning custody from the local authority rather than protecting them from harm.
My nan and granddad had to go to court to get me to come here and then I was about 4–5 when I came to live here. (Child moved from foster care to grandparents. Returned unsuccessfully to parent and restored to carers. Court made a residence order)

Pop went to court, I've been living here since. He won the court case. (Local authority supported grandfather in obtaining residence order some years after children were placed with him on care order)

While these children were at least aware that the court had been involved in some way, others were more confused about the whole process:
I remember auntie saying she went to the government and [they] said could she have us.

My mum called a solicitor and they thought it was my mum doing it [hurting me] and so he [the solicitor] sent me to live with my nan. (Care proceedings following bruising. Child moved to carers after mother failed residential assessment)

This child was still struggling to understand his move from home, 10 years ago:

I was actually doing quite well with my mum . . . I can't remember it but my mum told me the story. I'd like to know more about how the solicitor got in contact and sent me away and why I couldn't stay with my mum.

One child had very vivid memories of Social Services' involvement in the move:

Social Services came to take me and I remember my dad and his mate passing me backwards and forwards across the fence so that they couldn't take me. Then I hid under a table but they found me.

Others, however, were very vague: 'I think it was Mr M [the social worker] who decided'; eight made no mention of social workers at all.

Our findings chime with Cleaver's research (2000) on children in foster care, which highlighted children's 'lack of understanding (and) muddled views' (p 100). Twenty-seven per cent of children in her study had no idea why they were not living at home. Other research on kinship care also indicates that merely remaining within the family does not guarantee greater clarity. Thus:

- Messing (2005) found that children could not remember their move because they were too young or found it difficult to report a single point in transition to their kinship placements.
- Farmer and Moyers (2008) noted that most children either came up with no reasons for their need for care or said explicitly they did not understand what had led them to leave their parents' care.
- Aldgate and McIntosh (2006) found that two-thirds of children had no sense of personal history about the transition to kinship care.
- Doolan *et al* (2004) report that a number of children said they knew little about how the decision was made but highlighted the significant

relationship the child had with the care-giver prior to placement so that the move to kinship care was neither novel nor disruptive.

This last suggestion – that the existing familiarity that the children had with their carers in effect buffered them from the trauma surrounding their move – rings true for our interviewed children in that 10 of the 12 knew their carer well because of past episodes of full-time care (7) or weekend stays (3). It could be that the children we interviewed were understandably guarded in what they were prepared to disclose to the researchers about their background but there could also be some genuine confusion about quite complex events which tended to be talked about less and less with the passage of time. Five children said they did talk with their carers about why they were living with them, three said they sometimes did, and four said they did not. In contrast, the carers of nine of the children said in their interviews that they did talk with the children about this.

Does it matter?

Argent (2005) writes of the importance of continuity for children and how it is particularly easy for a child to lose the "thread" of their story. Aldgate and McIntosh (2006) ask what kind of support kinship children need to understand their past. It may be that there is an argument for life story work being more clearly on the agenda for kinship children. From the carer interviews, we understand that only two of the interviewed children (siblings) had had life story work completed. Another child mentioned that this was currently happening. However, only two of the remaining seven carers thought it might be useful. Three thought it was not necessary because the children had access to all the information they needed, citing for example, close contact with mother, baby photos and relevant paperwork.

Moreover, all but two of the interviewed children seemed satisfied with the information they had, prompting us to wonder whether story confusion mattered very much, or indeed whether it could be serving a positive function. Perhaps children placed within the family, particularly those who now have good relationships with parents from whom they were removed, need to reframe the reasons for their placement into a shape that makes sense to them and provides some emotional congruence between current and past relationships. This may explain why, despite the cases all being child protection ones, children could give stories that by-passed this element. This could be a positive strategy to make sense of things, and a life story book may not actually fit their needs as well as it does for children placed with non-kin. And of course, at the end of the day, they did have access to people in the family who would give their account of what had happened.

The two young adult interviewees also both suggested a desire to distance themselves from the details of their painful past, again suggesting this may be a coping mechanism:

I was told if I didn't go there I'd go into care. I don't know why I moved there. I think I chose them. I was going to school locally, I had friends round here. [Now] I've got my life and my kids, I don't care anymore [about the reasons]. As long as they don't take [my children] off me, I don't care.

I did life story work and when I went back to my aunt, she got the life story book out for me. I don't know if it's a good thing as you look at it as an adult and it brings back a lot of hurts and a lot of pain that you haven't felt for a long time.

It may be relevant in this context that seven of the 12 children (as well as both the young adults interviewed) had ongoing contact with their mothers who were now raising younger children without apparent Social Services involvement. Indeed, two of the children were actively hoping to return to their mother's care at some point soon. It may be problematic to cope comfortably with a past story of deficiencies in parental care against these more positive relationships.

Explaining to friends

Friends generally appeared quite accepting of the situation and children did not suggest that they felt particularly "grilled":

Some of my friends are interested but some aren't that interested.

They don't usually ask, they don't bother about it, a friend is a friend, like. People are curious, that's about it really.

Friends just accept it.

Where friends were more inquisitive, some children seemed to respond in a very matter of fact way:

They are quite interested . . . I tell them the story.

When I told Chrissie she was, like, 'you OK?' She was fussing over me and she wouldn't stop for like a couple of months and I go, Chrissie stop it . . . you don't have to be like that just because of what's happened. It happens to lots of kids nowadays when parents can't cope.

However, for three children (all girls) it was a sensitive area, perhaps with a degree of stigma, and they were cautious whom they told.

I only explained to Mel [best friend] and she keeps it to herself. I don't tell Billie as she'd tell everyone.

I just say that she's my auntie and people say, like, why? I don't tell them though.

It's hard, like. I used to just make it up because I was too scared. I still do sometimes but [now] I just say Mum and Dad never used to, like, get on, so that's why I live with my aunt.

Another child (whose self-scored SDQ had revealed problems with peer relationships) clearly felt very uncomfortable about this area and showed the red card (indicating she did not want to answer the question) when asked how she explained her position. This suggests that while most kin-placed children may be coping well with the situation, there may be some who could benefit with some help, perhaps in formulating a satisfactory "cover" story.

Research suggests that children living away from their parents can experience a degree of stigma (Stein and Carey, 1986; Aldgate and

Bradley, 1999). It is not yet clear how far kinship placement may mitigate against this. Aldgate and McIntosh (2006) noted that the children were conscious of being a "kinship child" and that this marked them out from many of their peers. Broad *et al* (2001) found that kinship children were more vulnerable to bullying and teasing. The children in Messing's study (2005), however, explicitly stated that kinship care placements reduced the stigma and trauma of explaining to friends their separation from a birth parent. Indeed, most reported that the listener did not have a reaction. Crumbley and Little (1997) noted that children could fabricate stories regarding the whereabouts of their parents.

Probably a cluster of features contribute to the feeling of "difference" for a child, including absence of parents, sibling separation, social worker presence as well as care arrangements. One boy we interviewed indicated that there were other aspects of his situation that proved more of a stigma: 'A social worker was more difficult to explain to my friends than being with Pap'.

Relationships with carers

Other research involving interviews with children in kinship care has reached very positive conclusions on the sense of well-being that the children felt about their placements. Doolan *et al* (2004) note the children feeling stable with committed carers. Broad *et al* (2001) reported that children felt loved, settled and safe and expressed a sense of emotional permanence. Altshuler's (1999) interviewees felt loved and cared for and this was considered to reflect the depth of the bond. Farmer and Moyers (2008) commented that most of their children had close relationships with their kinship carers. Aldgate and McIntosh (2006) noted that the children felt safe and loved, although one or two struggled with the legacy of their experiences of neglect.

There is little research evidence on children's views about the quality of their relationships in kinship care compared to children in non-related care. Wilson and Conroy (1999) report that children in kinship placements were more likely than children in non-kin placements to say they 'always' felt loved (94% compared to 82%). However, Gaudin and Sutphen (1993; cited in the *Report to the Congress on Kinship Foster Care*, US

Department of Health and Human Services, 2000) are reported to have found no differences in perceived levels of affection. A New Zealand study (Smith *et al*, 1999) found that there were very few unproblematic relationships in either type of care.

It was evident throughout our interviews with the children that they generally enjoyed warm and positive relationships with their carers. All of them, for example, reported being praised or rewarded if they did something well:

She'll praise me and that, she'll be really happy. If I've done something really good, she might buy a present or something. She'll say that's really good that you've done good.

He's pleased . . . he lets me play on the computer or gives me a treat. I can tell when he's pleased as he's jolly.

It will also be recalled from the earlier discussion about the ecomaps that all but one of the children placed their kinship carer in the innermost zone close to them.

One of our aims in the research was to assess the extent to which our kin-placed children were securely attached to their carers. However, while we had hoped to be able to use validated measures which would provide a standard of comparison with children in other circumstances, our enquiries failed to produce any which we considered would be appropriate or feasible to use (see Appendix A). Drawing on the attachment literature and existing measures of attachment, we therefore designed two short questionnaires which attempted to tap the key dimensions. The first comprised seven statements addressing children's sense of security, safety and belonging (listed in Table 8.3), the other 13 statements covering their perception of their carer (Table 8.4). The child was given three possible responses (true, sometimes true, not true).

As can be seen from Table 8.3, all the 12 children marked the 'I feel safe' statement as completely true for them and this seems to us a very important consensus. Given the children's histories, we might have expected them to be vulnerable to feeling at risk or unsafe, so their responses here are very encouraging.

Table 8.3
Security, safety and belonging

| | Children reporting statement true for them | | | | | |
| | Boys | | Girls | | All children | |
	No.	%	No.	%	No.	%
I feel I belong here	3	75	8	100	11	92
I feel safe	4	100	8	100	12	100
I feel wanted	1	25	8	100	9	75
I feel loved	3	75	8	100	11	92
I feel settled	3	75	8	100	11	92
I feel at home	3	75	8	100	11	92
I feel cared for	2	50	8	100	10	83
All the above	1	25	8	100	9	75
Overall score (maximum 7)	4.8		7.0		6.3	
(N = 12)	(4)		(8)		(12)	

All eight girls, but only one of the four boys, considered all the statements in the first questionnaire to be true for them. We wondered whether the girls did actually have a greater sense of belonging and attachment or were just more likely to idealise their situation. However, we also felt that the gender of carer/child might have an impact in that the three boys expressing ambivalence in at least one area were all placed with single female carers:

- a single boy with his female sole carer wanting to return to live with his mother and her boyfriend; he had a good relationship particularly with the latter;
- a boy (in an all female household) who placed himself closer to his father on the ecomap; he had put his kinship carer in the middle circle on the ecomap;
- a single boy living alone with his grandmother and posing her not inconsiderable behaviour challenges.

All three boys produced ambivalent responses to the statement 'I feel wanted' and two to the 'I feel cared for' category. The remaining four ambivalent responses related to four different statements. The most ambivalent child was longing to return to his birth parent and, although it is not possible to be certain, it seems likely that his responses reflected a process of mutual disengagement rather than inherent difficulties in the relationship with his carer.

Table 8.4
Children's perceptions of their carers

| | Children reporting statement true for them | | | | | |
| | Boys | | Girls | | All children | |
	No.	%	No.	%	No.	%
Loving	3	75	8	100	11	92
Encouraging	3	75	7	88	10	83
Helpful	3	75	7	88	10	83
Always has time for me	0	0	6	75	6	50
Patient	1	25	5	63	7	58
Easy to talk to	1	25	6	75	7	58
Fun	1	25	8	100	9	75
Interested in me	2	50	7	88	10	83
Fair	2	50	8	100	10	83
Makes me feel good about myself	2	50	7	88	9	75
Someone I can trust and rely on	4	100	8	100	12	100
Listens to me	3	75	8	100	11	92
Loves me no matter what I do	1	25	8	100	9	75
Overall score (maximum=13)	8.0		11.8		10.5	
(N=)	(4)		(8)		(12)	

The children were 100% in agreement that their carer was someone 'I can trust and rely on'. Again, this seems to us be an extremely important finding in terms of children's attachment and security. It echoes the finding of Aldgate and McIntosh (2006) that carers were seen by the children as trusted adults to whom they could turn with problems or worries.

The responses to the other statements were also, in general, very encouraging. However, there was again a marked gender difference, with girls reporting more positive perceptions. Only half of the girls expressed ambivalence on any statement and two were ambivalent about only one. In contrast, all four of the boys expressed ambivalence in at least one area and for eight statements more than one boy was ambivalent. Indeed, for every statement except one, the boys expressed more ambivalence than the girls. All the boys expressed some ambivalence about whether their carer always had time for them.

This again suggests that the boys may not be as close to their kinship carers as the girls were. One might suppose that the boys could be less compliant with their carers and that perhaps there was more conflict. However, the SDQ scores of the boys did not support this.

Two boys had the lowest scores on both questionnaires (one boy hoping to return to his mother and her partner, the other – who had placed his father closer to him than his carer on the ecomap – being the sole male in the household). Again one might hypothesise that boys placed in all female households with, perhaps older, lone relatives may have greater problems than girls in establishing a sense of belonging and close relationship with their carer.

Pros and cons of placement with relatives

We did not want to put children in a potentially difficult position by asking them directly about the pros and cons of living with their carer. So we opted for two indirect questions:

'At the moment, all over the country there will be children who are about to go and live with their gran, or their aunt/uncle because they can't live with their parents. If you were talking to one of them, what would you say were the good and bad bits about living with a relative?'

'If you were talking to the relative who was about to start caring for that child, can you think of any "top tips" (bits of advice) you could give them about what helps children?'

Some of the children responded by talking generally about kinship placements while others talked about their own particular experience.

Good bits

Broad *et al* (2001) reported that their interviewed children saw the advantages of their placements as being stability, avoidance of local authority care, being safe from adults, maintaining links with family, siblings and friends, sustaining their racial and cultural heritage and being supported with education. The positive theme of feeling safe is also echoed by Messing (2005).

From the carer interviews, we knew that seven of the interviewed children knew their kinship carer well before their move.[88] It was not therefore surprising that in our study, familiarity and confidence in the relationship with the relative was specifically mentioned by three children as being a 'good bit' in the placement.

> *Someone you know, you can trust and everything. It saves going, like, to strangers and places you feel uncomfortable with – it felt like that at foster parents. You know where you stand.*

> *With your auntie you know who you're living with and you can trust them and they're related. It's not a stranger you're going to, you know them since you were little and you can trust them with whatever you do.*

It is important to note, however, that some pointed out that even if children knew their carers well, it could still take time to settle in:

> *You feel like it's home **after a couple of years**.*

> *Once you get used to it, it's fine, it's fun **once you get used to it**.*

One young adult reminded us that a kinship care move did not necessarily mean a move to familiar adults. In describing her move she said:

> *It is quite a shock when you go to someone who is not a part of your life. I knew him as my dad's brother and my cousins but I didn't know them, we didn't go round there for dinner and we'd not stayed overnight before.*

---

[88] Of the 12 interviewees, five knew their relative well through previous long stays, one had stayed regularly for short periods before their move, one had had regular visits, while five had had only occasional visits or hardly any contact.

Nonetheless, she also felt that a placement with kin had been worthwhile as it:

Gave us the opportunity to stay together . . . it was right we went to the family where you've got some common ground.

One child from a minority ethnic family valued being placed with a relative of the same ethnicity, emphasising that 'you can do cultural things, activities'. Another child placed with an unfamiliar distant relative saw the main advantage of a kinship placement as avoiding the risks that could be associated with birth parent care:

If they're taking drugs or something, it's better for you to be out of that family because . . . you could, like, start taking drugs . . . but with [a related carer] . . . you're going to have a good education, you're going to grow up good.

Most of the children mentioned nurturing, caring qualities on the part of the kinship carer as being important qualities that would make a place-ment work. These seemed ordinary features of being a good parent such as kindness, helpfulness, and sensitivity, but perhaps also being especially attuned to the difficulties the child had previously experienced:

Just be very caring to the child because of what they've gone through and be careful what you say because you might say something and you might hurt them and just be loving to them, that's it really.

Pleasure and enjoyment were mentioned by a further two children with one 12-year-old reassuring that 'the good things are you will have just as much fun'. Others mentioned their carer's generosity:

If you're on your own [with grandparent] it's better, you won't get picked on or blamed for things. You get a TV and little bits and pieces you want because you know your Nan or aunt loves you . . . If I want something, my Nan will get it for me.

Interestingly, however, some children also warned against over-indulgence:

Don't give them anything they want. If [the child] achieves . . . encourage them to do it more . . . reward them and keep encouraging them to do it.

Bad bits

Negatives cited by the young people in Broad *et al*'s study (2001) included lack of freedom, financial hardship and difficulties accessing leaving care services. Doolan *et al* (2004) and Farmer and Moyers (2008) also report that finance was a concern to children. However, none of these issues were raised by any of the children in our study. Indeed, apart from missing their parents, most struggled to identify any "bad bits" about being in a kinship placement. As one put it:

Obviously for some people [there are bad bits] but not from my experience. We get along.

Health issues are a potential concern when children are placed with older kinship carers. However, the children in this study did not seem unduly concerned. Three children said they sometimes needed to provide support for their carer but did not appear to resent this. Indeed, their descriptions of this suggested a degree of relationship reciprocity rather than any sense that it was a burden:

Sometimes when you live with older people like Nan and Granddad you have to help them out more because they can't do everything on their own. (Girl aged 14)

I have to help out more now that I'm older as it's Pap but it's not a chore. (Boy aged 16)

One teenager was devoted to her grandmother who had a terminal illness, and envisaged that 'I'll probably be my nan's carer when I leave school . . . if I do work, I expect I'll be a nurse'. She had also thought about what would happen when her grandmother eventually died:

I won't be moving out . . . when she dies, I'm going to stay in the house with my granddad. When my nan goes – she's trying to stay until I'm 16 – I'll be upset for a couple of days but I'll get over it . . . you do get over it but it takes a short time to do it.

Another child, who was hoping to return home, said:

It's better to be with Mum as I'm closer to her. She's 27 or 28, it's better to keep young [have a young mum] so she won't pass away.

On the whole, however, children did not generally see the age of the relative as a disadvantage as long as they actively maintained a good degree of interest in them.

> *He's not old fashioned, I suppose he's up to date. He bought me a decent electric guitar, I enjoy playing the guitar and will do that for two hours every night.* (16-year-old boy placed with grandfather in his late 60s)

But it does seem that some children living alone with a grandparent could feel isolated:

> *Give them a telly if they are alone so they can sit and watch telly in their bedroom ... some children may think it's lonely [being only child with nan], some children will think it's OK. I've always been on my own so I don't know anything different.*

> *Don't leave them alone by themselves so they don't get bored. Make sure they have the phone numbers of their friends. I think Nan should spend more time with me, maybe go out together more. It's a bit more boring here as I'm not with my mum.*

The young women interviewees both had had experiences of being placed with grandparents at some point and felt, looking back, that the age gap had been difficult:

> *That's another thing – grandmas shouldn't do it because they haven't got the patience for it ... it's not fair as you want to have different lives. They [as an older person] want to go to car boot sales and things. Half of young people wouldn't be seen dead at a car boot sale. You don't want to live that granny life.*

> *There was that generation thing. We used to go shopping once a week, that was about it. It was all right at first. It was hard ... now and again there were patches when I was settled ... I could be helpful, depended what mood I was in. I did move out at one point ... and then I went back so it can't have been that bad.*

However, the latter interviewee qualified her comment by suggesting that it was not necessarily the age of the grandparent that made things difficult, but their degree of flexibility and understanding:

> *I got on all right with my grandfather. My granddad would listen to you but my nan wouldn't, she wanted things done her way and that was it, it is still the same.*

It did not seem that the age of the relative was by itself a good predictor of whether the child felt the kinship carer was interested and involved with them. One carer approaching his 70s (with little support from either birth parent) was perceived as active and interested by his teenage granddaughter, while a grandmother in her early 50s was perceived by the child as somewhat uninvolved and rather distant. Thought needs to be given as to how best to encourage and enable kinship carers to remain interested and active as children grow older.

Rules

Household rules as described by the children appeared striking for their ordinariness. Usually they related to basic standards of behaviour such as not taking things without asking, not jumping on the furniture, keeping bedrooms tidy, no fighting or bad language and being in at agreed times. Some children found the carers very easy going and flexible, and where they seemed fairer, the rules were perceived as fair:

> *My aunt sets rules that are fair, they're not can't do this, can't do that, there's always a reason why.* (Girl, 18 years)

> *They're fair . . . sometimes it may feel like it's unfair, but when you really think about it, you say to yourself they really care about me and that's why.* (Girl, 11 years)

The children's acceptance and approval of rules reflected the findings of Altshuler (1999) that the loving and caring offered by relatives seeps through into rules and expectations about the children's behaviour.

Parents

In the ecomaps, as highlighted earlier:

- 58 per cent of children put a parent within the circle nearest to them (four mothers, three fathers), indicating a close relationship;
- 33 per cent placed a parent (two mothers, two fathers) in the middle circle;
- 25 per cent placed a parent (one mother, two fathers) in the outer circle;
- A further 10 possible parents (five mothers, five fathers) were not placed on the ecomaps at all.

All the children's birth parents were separated from each other and in most instances had been for many years. All the children were aware of who their mother was and all but two their father. Ten had ongoing contact with a parent (seven with mothers and three with fathers), although none sustained contact of any significance with both parents. One child seldom had contact with either birth parent and one had no parental contact at all following legal disputes. Four children in two sibling groups had re-established contact with their mother after a considerable gap.

Interestingly, the seven children with maternal contact all had mothers who were now apparently successfully raising younger children, either those who had remained at home when the children moved to kinship care (3), or had been born later (4). The two young adults similarly had regular contact with mothers who were raising young half-siblings successfully. One also had contact with their father while the other's father was deceased.

Do children feel it is important to see their birth parents?

Doolan *et al* (2004) report that kinship placements enabled most children to stay in touch with at least one parent, that most children were positive about contact, and children who had lost touch with a parent expressed feelings of sadness about this.

The children in our study generally thought it was important to keep in touch:

Because you need to know the, like, truth really.

If you don't see them when you get older, you're going to think they don't want you, you're going to think, like, I'm living with my nan and granddad, my mum doesn't want to see me, whereas your mum would want to see you.

However, they also felt that the views of the individual child should take priority:

It depends on the child and what they're thinking; it depends on what the child wants.

It's up to them, it's entirely up to them, if they want to see their real mum and she wants to see them.

[It's] important [to see parents] but sometimes children don't wish to see them.

Relationships with mothers

As noted earlier, seven children had ongoing maternal contact and five did not. Most children appeared happy with the level that existed for them. For instance, one teenager enjoyed his informal and frequent contact:

I go down whenever, really, she doesn't mind me coming down. The relationship is all right. I can visit her whenever I like. I can go down by myself.

Another seemed to be quite accepting that his mother was not allowed any contact:

I'm quite happy about the way [it is] . . . I don't see my mum because I'm not even supposed to see [her] at all.

However, two girls – one with and one without contact – showed the red card, suggesting less comfortable feelings surrounding this. The child with contact (but with an ambivalent mother) seemed to be yearning for a more established relationship, stating, 'It goes well . . . I'd like to see her more'. The other, with a no contact order, had been subject to repeated court proceedings which had been very unsettling for her.

Two of the children had a marked sense of identification with their birth mother and were hoping to return to her care. They also remarked on their positive relationships with their mother's new partners although, for one, the transition between households could be painful:

I get on well with my mum's boyfriend. He lets me call him Dad. He'll make me feel happy. I am sad coming back here especially after the holidays. I feel happy there and feel down [here].

One of the young women whose placement had disrupted was close to her mother and found it very difficult to settle with her kinship carers. She recollected struggling with their antipathy towards her drug-using mother, stating that, 'They disliked my mum and they used to slag her off and stuff'. This difficult relationship resulted in the kinship carers' reluctance to host contact:

Contact was reduced because of our auntie and uncle as they didn't want her to come round . . . we had contact at the family centre after that – that was just horrible at the family centre . . . Who wants to see their parents with a social worker looking over you as if they're going to do something to you? I'd rather not see my mum at all. 'Cos that just makes me feel wrong, that just makes me feel wrong about seeing her. She did turn up but we didn't like the family centre and we stopped going in the end.

The relationship this young woman had with her mother survived these difficulties, demonstrating the strength of the bond for some children. Other children, while enjoying maternal contact, did appear to have a firmer primary identity with their kinship carer and appeared more distant from their mother.

Relationships with fathers

Research by Wineburgh (2000) suggests that children's self esteem can be negatively affected by a lack of relationship with or understanding about an absent father. There may be "father hunger", often hidden by anger or apathy. An active father (who can be a male care giver) provides a positive role model for children of both sexes. Flouri (2005) associates involved fathering with less criminality in boys and better mental health and educational attainment for girls.

Rowe *et al* (1984) and Cleaver (2000) found that generally mothers are more likely to keep in touch with children in care than fathers. In kinship placements, Messing (2005) reports that fathers were largely absent from children's lives, a source of sadness for some and anger for others, particularly girls. Boys yearned to have 'a big man'. Over half of the kinship children studied by Aldgate and McIntosh (2006) had no contact with their fathers (in contrast to 4 children out of 26 who never saw their mothers) and the majority of those with contact wanted more.

Only three of the interviewed children in our study (a sibling group placed with paternal relatives) had regular and frequent contact with their father. Despite his problems, they valued the contact and all three independently expressed a wish that the contact would be increased:

It's going good, yeah. For longer, if we could see him for longer and more often.

The remaining nine children (six with maternal relatives, three with paternal relatives) had no ongoing relationship. Six did have an adult male as a role model in the household and a seventh had a good relationship with his mother's new partner. Two children (one boy, one girl) lived with single female carers and had no contact with a father or father figure.

Fathers, therefore, were shadowy or invisible figures in the lives of most of the interviewed children. However, this did not mean the children were not interested. Indeed, some made quite poignant comments suggesting a sense of yearning for a relationship:

If you know where dad lives, try and get his number, try and find some way of getting in touch.

My father, I want to know more about my father and that's it.

I wish that I could see my real dad.

Their wish for contact resonates with research by Timms and Thoburn (2003), where over 60 per cent of children in care wanted to see their fathers.

Siblings

Seven of the 12 children interviewed formed three sibling groups. Without exception, the children who had been placed with siblings found this to be of positive benefit, echoing the comment of one child that placements with siblings were 'really important'. On the ecomap exercise, as reported earlier, whenever a child was placed with a sibling, they put them within the inner circle, indicating a close relationship. None regretted being with their sibling, even though they argued from time to time:

> *We get on well with each other. [We have] just little arguments but not that much because I guess we understand each other now because we're all older, we don't fight as much as we used to.*

> *We argue a lot! [But it's] very important to be together.*

One boy recognised that the complicated shared history he had with his younger sister was beneficial to them:

> *We are close obviously . . . we've not been apart all through things. It's really good, some one to talk to as well as someone to trust.*

Seven children had siblings and half-siblings living with their mothers with whom they had regular contact; as did both the young adults. This could be something of a mixed blessing:

> *They don't come and stay as they are a bit of a menace. They can be a bit of a problem as they get out of hand but I get on with them both quite well.*

> *It's actually quite fun being with my brothers even though they're quite rough.*

However, children appeared to enjoy their relationship with them and considered themselves close, despite their different histories. On the ecomaps, the children placed 15 of the 23 full- and half-siblings living with their mothers within the inner circle of the map.

It's good actually, at least you know who they are, they can make me feel happy.

It's really good, I get to see them grow up and when it's their birthday.

Social workers

Other studies of children in kinship care have suggested that children see social workers in a positive light. Doolan *et al* (2004) noted that overwhelmingly children wanted more direct contact and more of a relationship with social workers. Broad *et al* (2001) reported that children wanted better access to services accessed through social workers. Farmer and Moyers (2008) found that most children were enthusiastic regarding their current or former social worker, although 44 per cent had no memory of one. Aldgate and McIntosh (2006) found two-thirds of children saw their social worker as helpful. In the USA, Altshuler (1999) found the children had affection for social workers and appreciated their efforts.

As noted earlier, the children in our study rarely placed social workers on their ecomaps, only three being cited, by two children. Only one was an open case, although there were three other children in this position. A further four children had had recent social worker involvement. Eight therefore were able to comment on their involvement with social workers, as was one of the young adults.

One of the children and one young adult (who otherwise had fairly indifferent memories) recalled having enjoyed being taken out by social workers:

I remember she once took us out together to a park or somewhere . . . it was fun, it helped to take us out.

You got to go out with the social worker – swimming and bowling. Sometimes it's enjoyable.

Two felt social workers were generally helpful and useful to talk to when they had a problem.

I get on with her well. You can talk to her if you need anything or if you feel like you need to say something and if you're unhappy you can talk to her about it.

Quite good he is. He helps. He's the one that got the idea about the life story. Well, if you've got something worrying you and you can't talk to your parents, then you talk to them about it. Private stuff sometimes.

However, the same boy also had reservations about being in care: 'You have to have reviews at school as well, they're the bad parts about it really'. We could not but feel sorry for him appearing to have his reviews so obviously convened! The intrusiveness of having a social worker was echoed by two siblings who were pleased they were now on residence orders. One child advised social workers 'not to keep asking the same questions all the time'.

It used to get me annoyed as the social worker kept coming and asking questions all the time. It made me feel different, it was really annoying, the questions were really annoying.

Her brother, who commented that 'it got in the way a bit rather', felt that social services involvement made him feel more different from his peers than the fact he was living with his grandfather:

Friends would be a bit 'why do you have a social worker?' but it was OK . . . I was pleased it stopped, as I just wanted me and Pap.

This boy clearly felt less secure while on a care order and welcomed his legal status changing to a residence order with parental responsibility given to the grandfather:

There was always the possibility I'd be removed while [the social workers] came and I was in care. I was worried until Pap won the court case and it was sorted.

The future

Altshuler (1999) found that all the children in her study expected to be living with their carer in 12 months' time and did not anticipate returning to parental care. Doolan *et al* (2004) reported that the children felt secure and able to stay in their placements as long as they needed to. In contrast, Aldgate and McIntosh (2006) found that half of the kinship children interviewed were uncertain about the future of their placement (even though their carers were certain it was permanent). In Cleaver's study (2000) of the broader foster care population, 40 per cent of children were said to be confused about how long they would stay in their placements.

The interviewed children in our study, apart from two who were expecting to return to live with their mothers, had a real sense of attachment to and permanence with their kinship carers and expected to stay with them well into adulthood. When asked how old they thought they would be when they moved from the kinship carer, most thought they would remain there well into independence. One 16-year-old told us:

As long as I stay at school. I want to stay at school and hopefully go to university to get a music degree. [My home base will be] here.

Any concerns the children had about their futures appeared very normal, relating to education and job prospects. They also appeared to have encouragingly high expectations for their future:

I want to go to university and get my degree, maybe in law. (Girl, 11 years)

Be an English teacher. Do well in education. Be successful. (Girl, 13 years)

Working as a hairdresser. Hopefully I can get my own business and have my own salon and beauty parlour. (Girl, 18 years)

Their comments mirrored the findings of Broad *et al* (2001) that the children had a clear idea of employment and were keen to get qualifications.

Looking back as a young adult

The two interviews with the young women now in independent living raised some additional issues we want to note. Notwithstanding that both had had either a breakdown or at least a turbulent time in their kinship placements, the relationship with their carers had apparently weathered this and the carers remained part of the young adults' network. This reflects the findings in our kinship carer interviews that, even where placements had broken down or ended for other reasons, carers and children were active in keeping in touch with each other. Both the young people interviewed had a sense of identity with their kinship carers that extended into the long term:

> I'd done stuff for them and they'd done stuff for me ... been helpful ... now I'm the one they call in the middle of the night [if there's a problem]. My grandmother relies more on me.

> I went to see them this year just to say thanks and that and sorry for all that as I was bad to them. I wasn't an easy person to live with ... I never ever thought I would go and say thank you to them but I did ... we talked about the times we went through together – it wasn't all bad.

As with the younger children interviewed, there seemed little sense of hostility or anger with birth parents about what had happened. Indeed, what strongly came across from both the young adults was their eventual restored relationship with their mothers, with a real sense of belonging to and identity with a parent who has moved on:

> I think it got better with Mum when I had kids. Now I'm down there nearly every day.

> My family life now is better than it's ever been ... Me and Mum get on brilliantly now. I did try living with her but it didn't work. We go out for coffee, a glass of wine, it's fantastic. [Mum and boyfriend] have been together eight years. Mum's got a baby now ... we're a lot older, the baby brings us back together, if you see what I mean ... a new start to our family and it is a better family than we've had before.

Summary

Twelve children in continuing kinship placements plus two young adults in independent living were interviewed. On average, the 12 children had spent 4.9 years with their carer.

The children recounted a sense of ordinariness in placement. They were all fairly optimistic about how they were managing and none had abnormal self-reported scores on the SDQ. The children all appeared to have normal expectations about their future.

All the children evinced an overwhelming sense of safety in the placement and reliance and trust in the kinship carer and 10 displayed a real sense of permanence. All but one child considered themselves very close to their kinship carer and siblings. The children, especially the girls, described positive relationships and a sense of belonging. It is possible that the girls were more easily able to express positive emotional relationships but it could also be that gender may have an impact on a child's experience of kinship care, especially when a boy is placed with a single female carer. They appeared not unduly concerned about the age of their carer as long as their carers were interested in and involved with them.

The network of relationships and friendships that the kinship children identified appeared smaller when compared with children with a parent, especially if placed with a sole grandparent.

Most children retained good links with mothers and any siblings living with her. Children seemed able to embrace the two sets of relationships and move between the households, though the transition could be difficult. The young adults interviewed spoke positively of their restored relationships with mothers who were now more competent parents.

Fathers appear at risk of being lost, whether the child is placed with maternal or paternal family, and the children regretted this.

Social workers appeared very peripheral in the children's lives, even for the four remaining on care orders.

The children, on the whole, displayed no sense of anger or dissatisfaction that they lived within the extended family or about what had happened. Where a sense of difference exists, it can relate more to the existence of care order/social services' involvement rather than the fact that the child is with a kinship carer. This seemed more difficult to explain to friends.

9 Maintaining family links

Introduction

Current legislation and public policy in relation to substitute care emphasise the importance of preserving children's links with their birth families (Children Act 1989; DH 1989a and b, 1991). The research evidence that contact promotes children's well-being is not as strong as previously thought (compare Berridge, 1997 and Quinton et al, 1997). Nonetheless, in general, ongoing contact in some form is still considered to be potentially valuable for children (Sinclair, 2005). It can reduce the risk of placement breakdown and enhance the prospects for return home (Berridge, 1997; Sinclair, 2005). It is considered to be important in the development of children's sense of identity, may foster their sense of attachment, and is an additional form of social capital (Sinclair, 2005; Owusu-Bemphah, 2006).

Placement with kin, by definition, ensures that children remain in touch with at least one member of their family. The international research literature also generally suggests that it promotes the maintenance of other family links (Hunt, 2003a). Indeed, Greeff (1999, p 39) argues that 'the favourable results of many placements may be attributable to their built-in inclusiveness'. Kinship carers are reported to show a high level of commitment to contact, which they generally take responsibility for organising and supervising, and persist in maintaining despite sometimes considerable difficulties. There is also, however, evidence that contact can be problematic and difficult to manage (Hunt, 2003a).

As can be seen from Table 9.1, in many cases at least one parent (typically the father) was already out of the picture by the time the care proceedings ended (and usually long before). This largely reflects the prevalence of divorce and separation in the children's families (Chapter 3), although the fathers of six children were dead, as was one mother. It was extremely rare, however, for contact to be terminated (2%) or for only indirect contact to be ordered (4%). Thus, 86 per cent of children were expected to have face-to-face contact with at least one parent and 43 per

The intent to preserve family links: contact in the care plan

Table 9.1

Parental contact in the care plan

	Mother		Father		Either parent*		Both	
	No.	%	No.	%	No.	%	No.	%
Face to face	88	79	56	51	96	86	48	43
Contact LA discretion	2	2	0	0	2	2	2	2
Parent in carer's household	1	1	0	0	1	1	1	1
indirect contact only	2	2	3	3	4	4	1	1
All contact terminated	7	6	5	5	10	9	2	2
Parent dead/not in picture	11	10	47	42	50	45	8	7
(N=)	(111)		(111)		(111)		(111)	

* sums to >100 per cent because arrangements may be different for each parent

cent with both. Comparison with our sub-sample of kin-placed children (those less than five years old at the end of the proceedings) with children placed in non-kin substitute care (all under five) shows that parental contact was much more frequently envisaged in the kinship cases (98% compared to 27%), indicating that in intent at least, kinship placements are more likely to preserve parental links.

Plans also commonly provided for the continuation of sibling contact, with 82 per cent of children expected to see siblings with whom they had previously lived, and all contact being terminated in only six cases (14%). Perhaps oddly, however, the proportion was not higher than in our comparison group: all six of the non-kin-placed children with siblings with whom they had been living were expected to retain contact, compared to 85 per cent of the kin-placed children under five.

Frequency, venue and supervision

It was apparent from the levels of parental contact envisaged that contact was not seen as merely token; a real attempt was being made to preserve children's relationships. Almost half were expected to see a parent at least weekly and nine out of ten at least monthly (Appendix F Table F4). Again, however, relationships with fathers seemed more vulnerable, with just over a quarter expected to have weekly contact (compared to 47% of mothers) and less than half monthly (73%).

Few arrangements were covered by a contact order (19%) and only 40 per cent by a written agreement. While this might perhaps suggest a greater element of informality than might be customary for non-kin placements, this would be mediated by the involvement of the local authority through either a care or supervision order, many of which were made, at least in part, to assist with or control contact (Chapter 5). In total, there were only 12 cases without a contact, care, or supervision order in place at the end of proceedings.

Control was also exercised through other specific restrictions (Appendix F Table F4). In around half the cases the venue was specified – typically either the placement household (40%) or a facility such as a contact or family centre (52%). Contact at a parent's home was permitted in only 16 per cent of cases. In 63 per cent of cases, at least one parent's contact was expected to be supervised and in 20 per cent, both. Like Farmer and Moyers (2008) we found that carers were expected to play a significant role in this (65% of cases, compared to only 13% which were to be supervised by social workers, though contact/family centres were also important).

Did plans work out?

Who was seeing whom?

Parents
The most recent data available on each case indicated that, where it was envisaged, in a very high proportion of cases (88%) there was actually still some face-to-face contact, again confirming the potential of kinship care to preserve parental links. There were 11 in which all contact was known to have ceased (and a further eight where no data was available after the proceedings) (Table 9.2). Where other forms of contact were taking place (telephone, letter, e-mail), in almost all instances this was additional to

face-to-face contact. Only four mothers and two fathers were having only these forms of contact.

Table 9.2
Continuation of face-to-face parental contact where envisaged in care plan

	Maternal contact*		Paternal contact*		Either*	
	No.	%	No.	%	No.	%
All cases	69	83	30	59	79	88
(N=)	(83)		(51)		(90)	
Missing data	8		5		8	

*where contact with either envisaged in care plan

Only a minority of children (22%), however, were seeing both parents. Fathers continued to disappear from their children's lives. While 83 per cent of mothers expected to remain in contact did so, the figure dropped to 59 per cent of fathers (Appendix F Table F5). Mothers were more likely to be seeing their children if they had played a major part in the child's care prior to removal, but fathers were more likely to be doing so if they had not (though neither was statistically significant). Nonetheless, in either circumstance, fathers were less likely to stay in touch than mothers.

Girls were more likely than boys to be in contact with at least one parent (93% compared to 83%). There was little difference by gender in relation to maternal contact (87% compared to 83%), but the difference was larger in relation to fathers (65% girls; 54% boys) (Appendix F Table F5).

The overall figures for contact, however, are somewhat inflated by generally higher levels of contact in terminated placements, many of which ended with children returning to a parent, usually the mother. Ninety-seven per cent of children in terminated placements had contact with at least one parent up to the point the placement ended, compared to 82 per cent of those in continuing placements still in touch (Appendix F Table F5). However, although maternal contact levels were lower in continuing placements (73% compared to 97% in terminated placements), it was still the case that mothers were more likely to remain in touch than fathers in either type of placement (53% continuing; 67% terminated) (Appendix F Table F6). Even fewer children (14%) retained contact with both parents.

Farmer and Moyers (2008) report that 82 per cent of children placed with kin had contact with at least one parent. Sixty-eight per cent of children with a live mother with whom contact was permitted had contact with them and 49 per cent of those with a live father with whom contact was permitted had contact with them. Comparative figures for children placed with non-kin foster parents were 65 per cent and 31 per cent. Aldgate and Macintosh (2006) report that 85 per cent of kin-placed children with a live mother had contact with her compared with 43 per cent of those with a live father. Only 17 per cent had contact with both.

Siblings
Data on sibling contact was often only available for a limited period. However, the latest information we have on each case indicates that there was not a single child (of those expected to have contact) who was not seeing at least one sibling. Children were in touch with siblings with whom they had previously lived as well as other siblings. These figures are higher than those cited by both Farmer and Moyers (2008), who report that 61 per cent of children had contact with siblings, and those provided by Aldgate and McIntosh (2006) (83%). In part this is because we have excluded children who were not expected to have contact with siblings. The proportion of the whole sample is 78 per cent.

Extended family outside the care household
The latest information we have available indicates that at least 57 children were in face-to-face contact with one or more members of their extended families other than those in the carer's household (81% of those where data available). Indeed, our carer interviews indicated that children were in touch with a wide range of blood and step-relatives: aunties, uncles, cousins, grandparents, great-grandparents, great aunts. Some networks were particularly extensive, as this account by a carer indicates:

> The family doesn't keep in touch with mother but they have accepted Hayley. There is a big family network. Whenever we meet with family

*she is part of the family. She knows she has a place. We took her to
[country X] where the family come from several times, she has nearly
200 cousins and all the rest of it. We visit [country X] once every one
or two years. Her grandfather [in the UK] is very very glad she's with
me. She saw her great-grandmother on a regular basis and when she
died Hayley sang at her funeral. [The great-grandmother] died here
and we took the body to [country X]. Hayley sang at both services.*

Contact was more common with family members on the maternal side
(45% compared to 32%) as might be expected, given the larger number of
children placed with maternal carers. Eighty-three children were either
living with, or in face-to-face contact with a member of their maternal
extended family, compared to only 41 children living with, or in face-to-
face contact with a member of their paternal extended family. Only five
children (placed with non-kin carers) were not in touch with either side of
their family. However, only 17 (15%) children were in touch with both
(Table 9.3).

Of the 30 children who were not in face-to-face contact with their
mothers, at least 12 (40%) were not seeing members of the maternal
extended family either. A much smaller proportion of children without
paternal contact were also out of touch with the paternal family (seven of
76; 9%). Three of the 18 children with no parental contact, all placed with
non-family kin carers, were not seeing any of their extended family.

Table 9.3
Links with extended family*

	Maternal family		Paternal family		Both sides		Either side	
	No.	%	No.	%	No.	%	No.	%
All children	83	74	41	37	17	15	107	96
(N=)	(112)		(112)		(112)		(112)	

*cases where children were known to be in touch with one side of the family but
data were not available on the other were coded as having contact with one side at
least.

Changes in parental contact over time

Our data do not systematically cover changes in contact with siblings or extended family over time. As far as parents are concerned, with the exception of cases where children were returning to the contact parent, contact tended to diminish over time, as might be expected (Harwin *et al*, 2003). Thus, in the continuing and continuous cases, 93 per cent of children were having contact with at least one parent 12 months after the proceedings had concluded. Only 70 per cent of those for whom data were available were doing so more than five years on. Both maternal and paternal contact diminished: from 94 per cent of mothers at the 12 month point to 42 per cent more than five years on [76% to 38% fathers] (Appendix F Table F6).

Even where contact continued, it might become sporadic or diminish in frequency. The latest data available suggested this type of negative trajectory affected maternal contact for 49 per cent of children and paternal for 62 per cent (Table 9.4). Negative trajectories more commonly

Table 9.4

Contact trajectories

	Maternal contact		Paternal contact	
	No.	%	No.	%
Ceased	13	27	16	47
Became sporadic	7	14	3	9
Frequency reduced	4	8	2	6
Frequency increased	3	6	0	0
More restricted	0	0	1	3
Less restricted	6	12	5	15
Positive trajectory	6	12	5	15
Negative trajectory	24	49	21	62
Stable trajectory	19	39	8	24
(N=)		(49)		(34)
Negative trajectory – girls	12	55	7	44*
(N=)		(22)		(16)
Negative trajectory – boys	12	44	14	78*
(N=)		(27)		(18)

*p< 0.5

affected paternal contact with boys and maternal contact with girls, although the differences were only statistically significant in relation to paternal contact.

Positive trajectories (i.e. where contact frequency increased, or restrictions [on venue, frequency or supervision] were dropped) were relatively unusual – applying in only six cases of maternal contact (12%) and five (15%) of paternal. More optimistically, however, in the remaining cases regular contact was still continuing at the same levels of frequency and restriction. It is also important to point out that, while frequency did generally diminish over time, in many cases levels were still quite high. Three years post-proceedings, 48 per cent of children were having at least monthly contact with a parent and 28 per cent at least weekly (Appendix F Table F7). These figures are very similar to those reported by Aldgate and McIntosh (2006 [50% monthly; 32% weekly]).

The relevance of pre-existing bonds

We were not able to explore this question for all the children in the sample. However, we did ask the carers we interviewed whether, in their opinion, children had a close bond with either parent at the point they came into placement. This indicated that, even where contact was envisaged in the care plan, it was not typically a question of maintaining existing strong links but rather of building on what may have been fragile or non-existent foundations. Only 45 per cent of children were considered to have a close bond with their mothers and 19 per cent with their fathers. Strikingly, only one child had a close bond with both.

Contact was more likely to be maintained where there were perceived to be close bonds (Appendix F Table F8). Similarly, in the absence of such bonds, negative trajectories were more common. Perhaps more surprising are the number of fathers who managed to establish a bond with their children when none had existed prior to placement. Mothers, conversely, rarely did so.

Does it matter who the child is placed with?

Parental contact

Looking at all the cases where parental contact was envisaged in the care plan, it was clear that contact was more likely when children were placed with maternal relatives (Appendix F Table F9). The differences were most marked in the continuing and continuous cases:

- 88 per cent of children placed with maternal relatives were in touch with at least one parent, compared to 67 per cent of those placed with paternal relatives (a statistically significant difference);
- mothers were more likely to remain in touch where children were placed with their relatives (84% compared to 36% with paternal);[89]
- similarly fathers were more likely to remain in touch where children were placed with their side of the family (69% compared to 43% for maternal relatives);[90]
- mothers were less likely than fathers to retain contact with children placed with the opposite side of the family (36% compared with 43%);
- fathers were more likely to be in contact where children were placed with aunts or uncles rather than grandparents. Mothers were more likely to be in contact where children were placed with grandparents. In both cases, this is probably because of the greater preponderance of maternal grandparent carers.

Extended family

Children living with paternal carers were most likely to be having contact with other members of their extended family (Appendix F Table F10). Children with maternal carers were most likely to be having contact with members of the maternal family (80% compared to 14% paternal family) and those with paternal carers with their side of the family (47% compared to 43%) though the differences were smaller. This reflects, at least in part, the greater likelihood that fathers (and therefore probably their

---

[89] Farmer and Moyers (2008) report that 74 per cent of children placed with maternal relatives saw mothers, cf. 58 per cent living with paternal.

[90] Farmer and Moyers (2008) report that 75 per cent of children placed with paternal kin saw their fathers, cf. 27 per cent with maternal.

side of the family) were already out of the picture by the time the care proceedings ended.

Was contact in children's best interests?

Overall, despite attrition over time, the data indicate that, in line with other research, a good proportion of the children in kinship care in our study were able to sustain links with at least some members of their families. The question then arises, was that always in their best interests?

Did contact put children at risk?

Concerns about the ability of kinship carers to protect children from dangerous or unsuitable family members is a key theme in the research literature (Hunt, 2003a). Seventy per cent of the social workers interviewed in one US study, for instance, considered that kin-placed children were more at risk because of carers' problems in enforcing contact restrictions (GAO, 1999). Another reported that unauthorised contact was the most common problem contributing to the termination of placements and that many relatives did not understand or accept the risks or had divided loyalties (Terling-Watt, 2001). Farmer and Moyers (2008) report concerns about the child's safety or child protection issues in 39 per cent of kinship cases, slightly more than for children in non-kin placements. Hunt and Macleod (1999) found that 18 per cent of kinship carers had breached contact orders, although emphasising that there was no evidence that the children had actually been harmed as a result.

In view of these concerns, it was reassuring that there were only seven cases in this study (6%) where carers are known to have allowed unauthorised contact and that none of the children suffered harm as a result. Moreover, in five of the seven cases, face-to-face contact was permitted; the breach involved, variously, allowing a mother to take the child out (where she might meet the partner who had abused the child); allowing staying or unsupervised contact; and otherwise allowing contact other than that which had been agreed/ordered. In the remaining two cases (siblings) the father turned up at the house very distressed and the carer, the paternal grandfather, who had been responsible for Social Services involvement in the first place, let him in, but on only the one occasion. As he explained to us:

> I've only seen my son once since the no contact order was made at the end of the care proceedings. I keep in telephone contact with him. He is not allowed to see them although once he did come out of the blue. He said it was breaking his heart not seeing the children. I let him come in for a cup of tea. [The younger child] didn't know him. He said, 'Granddad, who was that man?'

In total, ten children may have been placed at risk because of contact. However, there were only two cases where this was the direct result of the carer's actions (one carer allowing a child to stay in a household where another family member was being investigated for child abuse; another allowing unsupervised contact). The remaining cases all concerned the actions of a parent who was having contact (allowing the child to have contact with the person who had abused them; poor care; or, in one case, taking the child with them to see a drug dealer).

These figures do not suggest that a substantial proportion of carers are cavalier about children's safety. Indeed, there were several examples where carers had quite clearly put children first. For instance, in the last case mentioned, the carer refused to let the parent take the child out on his own again, and on many occasions refused to allow contact when either parent turned up under the influence of drugs.

> I don't think it showed him a good way of life to be drunk or strung out on heroin. I wouldn't have them if they were out of it. I kept them apart so Kevin wouldn't get involved with it. I refused the contact a few times. They didn't like it. If you've got kids you should look after them, shouldn't you? My son used to moan as I wouldn't let him have Kevin so one day I let him have him when I was working. He took him down there [to see a drug dealer]. It was a ridiculous thing to do. He should have had more sense with a kid of that age. I wouldn't let him have him then. But I always had father here, I never turned him away.

Did children benefit from contact?

Contact with siblings

Our data do not allow us to be definitive about the value of contact with siblings for the whole cohort because this was rarely mentioned in case files. Where information was available, however, from whatever source, it generally presents a very positive picture. Thus, there were only three case files where sibling contact was noted as having negative elements for the child, compared to seven where it was entirely positive. None of the social workers interviewed mentioned any adverse aspects. The children interviewed indicated positive and close relationships with the siblings they saw (see Chapter 8). Similarly, the carers of all but two children were convinced of the benefits of contact, with none saying it was detrimental (although one was finding the sibling's presence every day during the holidays a bit much):

> It's important to them. They are very close kids and love one another dearly.

> They all enjoy it. They buy each other Christmas presents. There are lots of hugs and kisses when they leave.

However, there was one case where contact between siblings placed with different sides of the extended family proved extremely difficult, because of the hostile relationships between their carers. These problems had been anticipated in the care proceedings but a year later, the local authority applied to extend the supervision order because of the continuing stream of allegations and counter-allegations and the consequent complete cessation of contact. A meeting held to try to resolve the difficulties ended with one carer assaulting the other. In the end the children were only able to see each other once a fortnight during their contact with their mother.

In another case, it was reported that children were refusing to see their mother unless she brought their siblings, still living at home, to contact.

Contact with the extended family

Since files rarely mentioned contact with the extended family, and we did not specifically ask the children about this, our main source of data was the interviews with carers. These indicate that contact with relatives on the carer's side of the family was generally positive and problem-free (although there was one case where the carers had to leave the area because of harassment by others in the family):

They all have a good time when the family gets together on Sundays.

She feels loved and knows that she is part of this family.

She benefits from having them around, knowing who they are and where they are.

One carer also was very pleased that contact had been re-established with the other side of the family:

Mollie's enjoying discovering that side of the family. I don't know why it didn't come until now but I'm glad it has. At some stage I'm going to die, and if she's got relatives on that side as well, they can support her.

In others, however, contact seemed to be more problematic, either because of concerns about the contact itself, or because of difficulties in dealing with the relatives:

There were concerns that the grandparents had abused their own children so I was advised not to let them see her. I do but I don't leave them alone with her.

Will's grandmother visits three to four times a week but I have to be careful what I say. I am concerned about what information goes to father. He still doesn't know which school Will is at.

I've had a few clashes with them about them taking her places without telling me.

Grandmother is a very difficult lady to deal with, but we've coped.

Parental contact

As might be anticipated, any concerns about children's contact typically focused on parental contact.

As reported earlier, 95 children were known to have had some face-to-face contact with at least one parent since the care proceedings; 87 of them with their mothers and 47 with their fathers. For just over a third of these, the available evidence indicates that contact had been either positive (22%), or at least not detrimental (15%). Thus, all the children interviewed were positive about the contact they had (see Chapter 8). Carers reported children, variously, simply enjoying being with their parent, valuing the opportunity to see siblings; feeling part of their birth family; retaining or developing their sense of identity; maintaining, strengthening or building bonds; and being reassured about their parent's well-being:

They loved it, it made them really happy.

Yes, she feels part of their family. She loves her brother and step-brother. She sees other family there.

Yes, to be honest, I think she does [benefit]. A sense of knowing who she is.

Yes [she benefits] . . . because she would have suffered very much if she had been deprived – she worries enough now, it would be worse. She is glad to meet her mother's current partner and glad to think that someone's looking after her mother.

For most of the children in the sample, however, there was evidence that contact with at least one parent either had some negative elements (40; 42%) or was predominantly negative (20; 21%) (Table 9.5). Interestingly, these proportions are somewhat better than Macaskill's (2002) study of contact for adopted and fostered children, which found that for 57 per cent the experience was a mixture of positive and negatives and for 25 per cent, very negative. Farmer and Moyers (2008) also report a rather higher proportion of cases (31%) in which there was contact detrimental to the child. Nonetheless, our figures are disturbing.

One child's very mixed experience was eloquently described by her carer:

Father's contact is a two-edged sword – good in one way and bad in another. When someone is kept from you, as Annie felt it, you don't feel as if you are entire. You feel as if you've had a branch chopped off. [But] you can't trust him to do as he says so it's stressful for Annie, who can be in floods of tears. Contact started out as monthly but it's never been regular. Now she can see him two or three months running and then not for six months. There's no problem with the actual contact except that it's stilted and stiff. If instructed he can cope. [But] he's too close and clingy with her, she finds it embarrassing.

It was notable that while children's contact was just as likely to be positive with their father as their mother, maternal contact was twice as likely to have some negative elements or even be entirely negative. The poorer quality of contact some children were having with their mothers also emerged in our interviews with social workers.

Table 9.5
Impact of parental contact on the child

	Mother		Father		Either parent	
	No.	%	No.	%	No.	%
Positive only	29	34	16	34	21	22
Not harmful/difficult for child	8	9	16	34	14	15
Positive and negative aspects	19	22	10	21	40	42
Negative only	30	35	5	11	20	21
(N=)	(86)		(47)		(95)	

Recent UK research on children in kinship care (Aldgate and McIntosh, 2006; Farmer and Moyers, 2008) has described some of the difficulties contact can pose for children: being let down by unreliable parents; the upset of seeing and/or leaving a parent; having to confront parental short-comings; loyalty conflicts and confusion; and poor quality contact. There were instances of all these in our study too, as these quotes from carers indicate:

It did unsettle her, her behaviour worsened, she just got tricky all the time, she wouldn't do as she was told and said I wasn't her mum. We asked for contact with the siblings but not the mother. The social worker decided contact with mother should be at her house and that was when the problems got worse. Mother made promises that never happened.

No, [it wasn't beneficial] they came back crying. Social Services used to take the children and then come back with them as mother was drunk or had passed out somewhere. The kids got fed up with this. They tried different places for contact. The kids didn't like it in public because people were there and could see them. Social Services wanted it at a leisure centre and people knew them there and it was embarrassing for them as they were meeting their drunken mum.

She was very erratic and cancelled . . . She just sat in a corner while he got on and played with his toys. She didn't let him go near her and didn't speak to him.

Another recurrent theme in the literature is the poor relationship which can exist between some carers and parents (Hunt, 2003a). As Laws (2001, p 126) puts it: 'The situations described challenge an excessively cosy view of kinship care placements'. Farmer and Moyers (2008) write about relationships marred by parental hostility and resentment, open conflict, violence and threats of violence. Overall, they record conflict between carers and parents or other family members in 54 per cent of kinship cases, compared to only 16 per cent where children were placed with non-kin foster carers.

In our study there were examples of very good, positive relationships between parents and carers, including those on the other side of the family. Some were said to have always been good, others had improved over time:

We get on pretty well. I've always got on with her except for the odd occasion. She says I'm more of a mother [to her] than her own mother.

We have a good relationship now. Things have got much better. It was difficult because of what she was being led to believe about me. My daughter has come round a lot now, it took a lot of work.

Our relationship got stronger over time. There have been times when she has been resentful but that doesn't happen now.

In others, relationships were more ambivalent, but at least on the surface, civilised:

We are polite to each other now but that's as far as it goes.

He tolerated us and we tolerated him. It's only for Jimmy's sake.

However, relationships between carers and at least one parent were judged to be seriously strained or conflicted in over two-fifths of cases (Table 9.6).

Table 9.6
Conflict between carer and contact parent

	Mother		Father		Either parent	
	No.	%	No.	%	No.	%
Serious/persistent	36	41	7	15	40	42
Occasional/minor	8	9	5	11	11	12
None	43	49	35	75	44	46
(N=)	(87)		(47)		(95)	

In the most extreme cases, carers reported being harassed or even subjected to violence by parents or their partners. In other cases, the words used by carers, social workers, or the researchers summarising the data on case files speak volumes: 'difficult, awkward, strained, uneasy, resentful, hostile, antagonistic, aggressive, angry, undermining, acrimonious, estranged, interfering'. Overall, difficulties were much more likely to apply to relationships with mothers than fathers, and in particular, to mothers whose children were placed with paternal relatives (Tables 9.6 and 9.7).

Table 9.7
Parental conflict with carer by which side of the family child placed with

	Mother		Father	
	No.	%	No.	%
Maternal carer	19	34*	4	16
(N=)	(56)		(25)	
Paternal carer	17	61*	3	14
(N=)	(28)		(21)	

*p<.05

It is, of course, scarcely surprising that there should be this level of relationship difficulty. While many parents were probably relieved that they were not "losing" their children to non-kin care or adoption, others may have seen their relatives as contributing to their loss, perhaps by reporting them to Social Services in the first place (see Chapter 5). Carers too, could feel torn about this, as the following extract, referring to the relationship at the time of the care proceedings, shows:

Carer 1: *Stormy.*

Carer 2: *It was more strained. She's my daughter and it was so difficult. She's always relied on me, and even though I didn't like her very much I couldn't stop loving her. It's that awkward balance. It was very strained. Still is at times.*

Carer 1: *You're breaking one loyalty to form another. You could see that what you were doing would hurt her but it was protecting her at the same time.*

While some relationships seemed to be able to weather the trauma of the events leading to proceedings, others appeared to be permanently damaged:

We had a poor relationship with the parents after we reported the incident. Our relationship with parents has never recovered from this. Previously we would go and stay the weekend with them.

It had an impact on all the family in terms of anger, disgust, not with Fiona, obviously, with her mother. I am the only one who can just bear to see her. I'm sorry to word it like that but as she's my daughter but every time I see her I feel physically sick. The others feel it more. She allowed a man to abuse a child and when she knew it was happening, she just stood by him. So I take Fiona to see her and speak lovingly and she comes here for the reviews. She talks to Fiona every week [by phone] and I do all the proper things but I don't do them from the heart and I hate having to do them. I can't sympathise with that one thing. She may have been stupid but she wasn't that stupid, she wasn't so terrorised she couldn't leave the man and take those poor little children.

As time went on, parents could feel marginalised in their children's lives. Mothers seem to have reacted to this most keenly. According to carers, some fathers seem to have slipped fairly readily into more of an "uncle" role. Not so mothers:

> *She did find it quite difficult. She used to come round and feel that her position as a mother was almost a little redundant because Jess would come to me for so many things.*

> *Sometimes I think she resents me because I've got more control over them than she has. 'She's their mother; she should be doing this', but she can't. We get the nagging most of the time that she's the mother, she should have some say but if you do include her in anything, she says all the wrong things and she just upsets the children. All the bickering and talking in front of the children about them going back.*

For their part, some carers resented being made use of, or saw parents as having it easy:

> *She only phones if she wants me to do something.*

> *She [mother] thinks it's great – no responsibilities for her! We still feel angry that they're sitting there with one child, carrying on their drug life, getting all the money, getting all the help.*

The research literature on contact between children and their non-resident parents after separation or divorce clearly demonstrates that a key factor affecting children's experiences of contact is the relationship between their parents and that when those relationships are persistently hostile, particularly where there is overt conflict, contact can be harmful to children (Hunt, 2003b). While one must be wary about applying these findings to a different set of relationships, they should not be ignored. Although Bergerhed (1995) reports that the kin-placed children in her Swedish study seemed to be able to avoid becoming enmeshed in adult conflicts, not all children may be so fortunate (Hunt and Macleod, 1999). The files on one child in our study, for instance, noted:

> Continued conflict with mother re: contact. She continues to violate arrangements for contact and cause upset within the family. Puts child

in a difficult position by asking him to keep secrets from the grandparents.

Four of the eight interviewed social workers who reported conflicted relationships between carers and parents also said this was having an adverse effect on the child.

Taking account of poor adult relationships reduces the proportion of children in our sample likely to have experienced only unproblematic contact to less than a third (31%; Table 9.8). These figures are very similar to those reported by Farmer and Moyers (2008) where only 36 per cent of cases were problem-free. In our study, maternal contact again emerged as more difficult for children.

Table 9.8
Quality of contact for child

	Mother		Father		Either parent	
	No.	%	No.	%	No.	%
Positive contact, little/no conflict	22	26	16	34	16	17
Unproblematic contact, little/no conflict	8	9	15	32	13	14
Positive but conflict	7	8	0	0	4	4
Unproblematic contact but conflict	0	0	1	2	3	3
Positive & negative impact, little/no conflict	11	13	5	11	18	19
Positive & negative impact, conflict	8	9	5	11	22	23
Negative impact, little/ no conflict	9	11	4	9	6	6
Negative only, conflict	21	24	1	2	13	14
(N=)		(86)		(47)		(95)

Problematic contact

Did difficult parental contact continue?

Of the 95 cases in which children had had any parental contact, there were only 14 cases in which contact deemed to have a wholly (10) or partially (4) negative effect on the child ceased. Since there were only 36 cases in which ongoing contact appeared to be wholly positive, this means that in 45 cases (47%) children continued to be exposed to negative experiences. Indeed, if we factor in conflicted adult relationships, the proportion continuing to be subject to problematic contact rises to 55 per cent in all placements (Table 9.9). It should be noted, however, that there was a somewhat higher incidence of difficult contact in placements which had ended. In continuing placements, the proportion was 47 per cent. Children were more likely to have ongoing problematic contact with their mothers (55% compared to 31% with fathers). The data available from our carer interviews indicate that problem contact was more likely where children were not reported to have a close bond with their mothers prior to placement. This was not the case with fathers.

Table 9.9
Continuation of problematic contact*

	Mother		Father		Either parent		Continuing placements	
	No.	%	No.	%	No.	%	No.	%
Continuation of problematic contact	47	55	11	31	52	55	28	47
Negative/problematic contact ceased	12	14	5	14	14	15	11	18
Ongoing contact not problematic	26	31	20	56	29	31	21	35
	(85)		(36)		(95)		(60)	

*excludes cases where unproblematic contact ceased

Were contact difficulties predicted?

At the time of the care proceedings, professional concerns specifically relating to some aspect of contact were recorded in 37 cases. Most of these related to parental contact (30) but there were five cases where concerns related to the difficulties contact between siblings placed separately might present because of the hostility between the kin carers they were placed with, and in two where there were concerns about the other side of the child's extended family. There were, additionally, 18 cases where there were concerns about relationships between carers and parents which, while these were not specifically framed in terms of contact, were likely to impact on it.

In total, there were 35 cases where maternal contact was envisaged and some type of difficulty was anticipated (38%) and 19 cases (34%) where difficult paternal contact was anticipated (Appendix F Table F11).

These "predictions" about parental contact did not prove very accurate, particularly as regards maternal contact. Whether or not difficulties had been anticipated appeared to make no difference to whether mother's contact was problematic, or to its impact on the child, although serious/persistent conflict with the carer was more likely (but not statistically significant). However, anticipated problems *were* significantly associated with whether maternal contact ceased altogether, or followed a negative trajectory. Interestingly, this was not the case with fathers, although there was a trend in this direction. Differences between the groups were also apparent in relation to the impact on the child and conflict with the carer, but the only statistically significant difference was the extent to which contact was problematic.

Even where problems did materialise in cases where there had been specific concerns about contact, they were not necessarily the same problems as had been anticipated. For instance, in one case, the concerns were that the level of contact had been set too high, given that rehabilitation was not planned. The difficulties which actually occurred arose from the suspension of contact while the child underwent therapy for sexual abuse. Mother then made repeated (successful) court applications to get contact reinstated and increased in the face of hostility from the carer. Father dropped out of contact.

There were 14 cases (11 concerning maternal contact and 3 paternal) in which the specific concerns did prove partly or wholly justified. Typically, these related to conflict between carers and parents (11 cases), although in one case the problems were only temporary. In this case, the anxieties centred on the volatile relationship between the mother and maternal grandmother. In the event, as the researcher summarised in the file notes:

For the first three months mother made complaints about grand-mother's care; said she was angry with grandmother and wouldn't have contact at all. However, things settled down and after that a stable contact pattern did appear to become established.

For four children (two placements) there were worries that the parent with contact would allow the child to see the other (abusive) parent. Although this did not happen, in each case the contact parent allowed telephone contact. In two cases, concerns about the ability of carers to control the contact were borne out to some extent. In the first, a mother was allowed telephone contact instead of just supervised contact, and in another, the mother moved in with the carer (with the knowledge of Social Services) but was allowed to spend time with the child unsupervised, which had not been agreed.

In what was probably the most problematic case in the sample as far as contact was concerned, there had been multiple concerns: about mother's attitude to contact, her potential for disrupting the placement given her previous behaviour while the child was in foster care, the likelihood of conflict with the carer and her negative attitude to the child. The carer described the difficulties thus:

The whole idea of me having Maisie was that [mother] thought she would be able to come down whenever she wanted. All the problems started when I began to say no ... [And] when she came down, we weren't doing things as she wanted it. She would start and complain and make a fuss ... she started to use foul language in my house. She took Maisie out and she shouldn't. I had to call the police ... So they said she'd have to have supervised contact, which was once a month at the children's place, and every time she'd walk in and look at Maisie and say 'Isn't she black, isn't she ugly?' ... even though she was a baby at the time. She did this in front of the social workers so they could see what was happening . . . As Maisie got older, I would dress her up and encourage [her] that she was going to see her mother, but we'd wait and we'd wait, and [the social worker] had come all the way from [X] as well. Maisie was three or four, right until she was five. Mother just doesn't turn up. I had built it up with Maisie, this is your mother you know.

These difficulties resulted in multiple court applications by both the carer and mother and, eventually, the termination of contact and a ban on the mother making any further applications for five years.

One factor which might be expected to increase the likelihood of problematic contact, and in particular, conflict between parents and carers, is whether, by the end of proceedings, parents had come to accept the placement and/or the arrangements for contact. However, again there appeared to be no consistent link, with the problematic contact being more likely to arise in cases where parents at least *appeared* to accept the arrangements. Whether they actually did so, of course, is another matter. In the case described above, Maisie's mother had seemed to be in agreement with the placement which, as the carer pointed out, she had actually suggested in the first place.

Problems were not generally anticipated over sibling or extended family contact and there was generally little information about this. However, difficulties over sibling contact did materialise in four of the five cases in which they were predicted.

To what extent were the courts used to resolve contact issues?

In total, there were known to be further court proceedings over contact in 20 cases. Although most of these concerned cases where contact had been problematic (14, including 11 cases where problems had been serious or persistent), they only amount to one-third of all cases with contact difficulties. So there was no general rush back to court.

Table 9.10
Contact applications

| Outcome | Applicant | | | | | | | |
| | Mother | | Father | | Carer | | Social Services | |
	No.	%	No.	%	No.	%	No.	%
Successful	5	45	1	20	4	100	3	100
Unsuccessful	4	36	3	60	0	0	0	0
Withdrawn	0	0	1	20	0	0	0	0
(N=)	(11)		(5)		(4)		(3)	
Missing data	(2)		(0)		(0)		(0)	

In most instances (13), parents were the sole applicants, although in three cases it was Social Services (relating to one sibling group), and in three, it was the carers. In one case, there were applications (on more than one occasion) by both mother and the carer. In all, 14 parents made applications (11 mothers and five fathers) as did four carers, with Social Services being responsible for three (Table 9.10).

Applications by carers and Social Services invariably succeeded (Table 9.10). Six of these allowed face-to-face contact to be terminated, while in two the aim was to attempt to regularise mother's contact, which had become increasingly sporadic and unannounced. Mothers were successful with five applications, all to increase the amount of contact or to be allowed unsupervised contact. Three of their four unsuccessful applications were, respectively, to restore contact to its original weekly frequency after the carers had found it impossible to cope with this; to increase the frequency of contact and to be permitted staying in contact. There was only one case which concerned the restoration of contact (the carer stopped contact after the contact supervisor reported negative effects on the child). Unfortunately, the outcome of this application is not known.

Fathers were typically unsuccessful or did not pursue their application. Rather than reflecting any bias against fathers, however, this was probably due to the fact that all the unsuccessful applications were to obtain contact which had not been envisaged in the care plan. The successful application, in contrast, was to permit staying in contact.

Lost contact

Why did parental contact cease?

As noted earlier in this chapter, by the end of the care proceedings (and usually long before), at least one parent (typically the father) was either dead or had disappeared from the lives of 50 children. In a further 14, the court terminated contact. In the course of the kinship placement at least 14 children (12%) stopped having face-to-face contact with their mothers and 21 (41%) with their fathers. What explains this? In particular, what explains the fact that of the children who had remained in their placement continuously, and who had live parents, 11 (23%) were no longer seeing their mothers and 12 (40%) their fathers?

The loss of maternal contact

Maternal contact was terminated by court order for four children in (two) continuing placements. One carer stopped contact and one child (aged seven) refused to carry on seeing her mother who had been very unreliable about the contact arrangements and when she did turn up was often clearly under the influence of drugs. In four of the remaining cases, contact either never got established after the care proceedings (two children) or rapidly ceased. There was only one case in which contact slowly faded away.

Although the numbers in which maternal contact did cease were small, a number of factors did seem to be linked with discontinuation, namely: the child being placed with the paternal side of the family; contact being seriously conflictual or perceived to have an entirely negative effect on the child; the child being a boy; and the mother not having been the main carer prior to proceedings (Appendix F Table F12). The child's age made no difference.

The loss of paternal contact

The fathers who lost contact in continuing placements largely seem to have just drifted out of their children's lives. None of them were prevented from seeing their children by court order, and although one child did tell her father she did not want to see him again, this was only after he had not been in touch for some time. Nor was it associated with conflict with the carers. However, parental separation did seem to be a key factor, in total, affecting seven cases where fathers lost contact. One father dropped out of contact when his mother died – the grandparents used to have the child for the day and father would see the child at their house. Other possible factors include the child's gender, with boys seeming to be more vulnerable to loss of paternal contact, the child being less than five at the end of proceedings and placement with the other side of the family (Appendix F Table F13). As with mothers, in some cases contact either never seems to have been established after the court proceedings ended (two), or it started to fade very quickly (three).

Were children adversely affected by the loss of contact?

None of our various sources of data indicate that more than a very few children were overtly suffering because of their lack of contact with their parents. The social workers interviewed, for instance, described one child as 'hurt' and another as 'angry'. Ten were described as either indifferent, accepting or, just occasionally, curious. Moreover, eight children were said to see the lack of contact as a positive thing.

He says he doesn't want to see [his father] until he's older, to punch him.

The last [contact] was very traumatic. 'Mother' and 'fear' were 'interwoven' into her thoughts, she was worried about what she might do. The emotional demands on her – she just wants to be left alone.

He said he would never forget how she treated him – why would he want to see her? She hurt him so much – a terrible trauma.

Fifteen of the carers we interviewed were looking after children who had lost contact with their mothers (17 children). Only three of these children were said to be still upset by this, although some had been in the past. Eight were considered to be largely indifferent and five to be positively opposed or relieved that contact had ceased:

He is perturbed about it. He goes through phases. He's curious really.

When Charlie was in foster care and her contact was so erratic, he was a bit down about it that she'd let him down again. Now he's OK about it, he's never mentioned it. I said I'd never stop you from seeing your mum. I said if you want to send a card you do it. He just doesn't want to see her.

Kylie doesn't want to see her at all – she was terrified that if mother sees her she is going to try and take her away. Everything started to improve once she was told mother couldn't take her to court for the next five years . . .

Of the five children we interviewed who were not having any maternal contact, only one seemed to be bothered about this, holding up the red card when asked about contact (Chapter 8). As Aldgate and McIntosh (2006) also report, none expressed any wish to see their absent mothers.

Children were more likely to express a wish to see their absent fathers (Chapter 8). This again chimes with Aldgate and McIntosh's findings. This was also a somewhat stronger theme in the interviews with carers, most of whom were looking after children (25 in all) without paternal contact.

The social worker said, 'Is there anything you'd like me to do?' and she said, 'Yes I'd like you to find my father'. She's always wanted to know who her father is, of him, and that he's not as terrible as the mother.

Tim went through a spell at 13 years old wanting to know about his dad. We tried to find out things through his maternal grandfather. Then, when Tim was about 15 years old, he said my dad must know from people that I exist and it wouldn't be that hard to find out about me and he hasn't done that, so I'm not going looking for him.

One carer had responded to the child's longing to know her father by tracking him down. Unfortunately, this did not work out and after a while the child refused to see him again.

The dominant themes, however, remained either indifference, often where children had never known their fathers, or positive hostility:

Bea doesn't know him and Chris never raises the subject, I don't think he's bothered, probably doesn't want to see him if the truth is known. They've seen the bloke that lives with their mother and I don't think they're impressed with him.

She doesn't talk about him. He sent her a letter asking her to reply – she hasn't. She's of an age where she can decide.

He doesn't want it. He doesn't like his Dad

Facilitating contact

How committed were carers to contact?

The literature on contact after parental separation or divorce suggests that a key factor in whether contact happens or is a positive experience for the child is whether the person the child lives with not only accepts but positively facilitates contact (Hunt, 2003b). Much of the research on kinship care comments on the high level of commitment carers show towards the maintenance and promotion of contact and their persistence in the face of difficulties (Hunt, 2003a). There were examples in this study, too, of carers clearly acknowledging children's needs for contact, encouraging parents to stay in touch, and helping them make contact a positive experience for the child:

He's hard work. If I knew right at the beginning the sort of commitment I was going to have to make with Dad if he was going to have to have contact . . . Lily wants to know him but she says he's boring. I have to tell him everything. Last year I had to tell him, quite severely, to take her out on a day trip over the summer holidays. Do something with her. It took me three attempts, going through the granddad as well. I have to literally tell him to take her to the pictures, or something else. He hasn't got much commonsense. When they first started seeing each other, well even after a year, they were just standing there looking at each other. I got games out. I had to come down from bathing the little one and tell him what to do. It was embarrassing telling another adult how to play with their child . . . And Lily needs guiding. She was trying to say to dad, can you do this or that but he wasn't picking up the signals. Once I trained him and got him to understand her, it got better. So then I started moving him out of the house, getting him to take her to the park in the summer, then over the last year and a half I've insisted that he picks her up and takes her out. Basically, that's turned him into a McDonald Dad. They do go up to his place and watch videos occasionally. But it's still quite strained.

It was also clear that some carers were having to put their own feelings aside for the child's sake:

Every two months we go to London as mother lives in [X, some distance away] and we do an activity together, cinema, park, all kinds of things. We do them together. Mother has no sense so I just see to it that things are safe and not extreme. Also, she comes to reviews twice a year and I have to put her up when she comes. Notice I said 'have to' as I don't really like it to be so. Mother takes me for granted, slips back into the family. I still can't do it [because of the history] but she can.

Most of the social workers interviewed (12) also reported carers to have a supportive and encouraging attitude to contact, even when there were, or had been difficulties:

She was always open and wanted it to happen. Initially, she didn't know how to make it happen.

The grandparents had a difficult relationship with mother at the start because of the injuries. By 2004 it was much improved, grandmother felt contact should go on, they had a better relationship.

Even though it's difficult for them they encourage it, especially if [the eldest child] is reluctant.

She was historically unhappy about [father's contact] and had a difficult relationship with paternal grandmother. Now she fully encourages father's contact.

On the basis of our interviews with carers, however, we could not say that the active promotion of contact, rather than its tolerance, was a significant theme. In some instances, it seemed that carers were adopting a fairly passive approach (if the parent got in touch; if the child asked for contact):

I'd do anything to keep the peace. That's all I can say. Is it of benefit to Patsy? I suppose so. It's up to her to decide and she keeps on seeing her.

There are no regular, fixed contact arrangements. I've left it flexible because I don't feel I should bully them into going every other weekend. Most of the time mother ignores them and leaves us alone. They go when they feel ready to see her and I think that suits everybody. We don't ever say you can't go and see your mum. We don't encourage it but we don't stop them. If they want to go and see their mum they can, but if and when they want to.

This theme of apparent passivity was echoed in the social worker interviews in relation to four children. For example:

She's OK [about contact]. She will go with what the child wants.

She was happy if the child was happy [about it].

Active hostility to contact seemed to be fairly rare. However, concerns were noted in 11 case files. For instance:

Paternal grandparents do not want mother to see the child and don't think contact is in the child's best interests. (Mother's contact stopped within a month of the care proceedings.)

The maternal grandparents do not want the child to have contact with father because they feel he was the main instigator of the claims of sexual abuse (against them). (Sporadic contact continued for several years, then ceased.)

The child can be used as a pawn and contact withdrawn if a falling out with mother occurs. (Contact continuing.)

The social workers interviewed identified four cases where carers' attitudes could still be problematic. In the worst, the social worker told us:

It depends on the current situation – [her attitude] can be negative if the relationship is not good with mother at that point. Relationships can be volatile. They can slag each other off. [The carer] can be very blaming.

Finally, our interviews with carers also revealed some negative or at least ambivalent attitudes:

I don't think either had a right to see him because of what happened.

I can't understand the mother and why she couldn't look after the children. I tolerate her. I can't stand their father, I hated him and I still do.

I'd like to say no [it's not of benefit to child] but he does want to see her [mother]. The longer he doesn't see her the better he is.

Did carers receive the help they needed with contact?

Was the right legal framework in place?

As mentioned earlier, where parental contact was envisaged, it was relatively uncommon for this to be regulated by a contact order (21 of 98 children). However, since in most of the remaining cases (65) either a care or supervision order was in place, it might reasonably be considered that the power of the law, and more particularly the local authority, was there in the background, at least in the short term. There were only 12 cases, all residence orders without additional orders, where everything was dependent on the parents and carers managing agreed arrangements.

Table 9.11
Problematic contact by legal orders made in care proceedings

| | Problematic contact | | | | | | |
| | Serious/ persistent | | Some problems | | No problems | | |
	No.	%	No	%	No	%	(N=)
Contact order	7	39	6	33	5	28	(18)
Care order only	22	42	22	42	9	17	(53)
Residence and supervision orders	1	9	1	9	9	82	(11)
Residence order only	1	14	4	57	2	29	(7)

In general, it would appear that the decisions made at the end of the care proceedings about the appropriate form of legal protection for contact were broadly correct in the sense that those with the least legal protection were also least likely to experience serious or persistent problems with contact (Table 9.11). Moreover, in the two cases where contact was difficult for children, there is no reason to think that the specific problems would have been affected by a more powerful order. However, the very low incidence of problems in cases where supervision orders were made is striking, given that, in at least 11 cases, one of the reasons for making the order was anticipated difficulties with contact.

Were the right services provided?

Contact-related services were recorded in less than half the cases where contact was expected to take place. The most common form of assistance (37 cases) was the provision of staff time, either in the form of supervising contact or taking children to contact, followed by the provision of a neutral venue (29). Transport was provided in 24 cases and financial assistance with the costs of contact in 21. In nine cases, other forms of support were given. It is possible, of course, that less tangible forms of assistance, such as advice or relationship help were given, but not identified because they were just regarded as part of the relationship with the social worker. Nonetheless, it has to be pointed out that only four carers mentioned help of this nature.

In view of this, and given the extent of the problems over contact in our sample, we had expected to find, as some other researchers have reported, carers expressing the need for help with contact and relationships with parents (Russell, 1995; Laws, 2001; Richards, 2001). We were therefore surprised that, when asked what services might have been helpful, only one set of carers interviewed highlighted assistance with contact or with relationships with parents, and they were only referring to the early days of the placement:

> Carer 1: *It was difficult to arrange. Father was a violent person. We didn't really have much guidance at the time.*

> Carer 2: *We didn't have any guidance. Social Services more or less left it to us. We were telling Social Services what we were doing, not them telling us what we should be doing.*

Perhaps by the time of interview, where placements had been going for several years, carers had simply learned to cope on their own.

Summary

The majority of children were expected to have face-to-face contact with at least one parent. It was rare for contact to be terminated, but many children had already lost contact with a parent, typically a father, by the time the proceedings ended. Most children were also expected to retain contact with one or more siblings (where they had previously lived together) although, in respect of children under five, the proportion in touch with siblings was smaller in the kin-placed group.

At least one parent did stay in touch in most cases. However, very few children had contact with both parents and fathers were less likely to be in contact than mothers, even where contact had been envisaged. All children retained contact with at least one sibling with whom they had previously lived. Many children were also in touch with members of their extended families outside the care household. However, this was typically on the carer's side of the family; it was unusual for children to have contact with both sides.

Parental contact tended to diminish over time, and even where it continued, could become sporadic or less frequent. Such negative trajectories affected both maternal and paternal contact, though it was more common in the latter. Positive contact trajectories were rare.

Parental contact was more likely when children were placed with maternal relatives. A parent was more likely to stay in touch when the child was placed with their side of the family.

There was little evidence that parental contact was putting children at risk and none that they had actually been harmed.

Less than a third of cases had no problems at all with either child contact or the associated adult relationships. Problematic contact, however, was common, and in a substantial minority of cases, contact appeared to be entirely negative for the child. Maternal contact tended to be more difficult than paternal, particularly where children were placed with the paternal side of the family. In most cases where difficulties were evident, contact, particularly maternal contact, continued.

At the time of the care proceedings, difficulties over contact had been anticipated in many cases. However, in general, these predictions did not prove particularly accurate. Anticipated contact difficulties were associated with contact cessation or a negative maternal contact trajectory. In those cases where parental contact problems were accurately predicted, there tended to be difficulties relating primarily to adult relationships. There appeared to be no link between contact problems and whether parents had accepted the placement and/or the contact arrangements.

Only a minority of families went back to court to try to resolve difficulties over contact.

Fathers who lost contact seem to have just drifted out of the children's lives, often after they had separated from the mother. While some mothers did the same, there were more cases in which contact was terminated by the carer, the child, or the court.

There was little evidence that children were overtly suffering from the loss of contact.

While some carers were clearly making great efforts to facilitate contact, many seemed to be quite passive, leaving it up to the child or the parent. Active hostility, however, was quite unusual.

Less than half the cases where face-to-face parental contact was envisaged appear to have had any form of assistance with contact. However, very few carers indicated that they would have welcomed such help.

10 Conclusions

This project examined the outcomes of 113 kinship placements made following care proceedings which concluded between 1995 and 2001. For comparative purposes, we also collected data on 31 children, aged under five at the end of the proceedings, but placed with carers who were not members of their extended family or social network.

Our outcome measures – placement stability, quality, relationship with carer and child well-being – were derived from Objective 1 of the Quality Protects programme – secure attachment to safe and effective carers for the duration of childhood. We have also looked at decision-making, contact issues, support for placements and, importantly, the views of children and kinship carers. In this concluding chapter, we first look at the implications of key specific findings for policy and practice relating to kinship care and then, more broadly, consider what needs to happen if this form of care is to be used most effectively in the interests of children.

Key findings and their implications for policy and practice

Key point 1: There is scope for a more systematic exploration of the kinship option for all children prior to proceedings. This could lead to more/earlier placements.

- Only a third of the kin placements in our study were instigated by social workers. While this is considerably higher than the four per cent reported by Farmer and Moyers (2008), it still indicates a fairly reactive approach.
- Some children could have been placed earlier if there had been a thorough investigation of the potential for care within the extended family.
- Although placements which were not instigated by the carers did have poorer outcomes in terms of relationships, this was not invariably the case; sometimes the outcome was good even when children scarcely knew their future carers. This, therefore, cannot be used as a justification for a reactive approach.

- In 33 per cent of the cases where children were placed with non-kin carers there was no evidence that a kinship placement had been considered, while in a further 25 per cent, although relatives were identified, they were never fully assessed.
- The non-kin sample data also showed, however, that no matter how wide the net may be cast, in many families there does not appear to be a "bottomless pit" of willing and available relatives to care.
- There appears to have been little exploration of the kinship option before proceedings were instigated.
- Even in the cases where children were placed with kin who had been heavily involved with the child, and may even have reported their concerns to the local authority, the carers were rarely involved in the formal local authority decision-making processes.

Practice and policy messages from Key point 1

- Pre-proceedings "mapping" of significant relatives needs to be actively carried out for all children at risk of care, including their history of involvement with the child. Social workers need to contact family members, particularly those who have had direct involvement in the child's care prior to any move of the child to non-kin foster care. We welcomed the proposal in the Green Paper (DfES, 2006a[91]) that local authorities should be required to prepare a care plan at the outset of proceedings, and to explain why kinship care is not considered appropriate. This, together with the new duty in the Adoption and Children Act 2002 to consider relatives when decisions are being taken about adoption, should encourage the exploration of kinship care at an early stage.
- In addition, we wonder whether there is an argument for the local authority having a duty/right to approach relevant family members in advance of court action, if necessary without parental permission. A recent court decision[92] indicates that the courts are likely to take a

---

[91] Now also contained in the White Paper, *Care Matters: Time for Change* (DfES, 2007)

[92] *Birmingham City Council v S and Others* [2006] EWHC 3065 (Fam) – father and grandparents.

robust stance on this but the child in question was already subject to care proceedings.

- Records should be kept of efforts made to keep the child in the extended family, e.g. relevant assessment reports upon which decisions not to place are made should be easily accessible on files and should form part of the bundle of documents required by panels to endorse a care plan for permanent placement with non-kin. Such records should be retained to explain to the child in adulthood why they were not able to remain within their birth family. It needs to be noted in this context that case law has established that any family member putting themselves forward to care for a child needs to be properly assessed, even where that person is living abroad.[93]

- Social workers should be provided with training to enable them to examine their own values, attitudes and belief systems and how these impact on their practice decisions.

- The early processes of involvement of the child's extended family need to be further researched to understand better how decisions are made by local authorities at this critical time.

- We welcome the government's intention (DfES, 2007) to promote the use of family group conferences.

- We need to be realistic, however, about the extent to which kinship care can be extended. It is fanciful to assume that there are potential relative carers for every child. The successful expansion of kinship care may depend more on encouraging and supporting those relatives who already have shown some interest in and potential to care for the child than on recruiting extended family members who have had little or no involvement.

---

[93] See *Re J* 2003 FLR 114: Test for leave for residence order application – 59-year-old grandmother applied for leave, local authority said she was too old and wanted closed adoption. Grandmother refused party status by the court but appealed. Appeal upheld; court said judge needed full enquiry of the grandmother before dismissing her application, citing Human Rights Act. Also *Re A* (A child) Court of Appeal held that the judge had gone beyond the bounds of his discretion by denying the child the possibility of placement with his birth family on the basis of a six-hour visit by the social worker to Turkey. International Social Services was instructed to carry out a full assessment.

Key point 2: Kinship care can deliver Quality Protects Objective 1 for many children but it does not work for all.

- In terms of placement stability, the majority of placements (72%) were either continuing and stable (52%); terminated but had lasted as long as needed (7%); or continuing even though they appeared to be vulnerable (16%). Although 28 per cent had terminated prematurely, half the children concerned were retained within their family network, going to live with either a parent or other relatives.

- Seventy-six per cent of children had positive relationships with their carers. Indeed, even where placements had terminated prematurely, many carers still had quite positive and supportive relationships with the children they had cared for. All the children interviewed displayed an overwhelming sense of safety in the placement, reliance and trust in the kinship carer and (almost all) a close relationship with their carer.

- Most placements were safe. Only 10 per cent of placements (11) raised child protection issues, despite quite high levels of anxiety about this at the time of the care proceedings. Only three of the 11 cases involved actual abuse and one of these was not by the carer. However, there was one very serious case of sexual abuse. The most common problem (7 cases) was neglect.

- Many placements did raise some quality issues, with only 36 per cent being free of any concerns. However, only 20 per cent of placements had major concerns.

- Most children were doing well or reasonably well. For 47 per cent of children there were no concerns in any dimension of well-being and only 19 per cent had difficulties in three or more dimensions.

- Overall, the most pessimistic interpretation of the findings (our worst case scenario) indicates that only 23 per cent of placements scored positively on all outcome measures and 17 per cent on none. A more generous interpretation (our *best case scenario*) gives 58 per cent scoring positively on all measures and only 5 per cent positively on none.

These findings are encouraging, given that our kin-placed children had been exposed to many adversities pre-placement and their life chances were already seriously compromised. Indeed, the exposure to adversity for our under-five kin-placed children was the same as for our sample of under-fives placed with non-kin, dispelling the myth that it is the less damaged children who go into kinship care.

Practice and policy messages from Key point 2

- Kinship care is a viable option which should be promoted. We welcome its endorsement in *Care Matters* (DfES, 2006a) and *Care Matters: Time for Change* (DfES, 2007)
- It is not a panacea, however, to be used indiscriminately. Even in our *best case scenario*, only 58 per cent of placements met each element in Quality Protects Objective 1 and there was a core group of children (between 5% and 17%) whose placements did not score positively on any measure.
- Careful assessment is needed of the capacity of potential carers to meet the needs of children who have already experienced adverse life circumstances and the supports which will be necessary to enable them to do so most effectively.

Key point 3: Better or poorer outcomes are not solely dependent on individual circumstances; it is possible to identify some protective and risk factors.

- Eleven factors proved to have a statistically significant association with at least one of our outcome measures.
- Better outcomes were found where:
  - the child was young, had a low level of difficulties pre-placement, had lived with the carer on a full-time basis before, had not asked to live elsewhere;
  - the placement was with a single carer rather than a couple, the carer was a grandparent, there were no other children in the household other than the child's siblings, the placement was instigated by the carer.
  - there had been a pre-placement assessment, there had been a positive assessment of parenting capacity, and, counter-intuitively, there had been disagreement about the placement during the proceedings.

- The age of the child was a potent factor, being the only factor which was statistically significant across more than one outcome.
- The relationship between the child's age at the end of the proceedings and placement stability was marked: 44 per cent of placements of children over five did not last as long as needed compared with 11 per cent for the under-fives. Children in placements with positive ratings on all the outcome measures were younger at the end of proceedings (2.5 years) than those with only some positive ratings (4.9 years) or no positive ratings (9.3 years).
- Age itself was, in turn, associated with the child's level of exposure to prior adversities, pre-placement emotional and behavioural difficulties, and length of Social Services involvement with the family prior to the start of proceedings, although none of these in themselves were predictive of outcome.

Practice and policy messages from Key point 3

- The fact that two of the statistically significant factors related to assessment again emphasises the importance of this.
- The remaining factors which proved significant could be useful to practitioners in identifying placements which are potentially more vulnerable and likely to need more support.
- It may be useful to systematically screen for the child's level of difficulties using a tool such as the Strengths and Difficulties Questionnaire to provide early knowledge of the child's emotional and behavioural problems, and thus identify the placements most likely to need assistance.
- Placements of very young children appear to work out well. However, as in other forms of substitute care, the risk of poorer outcomes increases with age at placement. It should be assumed that these placements, *prima facie*, will need ongoing support.
- There is a need for disruption meetings where placements have terminated so that lessons can be learned from breakdowns.
- Research needs to be undertaken on placement breakdowns.

Key point 4: Assessment is important but problematic.

- Placements where some kind of assessment had been carried out prior to the placement of the child were more likely to be stable.
- The assessed parenting capacity of the kinship carers at the time of proceedings was associated with parenting capacity during placement and was an important predictor of placement quality.
- Professionals, however, were poor at predicting future concerns. Problems which had been anticipated rarely materialised; problems which arose had rarely been flagged.
- There is a conflict between the need to avoid children going into non-kin care and the need to complete some form of assessment prior to placement.
- Carers generally accepted the need for assessment but some were critical of the way it had been handled and many found it stressful.

Practice and policy messages from Key point 4

- A balance has to be struck between the respective values of pre-placement assessment and early placement with kin. A two-stage assessment process could be a way forward. Early rapid viability assessments could precede the decision to place the child. Subsequent exploration, with the carer, of the wider issues of caring should then follow. We would emphasise, however, that the initial assessment would need to be rapid, since otherwise any gains would be out-weighed by the potential damage to the child of first being placed with non-kin. This would have considerable resource implications.
- The importance of assessment has implications in terms of the practice experience and knowledge base of those professionals carrying out this task. The centrality of the assessment of parenting capacity suggests that family placement workers should be involved in the assessment process. However, there is a strong professional consensus that assessing kinship carers is different from assessing non-kin carers. This argues for assessments to be carried out by specialist kinship workers, as is increasingly the case in many local authorities.
- Whoever is to carry out the assessment needs access to appropriate tools, tailored to this form of care, and to training. We therefore

support the work the relevant government departments have already undertaken on this and urge that further work be expedited.

- Ways to make the assessment process less stressful for and more useful to carers need to be considered. The proposed two-stage process could help, in that once the carers are assured that the child will be placed with them they may feel more able to participate in a process which is then more about identifying possible vulnerabilities and working out ways of minimising their effect.

- Kinship carers may need to be helped to think through the implications of caring for themselves, the child and the family. Since they may be reluctant to do this with someone from an agency with decision-making power, the use of experienced kinship carers as mentors/ supporters should be considered.

- The relative inaccuracy of professional predictions about specific concerns in cases where placements were made raises questions about whether there are similar levels of error in cases where placements are rejected. This emphasises the need for evidence-based decisions rather than "professional hunches" as to what the difficulties will be.

- Assessment may not lead to more kinship carers being accepted or rejected but it should lead to better identification of their support and training needs. Kinship carers therefore would not only be more able to deal with difficult children but also have a better experience themselves as carers.

Key point 5: The support needs of kinship placements need to be more adequately addressed.

- Finance was an issue for many carers, with only just over a third having managed without any difficulty and several suffering financial strain. Carers with children on residence orders were more vulnerable to such difficulties. Carers had inconsistent experiences: the most fortunate receiving grants for start-up costs, extensions and special expenses as well as regular allowances; others receiving very little. Some children were remaining on care orders purely for financial reasons.

- Children in kinship placements have high levels of need, similar to children in non-kin placements, but their carers may be less well-equipped to meet those needs than non-kin adopters or foster carers. There was evidence of service gaps in many cases even while Social Services was still involved. In some cases it seemed likely that better provision might have prevented placements from terminating prematurely.

- Difficulties could arise in placements which had been going well and Social Services involvement had ceased. However, carers did not always know how to make contact if they needed help and some would be reluctant to do so.
- Placements made with carers living outside the placing authority appear to be particularly poorly served in terms of support.

Practice and policy messages from Key point 5

- There is an urgent need to ensure that kinship carers have adequate financial and material help. This would be most appropriately dealt with by the provision of a national carer's benefit, available as of right.
- Local authorities must improve the support available to kinship placements, either by providing it themselves, or, which might be more acceptable to some carers, through contracting out the service, as is already done in at least one authority (DfES, 2007). If the proposal that some work could be contracted out to "firms" of social workers working outside the local authority is proceeded with (DfES, 2006a), kinship care support would be a prime contender.
- When cases are closed, carers need to be given the name of a person who can be contacted in case of difficulty and informed when there is a change of personnel.
- Arrangements need to be made to ensure that out-of-authority placements receive proper local support. This might involve the placing authority spot-purchasing support and training packages.

Key point 6: Kinship care facilitates the maintenance of some family links and contact is usually safe but it is often difficult.

- Most of the children were in touch with at least one parent, usually their mother. Many also had good links with siblings and extended families. However, few children maintained contact with both parents or with both sides of the extended family.

- Contact typically followed a negative trajectory, diminishing over time.
- Problematic contact, especially with mothers, was common and, in a substantial minority of cases, contact appeared to be entirely negative for the child.
- Few carers reported having had any professional assistance with contact and it was unusual for contact difficulties to be returned to court. Carers sometimes seemed to be adopting a rather passive attitude to contact, rather than actively encouraging it.

Practice and policy messages from Key point 6

- It should not be assumed that because the child is in an extended family placement the family can manage the contact arrangements smoothly themselves.
- There needs to be more focus on contact planning at the assessment stage and perhaps more use of formal written agreements.
- Carers need access to sources of support, perhaps independent from the local authority, which they can tap into when difficulties do arise. They may also need help in actively facilitating contact.
- Consideration needs to be given to terminating or controlling contact which is actively damaging to the child.

Developing kinship care in the interests of children

Our conclusions from this project can be simply stated: kinship care can be a positive option for many children but it is not straightforward and requires careful assessment and adequate support. Therefore, if the full potential of kinship care is to be realised, there must be clear policies at both central and local government level, appropriate infrastructures must be developed, and adequate resources must be provided.

This call for action is not new but echoes the conclusions of many other commentators, and researchers on kinship care (see, for example, the contributors in Broad, 2001 and Greeff, 1999; Richards and Tapsfield, 2003; Broad 2004; Broad and Skinner, 2005; Sinclair *et al*, 2007; Farmer and Moyers, 2008). The scoping paper which Hunt prepared for the Department of Health in 2001 concluded that:

What appears to be needed is a policy which reinforces the Children Act objectives of keeping children within their extended families wherever this is in their interests but acknowledges the dilemmas and difficulties which the policy entails and enables it to be delivered to the benefit of children and their carers. It cannot be said that such a policy framework is currently in place (Hunt, 2003a, page 84.)

That paper identified a number of action points for central government, including: a cross-government initiative; addressing the issue of financial support; developing a framework for service provision; collecting information on the whole population of children living with relatives; commissioning and disseminating research. At a local level, policies should be developed on an inter-department and inter-agency basis. There was a need for better information, allocation of responsibilities for developing this area of work and creative thinking about service delivery. Social workers needed training in this challenging practice area. Above all, effective policies and practices had to grow out of valuing what kinship carers do, appreciating their difficulties and understanding that this form of care is unique and should not be forced into existing structures and practices.

Apart from the commissioning of research, however, little tangible in the way of action emerged, despite the sustained interest of individual civil servants. Four years later, Hunt was invited, along with Professor Elaine Farmer, to talk about kinship care to officials from a number of relevant departments. The meeting was very well attended and there appeared to be enthusiasm and a determination to move forward, in a co-ordinated way, on the policy front. Again, however, while much may have been going on in the background, nothing concrete materialised. At the point the draft report on this study was being finalised for submission to the DfES, the Green Paper *Care Matters* (DfES, 2007) was published. As reported in Chapter 1, while kinship care did secure a space (unlike in the earlier paper *Every Child Matters* (DfES, 2003)), it was fairly minimal and it seemed that this form of care might continue to be marginalised. Accordingly, our report, submitted in January 2007, concluded by repeating what Hunt had earlier set out as a strategy for kinship care (published in Hunt, 2006).

Developing a strategy for kinship care
Kinship care needs to become much more high profile and move up the agenda of government policy.

Three overall goals are suggested as a starting point for developing a strategy on kinship care:
* *Every child who cannot be cared for by birth parents has the opportunity to be cared for safely and effectively within their family/social network;*
* *Outcomes for all children cared for by relatives or friends are as good as possible/compare well with children in non-related care;*
* *Systems for dealing with all forms of family and friends care are transparent, family-friendly, experienced as fair and supportive and minimally intrusive.*

These could be supplemented by a set of objectives:
* *National/local policy covers the spectrum of kinship care arrangements;*
* *Kinship care is recognised/responded to as unique, in terms of opportunities and challenges;*
* *Policy and practice is evidence-based and clear-sighted, not clouded by prejudice, romanticism or determined primarily by budgetary considerations;*
* *Services and supports are adequate, appropriate, needs-led; encompass the whole family; contain an element of user choice; are based on participation and partnership; and are community-based.*

Establishing a dedicated working group or task force would . . . seem to be a productive first step, not least because it would give a clear message that kinship care is on the policy agenda. This needs to have cross-government membership because of the range of issues facing carers and its remit should cover all forms of kinship care, not just foster care. The task force should identify the issues to be addressed and establish a timescale and strategy for addressing them. It should, in particular, make recommendations for mapping the prevalence of different forms of kinship care across the country. Another clear priority would be addressing the financial issues.

Work needs to be done (either by the task force or the Department for Education and Skills) with relevant government departments to ensure their services are sensitised to kinship care; address issues relevant to their service; and are able to act as information and referral points for families. It is imperative to ensure that kinship care is included in central and local government thinking about family support and in the creation of new systems such as children's centres and extended schools.

Local authority departments with responsibility for children's services need to be given a stronger policy steer. There should be clear expectations about written policies and information for families; detailed operational guidance; and appropriate decision-making structures. Advice should highlight the need for services, staff training and support, reliable data across the range of arrangements, and sensitising and working with other agencies. Government should work towards developing detailed, dedicated guidance and, where necessary, regulations, for kinship care as a distinct form of care. This needs to cover assessment, standards, decision-making processes, support services, monitoring and finance.

There is also much that could be done in the way of facilitating local developments, for instance, by collecting and disseminating examples of innovative practice, evaluating existing schemes and setting up action research projects. An electronic national information network would enable practitioners to share experiences, problems and creative solutions. Kinship care needs to be included in social work training at both a basic and post-qualifying level and accessible training events need to be run across the country.

Finally, funding is needed for a dedicated programme of research. It is ironic that . . . the pro-kinship thrust of the Children Act was substantially due to unexpected research findings which pointed to the benefits of kinship care for children. Had this been treated as a fruitful starting point for further exploration and hypothesis testing, there might now be a solid basis for the development of policy. Instead, no major research was commissioned for more than a decade. Because the use of kinship care did not develop as rapidly as had been anticipated post-Children Act, we have not reached the position of jurisdictions such as the US, Australia and

New Zealand, where researchers have cautioned that the use of kinship care has far outstripped the knowledge base to support it. A number of studies have now been completed or are in progress. But they remain pitifully small and we are still over-reliant on studies carried out in other countries to help fill the many gaps which remain. Since kinship care takes many forms, with creative thinking it can be squeezed into research programmes in which it is not the central focus. In reality, it is more likely to be marginalised. Given that both adoption and residential care, neither of which affect substantial numbers of children, have had their own research programmes, the time is long overdue for kinship care to receive its fair share of research scrutiny.

Back in 2001, Hunt's scoping paper concluded that, although the research evidence for the benefits of kinship care was not strong, there was no reason to question the Children Act philosophy that, wherever it was possible and in their interests, children needing substitute care should be placed with their extended families or social networks. It was not advisable to 'mark time' awaiting better 'proof'. Action was needed now.

As reported in Chapter 1, some progress has been made and there is now stronger research evidence on some aspects of the subject. It is to be hoped that the 'policy framework for kinship care' promised in the White Paper, *Care Matters: Time for change* (DfES, 2007), and the Children and Young Persons' Bill going through Parliament means that, at last, kinship care is to get the more concentrated attention it so clearly needs and deserves.

References

Adamson, G. (1969) *When Auntie or Grannie is Mum*, Gabriola Island, Canada: New Society.

Aldgate, J. and Bradley, M. (1999) *Supporting Families Through Short-Term Fostering*, London: The Stationery Office.

Aldgate, J. and McIntosh, M. (2006) *Looking After the Family: A study of children looked after in kinship care in Scotland*, Edinburgh: The Scottish Executive.

Altshuler, S. J. (1998) 'Child well-being in kinship foster care: similar to, or different from, non-related foster care', *Children and Youth Services Review*, 20, pp. 369–388.

Altshuler, S. J. (1999) 'Children in kinship foster care speak out: "We think we're doing fine" ', *Child and Adolescent Social Work Journal*, 16, pp. 215–235.

Argent, H. (2005) *One of the Family: A handbook for kinship carers*, London: BAAF.

Beeman, S. and Boisen, L. (1999) 'Child welfare professionals' attitudes towards kinship foster care', *Child Welfare*, 78, pp. 315–357.

Bene, E. (1985) *Manual for the Family Relations Test*, 2nd edn. Slough: NFER.

Benedict, M., Zuravin, S. and Stallings, R. (1996) 'Adult functioning of children who lived in kin versus non-kin family foster homes', *Child Welfare*, 75, pp. 529–549.

Bergerhed, E. (1995) 'Kinship and network care in Sweden', in Thelen, H. (ed) *Foster Children in a Changing World: Documentation of the 1994 European IFCO conference*, Berlin: Arbeitskreis Zur Forderung Von Pflegekindern EV.

Berrick, J. D. (1997) 'Assessing quality of care in kinship and foster family care', *Family Relations*, 46, pp. 273–280.

Berrick, J. D., Barth, R. P. and Needell, B. (1994) 'A comparison of kinship foster homes and foster family homes: implications for kinship foster care as family preservation', *Children and Youth Services Review*, 16, pp. 33–63.

Berrick, J. D., Needell, B. and Barth, R. P. (1999) 'Kin as a family and child welfare resource: the child welfare workers perspective', in Hegar, R. L. and Scannapieco, M. (eds) *Kinship Foster Care: Policy, practice and research*, New York: Oxford University Press.

Berridge, D. (1997) *Foster Care: A research review*, London: The Stationery Office.

Berridge, D. and Cleaver, H. (1987) *Foster Home Breakdown*, Oxford: Blackwell.

Blaiklock, O. (2005) *Britain's Pensioner Parents: The quandry of parenting your grandchildren*, report from the office of Frank Field M.P.

Bourne, J. and Porter, D. (2001) *Life Changes when you take on Grandchildren: The experiences of a group for grandparent carers*, unpublished: Barnardo's Peepul Family Resource Centre, Croydon.

Brannen, J., Heptinstall, E. and Bhopal, K. (2000) *Connecting Children: Care and family life in later childhood*, London: Routledge.

Broad, B. (ed) (2001) *Kinship Care: The placement choice for children and young people*, Lyme Regis: Russell House Publishing.

Broad, B. (2004) 'Kinship care for children in the UK: messages from research, lessons for policy and practice', *European Journal of Social Work*, 7, pp. 211–227.

Broad, B., Hayes, R. and Rushforth, C. (2001) *Kith and Kin: Kinship care for vulnerable young people*, London: National Children's Bureau.

Broad, B. and Skinner, A. (2005) *Relative Benefits: Placing children in kinship care*, London: BAAF.

Burnette, D. (2000) 'Latino grandparents rearing grandchildren with special needs: effects on depressive symptomatology', *Journal of Gerontological Social Work*, 33, pp. 1–16.

Burton, L. M. (1992) 'Black grandparents rearing children of drug-addicted parents: stressors, outcomes and social service needs', *The Gerontologist*, 32, pp. 744–751.

Cabinet Office (2000) *Adoption: A new approach. A white paper*, London, Department of Health.

Calder, M. (1995) 'Child protection: balancing paternalism with partnership', *British Journal of Social Work*, 7, pp. 749–766.

Chamberlain, P., Price, J. M., Reid, J. B., Landsverk, J. A., Fisher, P. A. and Stoolmiller, M. (2006) 'Who disrupts from placement in foster and kinship care?' *Child Abuse and Neglect*, 30, pp. 409–424.

Chipman, R., Wells, S. J. and Johnson, M. A. (2002) 'The meaning of quality in kinship foster care: caregiver, child and worker perspectives', *Families in Society*, 83, pp. 5–6.

Chipungu, S. and Everett, J. (1998) *Children Placed in Foster Care with Relatives: A multi-state study*, U.S. Department of Health and Human Services.

Cimmarusti, R. A. (1999) 'Care-giver burden in kinship foster care', in Gleeson, J. P. and Hairston, C. F. (eds) *Kinship Care: Improving practice through research*, Washington DC: CWLA Press.

Cleaver, H. (2000) *Fostering Family Contact*, London: The Stationery Office.

Cox, C. B. (2000) 'Why grandchildren are going to and staying at grandmother's house and what happens when they get there', in Cox, C. B. (ed) *To Grandmother's House we go and Stay: Perspectives on custodial grandparents*, New York: Springer.

Crumbley, J. and Little, R. (1997) *Relatives Raising Children: An overview of kinship care*, Washington DC: CWLA Press.

Dannison, L. and Smith, A. (2003) *Can we Talk about Family? Commentary, Harvard family research project*, Available: www.gse.harvard.edu [Accessed 15.11.04]

Dench, G. and Ogg, J. (2002) *Grandparenting in Britain: A baseline study*, London: Institute of Community Studies.

Dench, G., Ogg, J. and Thomson, K. (1999) 'The role of grandparents', in Jowell, R., Curtice, J., Park, A. and Thomson, K. (eds) *British Social Attitudes, the 16th report*, Aldershot: Ashgate.

Department for Education and Skills (2003) *Every Child Matters*, London: Department for Education and Skills.

Department for Education and Skills (2005a) *Children Looked After at 31 March 2005*, London: Department for Education and Skills.

Department for Education and Skills (2005b) *Statistical First Release: Special educational needs in England, January 2005*, London: Department for Education and Skills.

Department for Education and Skills (2006a) *Care Matters*, London: Department for Education and Skills.

Department for Education and Skills (2006b) *Outcome Indicators for Looked After Children: Twelve months to 30 September 2005, England*, London: Department for Education and Skills.

Department for Education and Skills (2006c) *Statistical First Release: The level of highest qualification held by young people and adults in England 2005*, London: Department for Education and Skills.

Department for Education and Skills (2007) *Care Matters: Time for change*, London: Department for Education and Skills.

Department of Health (1989a) *The Care of Children: Principles and practice in regulations and guidance*, London: HMSO.

Department of Health (1989b) *Introduction to the Children Act: A new framework for the care and upbringing of children*, London: HMSO.

Department of Health (1991) *The Children Act 1989 Guidance and Regulations. Volume 3: Family placement*, London: HMSO.

Department of Health (1992) *Children Looked After at 31 March 1992*, London: Department of Health.

Department of Health (1995) *The Children Act 1989 Residence Orders Study: A study of the experiences of local authorities of public law residence orders*, London: Social Services Inspectorate.

Department of Health (1998) *The Quality Protects Programme: Transforming children's services (LAC (98) 28)*, London: Department of Health.

Department of Health (1999) *The Government's Objectives for Children's Social Services*, London: Department of Health.

Department of Health (2000) *Children Looked After at 31 March 2000*, London: Department of Health.

Department of Health (2001) *Children Act Report 2000*, London: Department of Health.

Department of Health (2002) *Friends and Family Care (Kinship Care): Current policy framework, issues and options. Discussion Paper*, London: Department of Health.

Department of Health/Welsh Office (1992) *Review of Adoption Law: Report to ministers of an interdepartmental working group*, Department of Health/Welsh Office.

Doolan, M., Nixon, P. and Lawrence, P. (2004) *Growing up in the Care of Relatives or Friends*, London: Family Rights Group.

Dowdell, E. B. (1995) 'Caregiver burden: grandmothers raising their high risk grandchildren', *Journal of Psychosocial Nursing*, 33, pp. 27–30.

Dubowitz, H., Feigelman, S. and Zuravin, S. (1993) 'A profile of kinship care', *Child Welfare*, 72, pp. 153–169.

Dubowitz, H., Feigelman, S., Zuravin, S., Tepper, V., Davison, N. and Lichenstein, R. (1992) 'The physical health of children in kinship care', *American Journal of Diseases of Children*, 146, pp. 603–610.

Dubowitz, H. and Sawyer, R. (1994) 'School behaviour of children in kinship care', *Child Abuse and Neglect*, 18, pp. 899–911.

Ehrle, G. M., Geen, R. and Clark, R. (2001) *Children Cared for by Relatives: Who are they and how are they faring?*, Washington DC: The Urban Institute.

Emick, M. and Hayslip, B. (1996) 'Custodial grand-parenting: new roles for middle-aged and older adults', *International Journal of Aging and Human Development*, 43, pp. 135–154.

Farmer, E. and Moyers, S. (2008) *Kinship Care: Fostering effective family and friends placements*, London: Jessica Kingsley.

Farmer, E., Moyers, S. and Lipscombe, J. (2004) *Fostering Adolescents*, London: Jessica Kingsley.

Farmer, E. and Parker, R. (1991) *Trials and Tribulations: Returning children from care to their families*, London: HMSO.

Farmer, E. and Pollock, S. (1998) *Sexually Abused and Abusing Children in Substitute Care*, Chichester: Wiley.

Finch, J. (1989) *Family Obligations and Social Change*, Cambridge: Polity Press.

Finzi, R., Cohen, O., Sapir, Y. and Weizman, A. (2000) 'Attachment styles in maltreated children: a comparative study', *Child Psychiatry and Human Development*, 31, pp. 113–128.

Flouri, E. (2005) *Fathering and Child Outcome*, Chichester: Wiley.

Flynn, R. (1999) *Kinship Foster Care: The forgotten face of kinship care: Making research count*, unpublished: University of Luton.

Flynn, R. (2001) 'Training materials for kinship foster care', in Broad, B. (ed) *Kinship Care: The placement choice for children and young people*, Lyme Regis: Russell House Publishing.

Flynn, R. (2002) 'Kinship foster care: research review', *Child and Family Social Work*, 7, pp. 311–322.

Fuller-Thomson, E., Minkler, M. and Driver, D. (1997) 'A profile of grandparents raising grandchildren in the United States', *The Gerontologist*, 37, pp. 406–411.

GAO (General Accounting Office) (1999) *Foster Care: Kinship care quality and permanency issues*, Washington DC: US General Accounting Office.

Gaudin, J. M. and Sutphen, R. (1993) 'Foster care vs extended family care for children of incarcerated mothers', *Journal of Offender Rehabilitation*, 19, pp. 129–147.

Gebel, T. J. (1996) 'Kinship care and non-relative family foster care: a comparison of caregiver attributes and attitudes', *Child Welfare*, 75, pp. 5–18.

Geen, R. (ed) (2003) *Kinship Care: Making the most of a valuable resource*, Washington DC: Urban Institute Press.

Giarrusso, R., Silverstein, M. and Feng, D. (2000) 'Psychological costs and benefits of grandparents raising grandchildren: evidence from a national survey', in Cox, C. B. (ed) *To Grandmother's House we go and Stay: Perspectives on custodial grandparents*, New York: Springer.

Goldberg, D. P. and Hillier, V. F. (1979) 'A scaled version of the General Health Questionnaire', *Psychological Medicine*, 9, pp. 139–145.

Goodman, R. (1997) 'The strengths and difficulties questionnaire: a research note', *Journal of Child Psychology and Psychiatry*, 38, pp. 581–586.

Gordon, A. L., McKinley, S. E., Satterfield, M. L. and Curtis, P. A. (2003) 'A first look at the need for enhanced support services for kinship caregivers', *Child Welfare*, 82, pp. 77–96.

Grant, R., Gordon, S. G. and Cohen, S. T. (1997) 'An innovative school-based intergenerational model to serve grandparent caregivers', *Journal of Gerontological Social Work*, 28, pp. 47–61.

Greeff, R. (ed) (1999) *Fostering Kinship: An international perspective on kinship foster care*, Aldershot: Ashgate.

Green, H., McGinnity, A., Meltzer, H., Ford, T. and Goodman, R. (2005) *Mental Health of Children and Young People in Great Britain, 2004*, London: Office for National Statistics.

Gullone, E. and Robinson, K. (2005) 'The inventory of parent and peer attachment – revised (IPPA-R) for children: a psychometric evaluation investigation', *Clinical Psychology and Psychotherapy*, 12, pp. 67–79.

Hall, E. (1999) *Where are they now? Outcomes for children made subject to care orders in 1995–6*, Durham and Darlington: Durham and Darlington GALRO Panel.

Hannah, L. and Pitman, S. (2000) *Oz Child's Kith and Kin Program*, Melbourne, Australia: Oz Child.

Harwin, J., Owen, M., Locke, R. and Forrester, D. (2003) *Making Care Orders Work: A study of care plans and their implementation*, London: The Stationery Office.

Hatmaker, C. (1999) *Project REFRESH: Research and evaluation of foster children's reception into environmentally supportive homes. Final Qualitative Report*, Cornallis, OR: Family Policy Program, Oregon State University.

Holloway, J. (1997) 'Outcome in placements for adoption or long-term fostering', *Archives of Diseases in Childhood*, 76, pp. 227–230.

Holtan, A., Ronning, J. A., Handegard, B. H. and Sourander, A. (2005) 'A comparison of mental health problems in kinship and nonkinship foster care', *European Child and Adolescent Psychiatry*, 14, pp. 200–207.

Home Office (1998) *Supporting Families: A consultation document*, London: Home Office.

Hunt, J. (2003a) *Family and Friends Carers: Scoping paper prepared for the Department of Health*, London: Department of Health.

Hunt, J. (2003b) *Researching Contact*, London: National Council for One Parent Families.

Hunt, J. (2006) 'Substitute care of children by members of their extended families and social networks: an overview', in Ebtehaj, F., Lindley, B. and Richards, M. (eds) *Kinship Matters*, Oxford: Hart Publishing.

Hunt, J., Drucker, N. and Gill, B. (2003) *Understanding Differences in the Hours Guardians ad Litem take to Complete Care Cases*, Oxford Centre for Family Law and Policy: University of Oxford.

Hunt, J. and Macleod, A. (1999) *The Best-Laid Plans: Outcomes of judicial decisions in child protection cases*, London: The Stationery Office.

Hunt, J., Macleod, A. and Thomas, C. (1999) *The Last Resort: Child protection, the courts and the 1989 Children Act*, London: The Stationery Office.

Inglehart, A. P. (1994) 'Kinship foster care: placement, service and outcome issues', *Children and Youth Services Review*, 16, pp. 107–122.

Jackson, S. and Thomas, N. (1999) *What Works in Creating Stability for Looked After Children?*, London: Barnardo's.

Janicki, M. P., McCallion, P., Grant-Griffin, L. and Kolomer, S. R. (2000) 'Grandparent caregivers: characteristics of the grandparents and the children with disabilities for whom they care', *Journal of Gerontological Social Work*, 33, pp. 35–55.

Jantz, A. R., Geen, R., Bess, R., Andrews, C. and Russell, V. (2002) *The Continuing Evolution of State Kinship Care Policies*, Washington DC: The Urban Institute.

Jendrek, M. P. (1994) 'Grandparents who parent their grandchildren: circumstances and decisions', *The Gerontologist*, 34, pp. 206–216.

Jordan, L. (2001) *Family and Friends Care: Developing practice*, London: Family Rights Group.

Kelley, S. J. (1993) 'Caregiver stress in grandparents raising grandchildren', *Image Journal of Nursing Scholarship*, 25, pp. 331–337.

Kelley, S. J. and Damato, E. G. (1995) 'Grandparents as primary caregivers', *MCN: The American Journal of Maternal Child Nursing*, 20, pp. 326-332.

Kelley, S. J., Whiteley, D., Sipe, T. A. and Yorker, B. C. (2000) 'Psychological distress in grandmother kinship care providers: the role of resources, social support and physical health', *Child Abuse and Neglect*, 24, pp. 311–321.

Laming, H. (2003) *Report of the Inquiry into the Death of Victoria Climbié*, London: The Stationery Office.

Laws, S. (2001) 'Looking after children within the extended family: carer's views', in Broad, B. (ed) *Kinship Care: The placement choice for children and young people*, Lyme Regis: Russell House Publishing.

Laws, S. and Broad, B. (2000) *Looking After Children within the Extended Family: Carers' views*, Leicester: Centre for Social Action, De Montfort University.

Le Prohn, N. S. (1994) 'The role of the kinship foster parent: a comparison of the role conceptions of relative and non-relative foster parents', *Children and Youth Services Review*, 16, pp. 65–81.

Macaskill, C. (2002) *Safe Contact? Children in permanent placement and contact with their birth relatives*, Lyme Regis: Russell House Publishing.

Malos, E. and Bullard, E. (1991) *Custodianship: The care of other people's children*, London: HMSO.

Mansfield, J. (1999) *Where are they now? An exploration of outcomes for children involved with the Manchester Guardian ad Litem Service*, unpublished dissertation, Diploma in Management Studies: Manchester Metropolitan University.

Margolin, L. (1992) 'Sexual abuse by grandparents', *Child Abuse and Neglect*, 16, pp. 735–741.

Masson, J. and Lindley, B. (2006) 'Recognising carers for what they do – legal problems and solutions for the kinship care of children', in Ebtehaj, F., Lindley, B. and Richards, M. (eds) *Kinship Matters*, Oxford: Hart Publishing.

McFadden, J. (1998) 'Kinship care in the United States', *Adoption & Fostering*, 22, pp. 7–15.

Meltzer, H., Gatward, R., Corbin, T., Goodman, R. and Ford, T. (2003) *The Mental Health of Young People Looked After by Local Authorities in England*, London: Office for National Statistics.

Messing, J. T. (2005) *From the Child's Perspective: A qualitative analysis of kinship care placements*, Berkeley, CA: National Abandoned Infants Assistance Resource Center, School of Social Welfare, University of California at Berkeley.

Millham, S., Bullock, R., Hosie, K. and Haak, M. (1986) *Lost in Care*, Aldershot: Gower.

Ministry of Justice, Judiciary of England and Wales (2008) *The Public Law Outline: Guide to case management in public law proceedings*, London: Ministry of Justice.

Minkler, M., Fuller-Thomson, E., Miller, D. and Driver, D. (1997) 'Depression in grandparents raising grandchildren: results of a national longitudinal study', *Archives of Family Medicine*, 6, pp. 445–452.

Minkler, M. and Roe, K. M. (1993) *Grandmothers as Caregivers: Raising children of the crack cocaine epidemic*, Newbury Park, CA: Sage.

Minkler, M., Roe, M. and Robertson-Beckley, R. J. (1994) 'Raising grandchildren from crack cocaine households: effects on family and friendship ties of African-American women', *American Journal of Orthopyschiatry*, 64, pp. 20–25.

Morgan, A. (2003) *Survey of Local Authorities in England: Policy and practice in family and friends care*, unpublished, London: Family Rights Group.

Murphy, M. (1988) 'Foster parents before relatives', *Social Work Today*, 22 Sept, p. 29.

Nixon, P. (2001) 'Making kinship partnerships work: examining family group conferences', in Broad, B. (ed) *Kinship Care: The placement choice for children and young people*, Lyme Regis: Russell House Publishing.

Nixon, S. (1999) 'Safe care, abuse and allegations of abuse in foster care', in Kelly, G. and Gilligan, R. (eds) *Issues in Foster Care: Policy, practice and research*, London: Jessica Kingsley.

Nixon, S. and Verity, P. (1996) 'Allegations against foster families', *Foster Care*, January 1996, pp. 11–14.

O'Brien, V. (2000) 'Relative care: a different type of foster care – implications for practice', in Kelly, G. and Gilligan, R. (eds) *Issues in Foster Care: Policy, practice and research*, London: Jessica Kingsley.

O'Reilly, E. and Morrison, M. L. (1993) 'Grandparent headed families: new therapeutic challenges', *Child Psychiatry and Human Development*, 23, pp. 147–159.

Office for National Statistics (2003) *Census 2001: National report for England and Wales*, London: Office for National Statistics.

Office for National Statistics (2004) *The Health of Children and Young People*, London: Office for National Statistics.

Osby, O. (1999) 'Child-rearing perspectives of grandparent caregivers', in Gleeson, J. P. and Hairston, C. F. (eds) *Kinship Care: Improving practice through research*, Washington DC: CWLA Press.

Owusu-Bempah, K. (2006) 'Socio-geneological connectedness: knowledge and identity', in Aldgate, J., Jones, D. P. H., Rose, W. and Jeffrey, C. (eds) *The Developing World of the Child*, London: Jessica Kingsley.

Peters, J. (2005) 'True ambivalence: child welfare workers' thoughts, feelings and beliefs about kinship foster care', *Children and Youth Services Review*, 27, pp. 595–614.

Pitcher, D. (1999) *When Grandparents Care*, Plymouth: Plymouth City Council Social Services Department.

Pitcher, D. (2001) 'Assessing grandparent carers: a framework', in Broad, B. (ed) *Kinship Care: The placement choice for children and young people*, Lyme Regis: Russell house Publishing.

Portengen, R. and Van Der Neut, B. (1999) 'Assessing family strengths – a family systems approach', in Greeff, R. (ed) *Fostering Kinship: An international perspective on kinship foster care*, Aldershot: Ashgate.

Pryor, J. (2006) 'Children and their changing families: obligations, responsibilities and benefits', in Ebtehaj, F., Lindley, B. and Richards, M. (eds) *Kinship Matters*, Oxford: Hart Publishing.

Quinton, D., Rushton, A., Dance, C. and Mayes, D. (1997) 'Contact between children placed away from home and their birth parents: research issues and evidence', *Clinical Child Psychology and Psychiatry*, 2, pp. 393–413.

Quinton, D., Rushton, A., Dance, C. and Mayes, D. (1998) *Joining New Families: A study of adoption and fostering in middle childhood*, Chichester: Wiley.

Richards, A. (2001) *Second Time Around: A survey of grandparents raising their grandchildren*, London: Family Rights Group.

Richards, A. and Tapsfield, R. (2003) *Funding Family and Friends Care: The way forward*, London: Family Rights Group.

Richards, L., Wood, N. and Ruiz-Calzada, L. (2006) 'The mental health needs of looked after children in a local authority permanent placement team and the value of the Goodman SDQ', *Adoption & Fostering*, 30, pp. 43–52.

Rittner, B. (1995) 'Children on the move: placement patterns in children's protective services', *Families in Society*, 76, pp. 469–477.

Rowe, J., Caine, M., Hundleby, M. and Keane, A. (1984) *Long Term Foster Care*, London: Batsford.

Rowe, J., Hundleby, M. and Garnett, L. (1989) *Child Care Now: A survey of placement patterns*, London: BAAF.

Rushton, A., Dance, C., Quinton, D. and Mayes, D. (2001) *Siblings in Late Permanent Placements*, London: BAAF.

Russell, C. (1995) *Parenting the Second Time Around: Grandparents as carers of young relatives in child protection cases*, Unpublished dissertation, University of East Anglia.

Ryburn, M. (1998) 'A new model of welfare: re-asserting the value of kinship for children in state care', *Social Policy and Administration*, 32, pp. 28–45.

Sands, R. G. and Goldberg-Glen, R. S. (2000) 'Factors associated with stress among grandparents raising their grandchildren', *Family Relations*, 49, pp. 97–105.

Sawyer, R. and Dubowitz, H. (1994) 'School performance of children in kinship care', *Child Abuse and Neglect*, 18, pp. 587–597.

Selwyn, J. and Quinton, D. (2004) 'Stability, permanence, outcomes and support: foster care and adoption compared', *Adoption & Fostering*, 28, pp. 6–15.

Shlonsky, A. R. and Berrick, J. D. (2001) 'Assessing and promoting quality in kin and non-kin foster care', *Social Service Review*, 75, pp. 60–83.

Shore, N. and Hayslip, B. (1994) 'Custodial grandparenting: implications for children's development', in Gottfried, A. E. and Gottfried, A. W. (eds) *Redefining Families: Implications for children's development*, New York, NY: Plenum.

Sinclair, I. (2005) *Fostering Now: Messages from research*, London: Jessica Kingsley.

Sinclair, I., Baker, C., Lee, J. and Gibbs, I. (2007) *The Pursuit of Permanence: A study of the English care system*, London: Jessica Kingsley.

Sinclair, I., Wilson, K. and Gibbs, I. (2000) *Supporting Foster Placements*, University of York report to the Department of Health.

Skuse, T., Macdonald, I. and Ward, H. (2001) *Looking After Children: Transforming data into management information, report of longitudinal study at 30.9.99, third interim report to the Department of Health*, Loughborough: CCFR.

Smith, A., Gollop, M. M., Taylor, N. J. and Atwool, N. (1999) *Children in Kinship and Foster Care: A research report*, Dunedin, New Zealand: Children's Issues Centre, University of Otago.

Spence, N. (2004) 'Kinship care in Australia', *Child Abuse Review*, 13, pp. 263–276.

Stein, M. and Carey, K. (1986) *Leaving Care*, Oxford: Blackwell.

Stelmaszuk, Z. W. (1999) 'The continuing role of kinship care in a changing society', in Greeff, R. (ed) *Fostering Kinship: An international perspective on kinship foster care*, Aldershot: Ashgate.

Stogdon, J. (2001) 'Comparing American and United Kingdom kinship care: a practitioner's view', in Broad, B. (ed) *Kinship Care: The placement choice for children and young people*, Lyme Regis: Russell House Publishing.

Strawbridge, W. J., Wallhagen, M. I., Shema, S. J. and Kaplan, G. A. (1997) 'New burdens or more of the same? Comparing grandparent, spouse and adult child caregivers', *The Gerontologist*, 37, pp. 505–510.

Sykes, J., Sinclair, I., Gibbs, I. and Wilson, K. (2002) 'Kinship and stranger foster carers: how do they compare?' *Adoption & Fostering*, 26, pp. 38–48.

Talbot, C. and Calder, M. (2006) *Assessment in Kinship Care*, Lyme Regis: Russell House Publishing.

Tan, S. (2000) *Friends and Relative Care: The neglected carers*, unpublished dissertation, PQ award in social work, Brunel University.

Terling-Watt, T. (2001) 'Permanency in kinship care: an exploration of disruption rates and factors associated with placement disruption', *Children and Youth Services Review*, 23, pp. 111–126.

Testa, M. F. (2001) 'Kinship care and permanency', *Journal of Social Service Research*, 28, pp. 25–43.

Timms, J. and Thoburn, J. (2003) *Your Shout! A survey of the view of 706 young people in public care*, London: NSPCC.

Triseliotis, J. (2002) 'Long-term foster care or adoption? The evidence examined', *Child and Family Social Work*, 7, pp. 23–33.

Tunnard, J. and Thoburn, J. (1997) *The Grandparents Supporters' Project: An independent evaluation*, Norwich: University of East Anglia/Grandparents' Federation.

US Department of Health and Human Services (2000) *Report to the Congress on Kinship Foster Care*, US Department of Health and Human Services.

Waldman, J. and Wheal, A. (1999) 'Training needs of friends and families who are foster carers', in Greeff, R. (ed) *Fostering Kinship: An international perspective on kinship foster care*, Aldershot: Ashgate.

Wasoff, F. and Martin, C. (2005) *Scottish Social Attitudes Family Module Report*, Edinburgh: Scottish Executive Social Research.

Waterhouse, S. (1997) *The Organisation of Fostering Services*, London: NFCA.

Waterhouse, S. (1999) 'The use of kinship placements in court proceedings', *Seen and Heard*, 9(4).

Waterhouse, S. (2001) 'Keeping children in kinship placements within court proceedings', in Broad, B. (ed) *Kinship Care: The placement choice for children and young people*, Lyme Regis: Russell House Publishing.

Waterhouse, S. and Brocklesby, E. (1999) 'Placement choices for children: giving more priority to kinship placements', in Greeff, R. (ed) *Fostering Kinship: An international perspective on kinship foster care*, Aldershot: Ashgate.

Webster, D., Barth, R. P. and Needell, B. (2000) 'Placement stability for children in out of home care: a longitudinal analysis', *Child Welfare*, 79, pp. 614–632.

Wedge, P. and Mantle, G. (1991) *Siblings Groups in Social Work: A study of children referred for permanent substitute family placement*, Aldershot: Avebury.

Wells, S. J. (1999) *Evaluating the Quality of Kinship Foster Care: Final report*, Urbana-Champaign, Il: University of Illinois at Urbana-Champaign.

Wheal, A. (2001) 'Family and friends who are carers: a framework for success', in Broad, B. (ed) *Kinship Care: The placement choice for children and young people*, Lyme Regis: Russell House Publishing.

Wilson, L. and Conroy, J. (1999) 'Satisfaction of children in out of home care', *Child Welfare*, 78, pp. 53–69.

Wineburgh, A. (2000) 'Treatment of children with absent fathers', *Child and Adolescent Social Work Journal*, 17, pp. 255–273.

Worrall, J. (1996) *Because we're Family: A study of kinship care of children in New Zealand*, unpubished Masters thesis, Massey University, Palmerston North.

Young, D. and Smith, C. J. (2000) 'When moms are incarcerated: the needs of children, mothers and caregivers', *Families in Society*, 81, pp. 130–141.

Appendix A: **Sample and methods**

The kinship sample

As indicated in Chapter 1, the research used an **existing** four-year cohort sample of all the children from two local authorities who were placed with members of their extended family or friendship network at the end of care proceedings which completed over the period 1.10.95 and 30.9.1999 (Waterhouse, 1999; 2001). This was supplemented by a **new** fifth- and sixth-year-cohort, from the same local authorities, of children whose proceedings completed in the year 1999–2001.

The original sample was collected, in two tranches, by Waterhouse, from data provided by two Guardian *ad Litem* and Reporting Officer panels of which she was a member.[1] The purpose of this survey was to ascertain the extent to which kinship placements were being used as a placement option for children subject to care proceedings.[2] Starting from basic information obtained from the panel, a telephone survey of guardians was conducted to obtain brief details about all the care cases they had completed over the sample period, including the child's placement at the end of proceedings and the nature of the final order. Details of the fifth- and sixth-year sample were again collected through short telephone surveys with guardians. As neither of the local authorities had systems for recording whether the children in their care, or who had been in their care, were in a kinship placement, the data collected from the guardians were the only way of identifying the sample we were interested in.

Using the basic details provided by the guardians, the local authorities were then able to try and trace these children through their systems. As expected, it was easiest to trace the children still on care orders and the initial information collected was the fullest through contact with the

---

[1] Since the original sample was collected, panels of guardians *ad litem* have become part of Cafcass.

[2] The court in such cases is under a positive duty to appoint a guardian unless satisfied that this is not necessary and in practice it would be extremely unusual for a child not to have a guardian. This means that the guardian service is a unique repository of data on all children coming before the courts in care proceedings.

social worker. For other children, sometimes the payment of a residence order allowance gave clues.

Recruiting the kinship sample

Since it was not possible for this research to be carried out without first gaining the consent of people about whom we would be collecting information (see access issues, Appendix B), it was necessary to develop a series of leaflets and letters giving details of the study. Using these materials, carers, parents and children over 18 years were contacted via the local authority and invited to take part in the study on an opt-out basis. Letters were sent recorded delivery to ensure that only the person named on the letter received it. If the child was still in placement, the carers were contacted before the parents to give them the opportunity to request that the parents were not contacted. It was our intention to see the case files before interviewing any of the parties involved but the carers were also given the option to be interviewed before the researchers saw the case files. If the carers and parents had not responded to the first letter and not opted out of the study, the files were seen by the researchers and follow-up letters were sent to re-invite them to be interviewed.

Total kinship sample obtained

Case file data

It was important to have data for a full cohort for at least the first four years of the sample. Therefore, in cases where the researchers were unable to view the case files because either the carers or the parents had opted out of the study, we were able to make provisions for data to be collected by a person employed by the local authority specifically for this purpose. This data was then passed on to us with all identifying information removed.

We experienced a small amount of sample attrition from the original figures collected by Waterhouse (1999; 2001), as there were seven cases where, on further investigation, we felt that the placement should no longer be classified as a kinship one.[3]

---

[3] For example, there was one case where a residence order was made to secure the placement of two siblings with their step-mother with whom they had been living for a significant period of time without the presence of their father.

Table A1

Case file data collected by year and local authority

	Authority A	Authority B	All cases
Year 1 (95/96)			
Data collected by researchers	5	0	5
Anonymised data received	1	2	3
Total	6	2	8
(Missing/lost files)	(0)	(2)	(2)
Year 2 (96/97)			
Data collected by researchers	4	6	10
Anonymised data received	0	4	4
Total	4	10	14
Missing/lost files	(0)	(1)	(1)
Year 3 (97/98)			
Data collected by researchers	9	10	19
Anonymised data received	0	1	1
Total	9	11	20
Missing/lost files	(0)	(0)	(0)
Year 4 (98/99)			
Data collected by researchers	8	6	14
Anonymised data received	9	6	15
Total	17	12	29
Missing/lost files	(0)	(0)	(0)
Year 5 (99/00)			
Total	11	13	24
(Lost to sample[4])	(5)	(4)	(9)
Year 6 (00/01)			
Total	10	8	18
(Lost to sample)	(5)	(3)	(8)
All Years (95–01)			
Total	57	56	113
(Lost to sample)	(10)	(10)	(20)

---

[4]   i.e. consent refused for researchers to access files; files missing or lost by local authority.

In total, we were able to collect case file data on 113 cases over the six sample years. With regard to the first four years of the sample, we were able to collect case file data for 71 children, which represents 96% of the four-year cohort (with the local authorities being unable to locate the remaining three sets of case files). Appendix C details the basic inform-ation about the sample and provides comparison figures with Farmer and Moyers (2008) and our non-kin sample where applicable.

Interviews with carers
We were able to achieve a total of 37 interviews with carers, which provided information on 48 children. The cases where we were able to interview carers were strikingly similar to those where we were unable to do so (Appendix D).

Interviews with parents
Attempts were made to interview parents in both ongoing and terminated placements. However, our efforts were largely unsuccessful and we were able to interview only two parents (both mothers).

Interviews with social workers
We carried out 24 interviews with social work professionals in relation to 33 children. We were able to interview the social workers in all 18 of the continuing placements where the child was still on a care order. We also interviewed a worker who had had current or recent involvement in seven cases with residence orders and one with an adoption order. Additionally, there were six cases that had ended, where we were able to interview a social worker (4 rehabilitations and 2 breakdowns).

Interviews with children and young people
During the carer interviews, we asked them if they thought the child/ren they were caring for might be willing to be interviewed. This was only asked in cases where the child was still in placement and they were at least eight years old. (This latter criterion was determined by a ruling by the President of the Family Division, whose permission has to be sought where children have been through care proceedings.) We were also able to

interview two young women, both aged 20 and now living independently. One had responded positively to the information we sent out directly to young people now aged 18 and above. The other arrived at her mother's house during the parent interview and agreed that we could interview her at a later date. In neither case had we interviewed the kinship carer.

The interviewed children accounted for one-third of all children over seven whose carers were interviewed (and 11% of all children in the cohort). They were unlikely to be representative of the cohort as a whole because of the selection process, viz:

- the carers had been traced (and were therefore more likely to be at a stable address) and had agreed to be interviewed themselves;
- interviews were only sought where carers agreed, children were still in placement, and they were at least eight years old.

Table F3 in Appendix F sets out some of the points of similarity and difference. It shows that the interview sample over-represented girls, children in longer placements, children placed with paternal relatives and relatives other than grandparents, those from minority ethnic groups and those on residence orders rather than care orders; children where proceedings were initiated because of abuse rather than neglect and proceedings starting with emergency action. The interviewed children also did slightly better on our overall outcomes measure.

The interviewed children themselves also appeared to be doing rather better than the average for the 28 children whose carers were interviewed. Carer-completed assessments of child well-being using the Strengths and Difficulties Questionnaire (Goodman, 1997) (see below) placed 25 per cent of the *interviewed* children in the abnormal category compared with 39 per cent of the *non-interviewed*.

The non-kin sample

The research also involved a small comparison group of 31 children placed away from their parents in non-kin care who were also the subject of care proceedings. These children were drawn from the first three years of the sample – to maximise follow-up time – and were under five at the end of proceedings so that they could be compared with the larger majority of the kinship sample who were under five at the end of proceedings.

Basic details about these children were collected by Waterhouse in her original study (1999; 2001). A random sample of 31 was then selected (using the SPSS select random cases function) from this group of approximately 200 children. No more than one child from a sibling group was selected to maximise the variety of data collected, and the number of children who had siblings also involved in proceedings was approximately the same as that found in the sub-sample of kinship children under five at the end of proceedings.

Methods

A range of methods was used to collect data about the kinship sample whilst only information from the case files was collected for the non-kin sample.

Case files

A structured case proforma was used to collect data from the local authority files. This was based on a schedule previously used in a study of outcomes in care proceedings (Hunt and Macleod, 1999) adapted to the particular circumstances of kinship placements, and on the proforma developed by Farmer and Moyers (2008) for their study.

Topics covered by the proforma included: basic information about the case; the background to the care proceedings; placement history up to the index placement; pre-placement adversities including child well-being and behaviour; decision making; details of the index placement; services and supervision; placement continuity, stability and quality; contact patterns; child outcomes and any post-placement information.

Key documents found on the files that were of particular use were guardian reports; statements from the local authority, parents and some-times kinship carers submitted as part of the court process; and LAC review documents. However, there were a small number of files where there was a dearth of information, which resulted in a limited amount of data being collected in these cases. Additionally, a few case files had been lost by the local authority resulting in partial pictures for a couple of children.

The same case proforma was used with the non-kin sample with certain sections which were not applicable omitted.

Interviews with social workers

The file analysis was supplemented by structured, mainly telephone, interviews with the current social worker where there was still Social Services involvement. These included questions about the history of the placement, the child's situation and well-being and input from Social Services. General questions were also included to canvass social workers' views about kinship care, and its use and management by the local authority.

Interviews with carers

Kinship carers in both current and terminated placements were interviewed and the interview proforma had to be designed to reflect this. In developing the schedule we drew on those developed by Farmer and Moyers (2008), Aldgate and McIntosh (2006), Pitcher (1999) and Sinclair *et al* (2000). The final schedule was semi-structured, using a mix of closed and open-ended questions and covered topics such as: the carer's household and circumstances; how the placement came to be made; subsequent events (including why the placement ended if applicable); the child's well-being; parental and extended family contact; support from family, friends and Social Services.

We also used two standardised tests in these interviews: the General Health Questionnaire (Goldberg and Hillier, 1979) and the Strengths and Difficulties Questionnaire (SDQ) (Goodman, 1997). The General Health Questionnaire is a brief 12-item instrument which measures general psychological health in adults. The SDQ is a widely used behavioural screening questionnaire suitable for completion in relation to children 3–16 years old. It assesses child functioning in five domains: emotional symptoms, behaviour problems, hyperactivity, peer problems and pro-social behaviour. Added together, these items generate a total difficulties score (based on 20 items) and a separate pro-social score based on five items. The SDQ has been tested against typical populations of children in the community so that 80 per cent of all child populations would have a score placing them in the "normal range", i.e. low needs/difficulties, 10 per cent would have borderline needs/difficulties and 10 per cent would have high needs/difficulties.

Interviews were carried out face-to-face except for the two carers who lived abroad who completed a modified questionnaire by post. To encourage participation, carers were offered a small honorarium (£20 of gift vouchers).

Interviews with parents

As we were only able to achieve two interviews with parents, they were largely unstructured, with guidance from general themes we had identified from our knowledge of the particular cases in question.

Interviews with children and young people

The child interviews contained the following elements:
- a qualitative semi-structured questionnaire;
- the completion of an ecomap by the child during the interview (see below);
- self-completed SDQ;
- two brief self-completed questionnaires designed by the research team (see below).

The questionnaire covered the following areas:
- the child's understanding of their story and how they explained their situation to friends;
- the child's relationship/friendship networks;
- pros and cons of living with relatives and "top tips" for relative carers;
- relationships with carers, other family members including parents and siblings, and social workers;
- the child's aspirations for the future.

All the children agreed that the interviews could be taped. They were given a red card to use if they did not wish to answer a question, an idea adopted from Aldgate and McIntosh's research (2006).

For the two young adults, an abridged version of the schedule was used. The interviews were also taped.

The researcher designed self-completion questionnaires

We sourced validated attachment measures to use with the children themselves during interviews. Attachment measures we considered using included:

- Bene-Anthony Family Relations Test (Bene, 1985);
- The Inventory of Parent & Peer Attachment – Revised for Children (Gullone and Robinson, 2005)
- Measure devised by the Institute of Psychiatry for use with children subject to care proceedings (unpublished)
- Attachment Style Classification Questionnaire (Finzi *et al*, 2000)

Some of these were unsuitable because of length or target age group. One test focused primarily on peer relationships. Our search proving unsuccessful within our time constraints, we devised our own brief questionnaires based on important positive relationship features from other attachment questionnaires.

The Ecomap

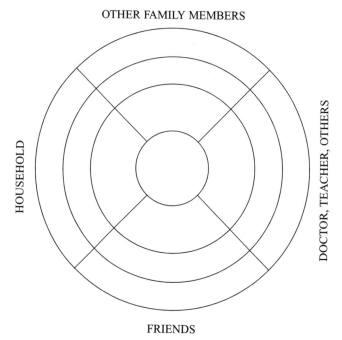

Appendix B **Access issues**

Gaining the required permissions and access agreements for this study was far from straightforward, complicated by differing legal interpretations and lack of an overarching agreed procedure that researchers must follow. The difficulties we encountered, detailed below, resulted in significant delay to the timetable but did not, in the end, compromise the quality of the work.

It has been the norm in the past for researchers to be granted access to local authority case file data without having to seek permission directly from the service users (e.g. Farmer and Moyers, 2008). However, the implementation of the Data Protection Act 1998 has resulted in increased consideration of confidentiality and access issues and this is no longer the case in many local authorities. This was the first stumbling block we encountered in one of our local authorities, which felt that clients should be contacted and asked to participate in the research. However, due to the nature of this study, there was an issue of who should be contacted as the children were variously still on care orders, with relative carers on residence orders, with a parent or their current location being unknown. Extensive discussions with this local authority and our advisory group centred on the issue of whether consent should be on an opt-in or opt-out basis. Eventually it was agreed that we could proceed with opt-out consent. **It is important to highlight that, if it had been necessary to proceed with opt-in consent, we would not have secured a single case for the study as there were no cases where both the parents and carers positively consented to be part of the study.**

It was agreed that carers should be contacted first where the child was still with them, followed by the parents if the carers had no objections. Where the child had returned home or moved to another placement, the carers and the parents were contacted simultaneously. Additionally, any children who were over 18 were also contacted. This process was followed in both local authorities. We wrote clear and informative leaflets and letters for this purpose, which were checked by both our advisory group and the local authorities. The letters were sent recorded delivery to ensure that only the addressee received the letter and the recipients were given two weeks to respond.[5] In one local authority the absence of parents' addresses and sometimes the kinship carers' addresses from the electronic database was fairly significant. Therefore, in cases where these data were missing, it was necessary for a local authority employee to access the file to obtain this information.

In order to boost our existing sample (1995–1999) to around 100, we wanted to identify a sample of children going through care proceedings between 1999 and 2001. We wanted to follow the same procedure of seeking assistance from guardians as had been done with the first four years of the sample. However, Cafcass now had assumed responsibility for the guardian service and the local service managers were now not able to give this agreement (as had happened several years before under the autonomous panel system) requiring permission to be sought from Cafcass headquarters. It was imperative that this additional sample was identified through the guardians as neither the local authority nor Cafcass held records that enabled them to complete this task. This again was initially problematic because of issues to do with the Data Protection Act 1998 and the Human Rights Act 1998. Permission was granted for us to do this in early 2004.

As there were court papers located on local authority files, a Privileged Access Agreement (PAA) issued by the Department of Constitutional Affairs was required to permit the researchers to access these papers. Under past practice this had been sufficient. In the course of the research, however, it emerged that this previous interpretation of the law may not have been correct. One local authority required us to seek the permission of the individual courts involved. After a period of considerable uncertainty and delay, the position was only clarified by an

---

[5] This apparently straightforward task of sending out letters was complicated by an unofficial postal strike in early 2004. This impacted on the progress of the study as a number of letters were sent out at the beginning of the strike and remained at the sorting office for the duration of the strike. This meant that when the letters were finally delivered, the date for returning the form had passed. Therefore, another batch of letters had to be sent, delaying progress by over two weeks.

amendment to the Children Act which, inter alia, covered researcher access to court papers, restoring the status quo ante.

We ran into further difficulties once the data collection had been in full swing for over six months. A concern raised by a social worker in one local authority necessitated the re-visiting of the access issues in terms of ensuring that the correct permissions were in place. Indeed, at one point we were told that it would be necessary for us to seek the permission of anyone who had contributed to the case file, which, given the number of people involved and the lapse of time since these cases had started, would have made the research impossible to carry out. Fortunately, eventually reason prevailed and we were only required to sign a confidentiality agreement detailing our responsibilities with regard to the data we were collecting. This issue was one that caused particular delay to the project.

In each local authority we were assigned a contact (a member of support staff) to identify addresses and social workers and to locate files, amongst other things. However, due to staffing changes, these contacts changed and whenever this happened there were significant delays in re-assigning contacts, meaning work in the authority could not be carried out during these periods.

Appendix C **Basic information on the sample**

Where possible, comparative data from Farmer and Moyers (2008) are presented.

Child's characteristics and history

Table C1

Child's characteristics and history: comparison with Farmer and Moyers (2008)

| | This study | | Farmer & Moyers | |
	No.	%	No.	%
Age[6]				
Under 5	55	49	23	16
5–9 years	38	34	39	28
10–14 years	20	18	59	41
15+ years	0	0	21	15
Gender				
Male	59	52	69	49
Female	54	48	73	51
Ethnicity[7]				
White British	94	83	120	85
Other ethnicity	19	17	22	15
Previous kin placement				
Yes	55	49	122	86
No	57	51	20	14

---

[6] Our study: at the end of proceedings; Farmer & Moyers: at the time of selection (July 2000).

[7] Data from the 2001 Census (Office for National Statistics, 2003) shows that people with black and minority ethnic backgrounds made up 7.9 per cent of the population. However, children of black and minority ethnic origin represented 21 per cent of the looked after children population in 2005 (DfES, 2005a).

- All of our sample had British nationality and had been born in the UK
- 57 per cent of 81 children where this could be established were actively involved in practising a religion. Forty (49%) were Christian and 4 per cent (3) either Muslim or Hindu.

Siblings

- 51 children were the sole subjects of proceedings (20 of these were believed to be only children).
- 30 sets of proceedings involved siblings but not all the sibling group members were in our cohort if, for example, they remained with a parent or were placed for adoption.
- 62 of the children in the 30 sibling proceedings were in our kinship cohort:
  - 27 (43%) were placed with all of their siblings involved in the proceedings;
  - 16 (26%) were placed with some siblings involved in proceedings;
  - 19 (31%) were not placed together at all.

Parents

- 91 per cent of fathers were identified – 44 per cent had parental responsibility at the end of proceedings.
- 80 per cent of parents were never married to each other; 11 per cent were married; and 8 per cent divorced/separated at the end of proceedings.
- Only 10 per cent of parents were living together at the end of proceedings; 53 per cent had split up; 30 per cent had never lived together; 8% had had an unstable on/off relationship.
- 94 per cent of mothers and 83 per cent of fathers were born in the UK.
- The mean age of mothers at the end of proceedings was 27 years; fathers were on average 30 years old.

Pre-placement adversities

Table C2

Mean number of adversities in each domain

Adversity domain	Mean		
	Authority A	Authority B	All cases
Parental circumstances	4.3	4.1	4.2
Environmental factors	4.7	4.6	4.7
Bereavement	0.4	0.2	0.3
Instability	1.7	1.8	1.7
Child difficulties	1.7	1.6	1.6
Abuse/child protection concerns	2.5	2.5	2.5
All adversities	15.2	15.0	15.1

We considered a large number of factors in order to determine the level of adversity the children had been exposed to before they moved to their kinship placements. Many of the questions asked related to whether the child had lived with a parent or parent figure who had a particular problem, as we felt the problem would have little effect on the child if they had not lived with the parent. However, the result of this is that our figures underestimate the extent of the problems the parents had. We categorised the adversity factors into six areas based on adversity type. The mean number of adversities experienced in each domain are shown in Table C2. There was very little difference between the two local authorities in the level of pre-placement adversity experienced.

Parental circumstances

These were adversities that related to the demographic characteristics of the parents or to problems that were inherent in the parents.

Table C3

Summary of adversities in the parental circumstances domain

| | Adversity present | | | Farmer and Moyers | |
| | This study | | | Kin sample | Non-kin sample |
	Total	No.	%	%	%
Mother under 21 at child's birth	112	54	48		
Mother no qualifications	78	69	88		
Father no qualifications	48	25	52		
Parent had previous child removed	111	20	18		
Parent has psychological/ psychiatric problems	112	65	58	44	45
Parent has physical problems	112	4	4	15	18
Parent has learning difficulties	113	15	13		
Parent has addiction problems (drugs and/or alcohol)	111	64	58	60	51
Parent in care as a child	106	38	36	13	23
Parent had poor early experiences	108	73	68		
Parent involved in criminal activity	112	50	45	42	44
None or one of these adversities present	113	3	3		
2 or 3 of these adversities present	113	35	31		
4 or 5 of these adversities present	113	51	45		
6+ (max 8) of these adversities present	113	24	21		

Environmental factors

Factors which would contribute to the child living in a less than ideal environment were grouped together.

Table C4

Summary of adversities in the environmental factors domain

		Adversity present			
		This study		*Farmer and Moyers*	
				Kin sample	*Non-kin sample*
	Total	*No.*	*%*	*%*	*%*
Lived with another child close in age	113	30	27		
Lived in a household with large number of children	113	57	50		
Lived in a one-parent family	113	92	81		
Parent socially isolated	103	61	59		
Parent on benefits	96	85	89		
Inadequate housing	98	49	50		
Temporary accommodation	100	56	56		
Child experienced racism inside or outside household	113	4	4		
Pre-natal exposure to drugs/alcohol	113	35	31	11	8
Child understimulated	109	26	24		
Domestic violence	111	73	66	52	52
None or one of these adversities present	113	6	5		
2 or 3 of these adversities present	113	24	21		
4 or 5 of these adversities present	113	45	40		
6+ (max 8) of these adversities present	113	38	34		

Bereavement/loss

Table C5
Summary of adversities in the bereavement/loss domain

				Adversity present	
		This study		Farmer and Moyers	
				Kin sample	Non-kin sample
	N	No.	%	%	%
Death of a parent	113	5	4	13	14
Loss of a parent through divorce/ separation	113	30	27		
Death of a sibling	113	1	1		
Any of these	113	36	32		

Instability

The lives of these children were characterised by high levels of instability of care or household arrangements. On average, the children had experienced four different care arrangements prior to their kinship placement (min 0, max 15) and had lived in an average of five residences (min 0, max 24). However, surprisingly, this is not correlated with the child's age at the end of proceedings. This information was used to produce a researcher rating of the stability of care arrangements prior to the kinship placement.[8] Only 12 per cent of children had had stable care arrangements prior to placement, 31 per cent had had "middling" care arrangements, 17 per cent had had unstable care arrangements and 40 per cent had had very unstable care arrangements. Fifty-three percent of children had been looked after prior to the index placement.

---

[8] Stable = child continuously with parent/primary carer
   Middling = at least one major change of carer or some moves/disruptions
   Unstable = at least two major changes of carer
   Very unstable = serial disruptions, moves, previous care spells.

Table C6
Summary of adversities in the instability domain

	Total	No.	%	Kin sample %	Non-kin sample %
		This study		*Farmer and Moyers*	
Frequent changes of residence	109	54	50		
Multiple separations from main caregiver	113	33	29	59	64
Many changes in composition of household	113	46	41		
Unusual number of school moves	55	20	36		
None of these	113	10	9		
One of these	113	40	35		
Two of these	113	38	34		
3+ of these (max 4)	113	25	22		

Child difficulties

These were problems that were specifically related to the child's health, development and well-being.

In order to assess well-being factors such as emotional and behavioural development, we noted down any information on the files about any difficulties the child had within four of the Strengths and Difficulties Questionnaire (Goodman, 1997) domains (behavioural problems; hyperactivity; emotional symptoms; peer problems) plus sexualised behaviour. There was a dearth of information of this nature on the files, in part due to the young nature of our sample, but we were able to gather information for 77 children. From the information obtained we were able to rate whether the child did or did not have problems in each of the five areas considered.

Table C7
Summary of adversities in the child difficulties domain

				Adversity present	
		This study		*Farmer and Moyers*	
				Kin sample	*Non-kin sample*
	N	*No.*	*%*	*%*	*%*
Concerns about child's physical growth as a baby/preschooler	108	14	13		
Child particularly difficult to manage as a baby/preschooler	111	13	12		
Child bullied by peers	106	10	9	17	23
Child has long-term health condition/physical disability	112	12	11	42	50
Child has learning difficulties/ developmental delay	113	12	11		
Child statemented	84	8	10	23	28
Behavioural problems	77	37	48		
Hyperactivity	77	6	8		
Emotional symptoms	77	45	58		
Peer problems	77	19	25		
Sexualised behaviour	77	7	9		
Child has none of these difficulties	112	34	30		
Child has one of these difficulties	112	32	29		
Child has 2–3 of these difficulties	112	27	24		
Child has 4+ (max 8) of these difficulties	112	19	17		

Child protection concerns

Table C8
Summary of adversities in the abuse/child protection concerns domain

| | | This study | | Adversity present
Farmer and Moyers | |
| | | | | Kin
sample | Non-kin
sample |
	N	No.	%	%	%
Child ever on Child Protection Register	111	90	81	70	72
Sexual abuse	113	6	5	13	12
Physical abuse	113	32	28	35	38
Neglect	113	86	76	68	61
Emotional abuse	113	36	32	22	26
Child inappropriately exposed to sexual activity	113	10	9	16	15
Parent a Schedule 1 offender	112	8	7		
Other person in close contact a Schedule 1 offender	112	17	15		
None of these adversities	113	2	2		
One of these adversities	113	15	13		
Two of these adversities	113	44	39		
3+ (max 6) of these adversities	113	52	46		

Carer and placement characteristics

- The mean age of the main carer at the point the proceedings ended was 45 years (range 19 to 69).

- In 73 per cent (79) of cases, either the main carer or partner were in employment at the point the proceedings ended. Of the remaining 30 cases, there were 11 cases where either a single carer or both of a couple of carers were retired and a further four cases where a single carer had a disability or chronic illness and could not work. Despite this apparently high level of household employment, there were 28 cases (of 97 where this was known) where the main carer had given up their job to take on the care of the child.

- In 26 per cent (29) of cases, there were adults other than the main carer

Table C9

Carer and placement characteristics

	This study		Farmer and Moyers	
	No.	*%*	*No.*	*%*
Relationship of carer to child				
Grandparent(s)	70	62	66	45
Aunt(s)/uncle(s)	29	26	46	32
Other relative	8	7	7	5
Other adult known to child	6	5	25	18
(e.g. friend carer)				
Side of the family				
Maternal	71	66	73	66
Paternal	37	34	37	34
Lone/couple carers				
Couple carers	80	71	103	73
Lone carers	32	29	39	27
Matched ethnicity[9]				
Matched ethnicity	97	100	117	99
No similarity in ethnicity	0	0	1	1
Placement overcrowding[10]				
Definitely overcrowding	25	22	31	22
Probably overcrowding	1	1	19	13
No overcrowding	86	77	92	65
Other children in household[11]				
Yes	78	69	94	78
No	35	31	26	22
Financial hardship[12]				
Yes	29	29	48	75
No	71	71	16	25

[9] Excludes children of dual heritage.

[10] At the start of the placement.

[11] In addition to index child.

[12] Farmer and Moyers caution that data were only available on 45 per cent of kin case files about financial circumstances.

	This study		Farmer and Moyers	
	No.	%	No.	%
Carer health difficulties[13]				
Yes	22	20	29	31
No	88	80	64	69
Change of school on moving to placement[14]				
Yes	34	55	38	38
No	28	45	63	62

and partner living in the household. In the majority of these cases (20), these were adult children of the carers.

• 85 per cent (96) of placements were inside the local authority boundary. Two of the placements outside the local authority boundary were abroad.

---

[13] Disability or chronic illness; Farmer and Moyers caution that data were only available on 65 per cent of kin case files about carer health difficulties.

[14] 44 per cent of our sample (48) were not of school age before moving to the placement.

Appendix D Characteristics of carer interview sample

On the whole, as the tables set out below show, there appeared to be little difference between the interviewed and non-interviewed carers in terms of either the carers themselves or the children they were caring for. The children whose carers were interviewed, however, had significantly fewer pre-placement adversities overall and more specifically in the domains of parental circumstances, bereavement/loss and child difficulties. We also interviewed significantly more paternal relatives than were in the rest of the sample. Other differences were not statistically significant.

Table D1
Child's characteristics and history

	Carer interviewed sample		Remainder of sample	
	No.	*%*	*No.*	*%*
Age[15]				
Under 5	25	53	33	47
5–9 years	16	34	24	34
10–14 years	6	13	14	20
Gender				
Male	25	53	38	54
Female	22	47	33	47
Ethnicity				
White British	38	81	61	86
Other ethnicity	9	19	10	14
Previously cared for by index carer full time				
Yes	15	32	21	30
No	32	68	48	70

---

[15] At end of proceedings.

Table D2
Pre-placement adversities

	Carer interviewed sample Mean	Remainder of sample Mean
Parental circumstances**	3.8	4.5
Environmental factors	4.7	4.7
Bereavement/loss**	0.2	0.4
Instability	1.7	1.8
Child difficulties**	1.2	1.9
Abuse/child protection concerns	2.3	2.6
All adversities**	13.9	15.8

** $p < 0.05$

There was little difference between the mean age of the main interviewed carer at the end of proceedings and that of the non-interviewed carers (44.9 years cf. 44.5 years).

Outcomes

The children whose carers were not interviewed had slightly higher levels of child difficulties in the placement than those whose carers were interviewed but the difference was not statistically significant.

Table D3

Carer and placement characteristics

	Carer interviewed sample		Remainder of sample	
	No.	*%*	*No.*	*%*
Last known legal order				
Care order	20	43	27	39
Residence order	24	49	38	54
Adoption order	4	9	5	7
Relationship of carer to child				
Grandparent(s)	29	62	45	63
Aunt(s)/uncle(s)	14	30	16	23
Other relative	2	4	6	9
Other adult known to child (e.g. friend carer)	2	4	4	6
*Side of the family***				
Maternal	23	51	52	76
Paternal	22	49	16	24
Lone/couple carers				
Lone carers	13	28	19	27
Couple carers	34	72	52	73
Other children in household[16]				
Yes	23	49	49	69
No	24	51	22	31
Other adults in household				
Yes	15	32	19	27
No	32	68	52	73
Placement location				
Inside LA boundary	37	79	62	87
Outside LA boundary	10	21	9	13

** $p = 0.005$

---

[16] In addition to index child or siblings.

Table D4
Outcomes

	Carer interviewed sample		Remainder of sample	
	No.	%	No.	%
Placement stability				
Lasted as long as needed/stable and continuing	24	59	38	54
Continuing but vulnerable	9	22	9	13
Did not last as long as needed	8	20	23	33
Placement quality				
Problem-free	12	29	28	40
Some concerns	23	56	26	37
Major concerns	6	15	16	23
Relationship quality				
Problems in relationship with carer	7	17	20	29
No problems in relationship with carer	34	83	50	71
Overall outcome measure				
Positive ratings on all outcome measures	10	24	15	21
Some positive ratings on some outcome measures	27	66	40	57
No positive ratings on any outcome measures	4	10	15	21

Support

Table D5
Support

	Carer interviewed sample		Remainder of sample	
	No.	%	No.	%
Rating of overall support				
Good support	10	25	21	42
Some support	19	48	22	44
Little or no support	11	28	7	14

Comparison with the sample of children placed with non-kin carers

Table E1
Child characteristics

	Kin under five		Non-kin	
	No.	%	No.	%
Gender				
Male	29	53	17	55
Female	26	47	14	45
Ethnicity				
White British	49	89	26	84
Other ethnicity	6	11	5	16
Religion				
Christian	17	44	10	33
Muslim	0	0	1	3
None	22	56	19	63
Previous kin placement				
Yes	22	40	6	19
No	33	60	25	81

All of the kinship sample of under-fives had British nationality and were born in the UK. All of the non-kin sample had British nationality but one child was born in Europe and came to the UK aged two.

Siblings

Eight children in the non-kin sample (26%) also had siblings subject to the same set of proceedings as them. Six of these children were placed with all of their siblings involved in the same set of proceedings and two were placed with some of their siblings involved in proceedings.

In the kinship sample of under-fives, there were 19 children (36%) who also had siblings involved in the same set of proceedings. Nine children were placed with all of their siblings involved in the same set of proceedings, six children were placed with some of their siblings involved in proceedings and six children were placed with none of their siblings involved in the proceedings.

Parents

The mean age of the non-kin sample children's mothers at the end of proceedings was 27 years with the mothers of the kinship under-five sample being, on average, 23 years.[17]

The mean age of the non-kin sample children's fathers at the end of proceedings was 34 years with the fathers of the kinship under-five sample being, on average, 28 years old.[18]

Table E2
Parental characteristics

	Kin under five		Non-kin	
	No.	%	No.	%
Mothers				
Born in UK	53	96	31	100
Fathers				
Identified	52	95	26	84
Had PR at end of proceedings	22	42	14	45
Born in UK	40	93	21	93
Parents marital status[19]				
Married to each other	6	11	9	29
Divorced/separated	6	11	2	7
Never married to each other	43	78	20	65
Parents relationship status[20]				
Living together	8	15	7	23
Split up, not living together	24	44	9	29
Never lived together	15	28	8	26
On/off relationship	7	13	6	23

[17] $t = 2.97$, $df = 84$, $p = 0.004$.
[18] $t = 2.87$, $df = 69$, $p = 0.005$.
[19] At end of proceedings.
[20] At end of proceedings.

Pre-placement adversities

The level of pre-placement adversity experienced by the non-kin sample and the sample of kin placements under five at the end of proceedings was very broadly similar. (Shaded rows indicate where the occurrence of the adversity is higher in the kinship sample.)

Table E3
Pre-placement adversities, comparison of kin and non-kin placements

	Kin under five			*Non-kin*			
	N	No.	%	N	No.	%	Sig
Parental circumstances							
Parent in care as a child	54	27	50	31	7	23	p=0.013
Parent has physical problems	55	1	2	31	5	16	p=0.021
Mother under 21 at child's birth	55	28	51	31	9	29	p<0.05
Parent involved in criminal activity	55	21	38	31	6	19	NS
Father no qualifications	25	13	52	18	12	67	NS
Mother no qualifications	41	35	85	28	20	71	NS
Parent had previous child removed	55	9	16	31	9	29	NS
Parent has addiction problems (drug/alcohol)	54	26	48	31	12	39	NS
Sibling removed from parent's family	54	5	9	29	0	0	NS
Parent had poor early experiences	55	32	58	30	20	67	NS
Parent had history of being cared for by relatives	54	4	7	31	1	3	NS
Parent has psychological/ psychiatric problems	54	29	54	31	16	52	NS
Parent has learning difficulties	55	6	11	31	4	13	NS
Environmental factors							
Parent on benefits	48	40	83	30	18	60	p=0.022
Pre-natal exposure to drugs/alcohol	55	16	29	31	5	16	NS

	Kin under five			Non-kin			
	N	No.	%	N	No.	%	Sig
Parent socially isolated	52	31	60	31	15	48	NS
Lived with another child close in age	55	14	26	31	5	16	NS
Domestic violence	55	28	51	31	13	42	NS
Lived in a one-parent family	55	40	73	30	20	67	NS
Temporary accommodation	53	22	42	27	13	48	NS
Child subject to racism inside or outside household	55	1	2	31	2	7	NS
Lived in a household with large number of children	55	14	26	31	7	23	NS
Inadequate housing	51	21	42	28	11	39	NS
Child understimulated	54	13	24	31	7	23	NS
Bereavement and Loss							
Loss of a parent through divorce/separation	55	12	22	31	5	16	NS
Death of a sibling	54	0	0	25	1	4	NS
Instability							
Many changes in composition of household	55	11	20	31	2	7	NS
Unstable care arrangements (rated middling, unstable or very unstable)	54	45	83	24	23	96	NS
Multiple separations from main caregiver	55	11	20	31	9	29	NS
Frequent changes of residence	55	23	43	30	12	40	NS
Child difficulties							
Concerns about child's physical growth as a baby/ preschooler	55	9	16	31	7	23	NS
Child has long-term health condition/physical disability	55	9	16	31	7	23	NS
Child has learning difficulties/developmental delay	55	4	7	31	4	13	NS

	Kin under five			Non-kin			
	N	No.	%	N	No.	%	Sig
Child particularly difficult to manage as a baby/ preschooler	55	4	7	31	3	10	NS

NS = not significant

Appendix F **Supplementary tables**

Table F1
Consideration of kinship placement

| | Kinship placement considered before proceedings | | | | | | Kinship placement considered during proceedings | | | | | | Kinship placement considered at any time | | | | | |
| | LA A | | LA B | | All cases | | LA A | | LA B | | All cases | | LA A | | LA B | | All cases | |
	No.	%	No.	%	No.	%	No.	%	No.	%	No.	%	No.	%	No.	%	No.	%
Explored but relatives rejected	0	0	0	0	0	0	2	15	3	17	5	16	2	15	3	17	5	16
Explored but no willing relatives	2	15	1	6	3	10	6	46	6	33	12	39	6	46	6	33	12	39
Considered but not pursued	0	0	3	17	3	10	2	15	4	22	6	19	2	15	5	28	7	23
No evidence that considered	10	77	14	78	24	77	3	23	5	28	8	26	3	23	4	22	7	23
N/A Child already with relative	1	8	0	0	1	3	0	0	0	0	0	0	0	0	0	0	0	0
N =	13		18		31		13		18		31		13		18		31	

Table F2

Duration of continuous Social Services involvement post-proceedings

	0–6 months		7–12 months		1–2 yrs		2–3 yrs		3–4 yrs		5+ yrs		
	No.	%	No.	%	No.	%	No.	%	No	%	No.	%	(N=)
Ongoing support not envisaged after proceedings	8	73	2	18	1	9	0	0	0	0	0	0	(11)
Case subsequently closed while child in placement													
Care order	0	0	1	5	3	14	3	14	8	38	6	29	(21)
Supervision order	0	0	8	42	7	37	4	21	0	0	0	0	(19)
Residence order alone	1	33	1	33	0	0	1	33	0	0	0	0	(3)
Case remained open while child in placement													
Care order	1	2	4	9	4	9	4	9	1	2	32	70	(46)
Supervision order	0	0	0	0	3	60	0	0	1	20	1	20	(5)
Residence order	0	0	1	100	0	0	0	0	0	0	0	0	(1)
All cases													
Care order	1	2	5	8	7	10	7	10	9	13	38	57	(67)
Supervision order	0	0	8	33	10	42	4	17	1	4	1	4	(24)
Residence order only	10	63	4	25	1	6	1	6	0	0	0	0	(16)
Total	11	10	17	16	18	17	12	11	10	9	39	36	(107)

Table F3

Characteristics of interviewed and non-interviewed children

	Interviewed children (N=12)	Non-interviewed children (N = 101)
Mean age at end of proceedings (years)	4.9	5.2
Continuous placement	83%	95%
Mean length continuous placements (years)	8	5.6
Boys	33%	54%
Girls	67%	46%
Child White British	67%	85%
Main carer White British	67%	93%
Mean age of main carer at placement (years)	43	45
Relationship to child		
Maternal relative	50%	65%
Grandparent carer (including step)	50%	63%
Aunt/uncle	42%	24%
Other adult	–	6%
Reasons for proceedings (some multiple categories)		
Neglect	50%	62%
Physical abuse	33%	25%
Emotional abuse	17%	34%
Sexual abuse	8%	4%
Whether proceedings started with emergency action		
Emergency order	50%	25%
Agreed emergency placement	33%	26%
Emergency action re other children	–	5%
Did not start with emergency action	17%	14%
Order at end of proceedings		
Care order	50%	62%
Residence order	50%	38%
Overall outcome category		
All good outcomes	17%	23%
Middling	75%	57%
All bad	8%	18%

Table F4
Contact frequency, venue, supervision

	Mother		Father		Either parent*		Both	
	No.	*%*	*No.*	*%*	*No.*	*%*	*No.*	*%*
Frequency								
At least weekly	29	47	10	27	34	47	5	20
2–4 weekly	22	36	17	46	31	42	13	52
Less than this	11	18	10	27	12	16	7	28
(N=)		(62)		(37)		(73)		(25)
Venue								
Specified	43	49	15	29	51	53	7	7
(N=)		(87)		(52)		(97)		(97)
Parent's home	4	10	3	20	7	16	0	0
Placement	13	32	6	40	17	40	2	5
Other relative's home	4	10	0	0	4	10	0	0
SS venue/family centre	20	49	6	40	22	52	4	10
(N=)		(41)		(15)		(42)		(42)
Supervision								
Contact to be supervised	53	64	25	47	59	63	19	20
(N=)		(83)		(53)		(94)		(94)
Supervised by								
Carer	28	53	11	48	35	65	4	7
Contact centre/ family centre	19	36	10	44	22	41	7	13
Social worker	5	9	2	9	7	13	0	0
Other relative	1	2	0	0	1	1	1	1
(N=)		(53)		(23)		(54)		(54)

*May sum to >100 per cent since arrangements may be different for each parent.

Table F5

Continuation of face-to-face parental contact where envisaged in care plan

	Maternal contact*		Paternal contact*		Either*	
	No.	%	No.	%	No.	%
All cases	69	83	30	59	79	88
(N=)	(83)		(51)		(90)	
Missing data	8		5		8	
Mother previously main/shared carer	59	84	24	56	65	89
(N=)	(70)		(43)		(73)	
Mother not previously main/shared carer	8	73	6	75	12	80
(N=)	(11)		(8)		(15)	
Father previously/ main/shared carer	19	83	11	46	23	85
(N=)	(23)		(24)		(27)	
Father not previously main/shared carer	8	73	3	60	9	75
(N=)	(11)		(5)		(12)	
Continuing & continuous placements	36	73	18	53	45	82
(N=)	(49)		(34)		(55)	
Missing data	8	4	8			
Terminated & continuous placements	29	97	10	67	30	97
(N=)	(30)		(15)		(31)	
Missing data	0		1		0	
Boys	38	83	15	54	40	83
(N=)	(46)		(28)		(48)	
Missing data	5		3		5	
Girls	31	84	15	65	39	93
(N=)	(37)		(23)		(42)	
Missing data	3		2		3	

*where contact with either envisaged in care plan

Table F6

Face-to-face parental contact in continuing and continuous cases

	12 months on		3 years on		5 years on		>5 yrs	
	No.	%	No.	%	No.	%	No.	%
Maternal contact	44*	94	31	89	17	65	13	52
(N=)	(47)		(35)		(26)		(25)	
Missing data	10		22		29		28	
This time not elapsed	0		0		2		4	
Paternal contact	26	76	18	64	12	48	10	38
(N=)	(34)		(28)		(25)		(26)	
Missing data	4		10		12		10	
This time not elapsed	0		0		1		2	
Face-to-face contact with either parent	51*	93	39	95	24	80	21	70
(N=)	(55)		(41)		(30)		(30)	
Missing data	8		22		31		29	
This time not elapsed					2		4	
Face-to-face contact with both parents	17	31	10	24	5	17	3	10
(N=)	(55)		(41)		(30)		(30)	
Missing data	8		22		31		29	
This time not elapsed					2		4	

** includes two cases where mother lived with carer and child

Table F7
Frequency of parental contact

	12 months on*		3 years on		5 years on		>5 yrs	
	No.	%	No.	%	No.	%	No.	%
Maternal contact								
At least weekly	16	38	9	29	3	18	3	23
At least monthly	24	57	12	39	6	35	6	46
(N=)	(42)		(31)		(17)		(13)	
Paternal contact								
At least weekly	5	19	3	16	2	15	3	27
At least monthly	13	48	9	47	6	46	8	73
(N=)	(27)		(19)		(13)		(11)	
Contact either parent								
At least weekly	20	40	11	28	5	20	6	29
At least monthly	32	64	19	48	12	48	13	62
(N=)	(50)		(40)		(25)		(21)	
	2							

*excludes two cases where parent living with carer and child

Table F8
Contact and bonding between parent and child

	Mothers				Fathers			
	Close bond		Not a close bond		Close bond		Not a close bond	
	No.	%	No.	%	No.	%	No.	%
Contact continued	13	93	11	69	3	75	9	53
(N=)	(14)		(16)		(4)		(17)	
Negative trajectory	4	29	9	56	1	25	12	71
	(14)		(16)		(4)		(17)	
Close bond now*	5	83	2	17	0	0	6	60
	(6)		(12)		(4)		(10)	

*continuing placements only

Table F9
Continuation of parental contact by familial links

	Maternal contact*		Paternal contact*		Either parent**	
	No.	%	No.	%	No.	%
Any contact	36	92	18	33	45	82
(N=)		(39)		(54)		(55)
Missing data	8	4	8			
Maternal relative	32	84***	9	82	35	88
(N=)		(38)		(11)		(40)
Missing data	7	3	7			
Paternal relative	4	36***	9	69	10	67
(N=)		(11)		(13)		(15)
Missing data		1		1		1
Grandparent	30	79	12	48	34	87
(N=)		(38)		(25)		(39)
Aunt/uncle	4	57	6	67	9	75
(N=)		(7)		(9)		(12)

*where envisaged in care plan
**where contact with either parent envisaged in care plan
***SS difference in mother's contact according to side of family: p= .001

Table F10
Contact with extended family other than care household

	Maternal relative		Paternal relative		Any relative	
	No.	%	No.	%	No.	%
Maternal carer	32	80	7	14	34	81
(N=)		(40)		(49)		(42)
						–
Paternal carer	9	43	16	47	18	100
(N=)		(21)		(34)		(18)
						–
Other carer	5	50	2	18	5	50
(N=)		(10)		(11)		(10)

Table F11

Were contact difficulties anticipated?

| | Difficulties with maternal contact anticipated | | | | Difficulties with paternal contact anticipated | | | |
| | Yes | | No | | Yes | | No | |
	No.	%	No.	%	No.	%	No.	%
Contact problematic	10	33	18	35	1	8	4	12
Some problems	10	33	16	31	6	50	5	15
No problems	10	33	17	33	5	42***	25	74
(N=)	(30)		(51)		(12)		(34)	
Negative impact on child	10	33	18	35	1	8	4	12
Mixed impact on child	6	20	13	26	5	42	5	15
Positive/neutral	14	47	20	39	6	50	25	74
(N=)	(30)		(51)		(12)		(34)	
Serious/persistent conflict	16	53	19	37	4	33	3	9
Minor/sporadic conflict	1	3	7	13	0	0	5	15
No conflict	13	43	26	50	8	67	26	76
(N=)	(30)		(52)		(12)		(34)	
Contact ceased	10*	32	4	8	10	58	11	32
Contact continued	21	68	48	92	7	41	23	68
	(31)		(52)		(17)		(34)	
Negative trajectory	18**	58	15	29	13	77	16	47
Stable trajectory	10	32	21	40	3	18	13	38
Positive trajectory	3	10	16	31	1	6	5	15
(N=)	(31)		(52)		(17)		(34)	

*SS p=.004; **SS p=.016; ***SS p=.046

Table F12
Factors linked with cessation of maternal contact post-proceedings

	Condition applies		Condition does not apply		Statistical significance
	No.	%	No.	%	
Child placed with paternal side of the family	7	64	6	16	.002
(N=)		(11)		(38)	
Contact perceived to have purely negative effect on child	9	56	3	9	.000
(N=)		(16)		(32)	
Serious/persistent conflict with carer	8	38	4	15	Trend, almost SS.065
(N=)		(21)		(27)	
Mother not previously had care of the child	3	33	10	26	Trend, not SS
(N=)		(9)		(38)	
Child is a boy	8	30	5	23	Trend, not SS
(N=)		(27)		(22)	

Table F13
Factors linked with cessation of paternal contact post-proceedings

	Condition applies		Condition does not apply		Statistical significance
	No.	%	No.	%	
Child placed with maternal side of the family	11	55	1	10	<.05
(N=)		(20)		(10)	
Child is a boy	8	57	4	25	Trend, not SS
(N=)		(14)		(16)	
Child <5 at end of proceedings	8	53	4	27	Trend, not SS
		(15)		(15)	

Index

Note: page numbers followed by n indicate footnotes.